MOON

S0-CFM-052

July 3, 2023

Annie, Lucas, & Eloise —
I hope you enjoy
exploring Chicago.
Kind regards

TAKE A HIKE
CHICAGO

BARBARA I. BOND   *Barbara I Bond*

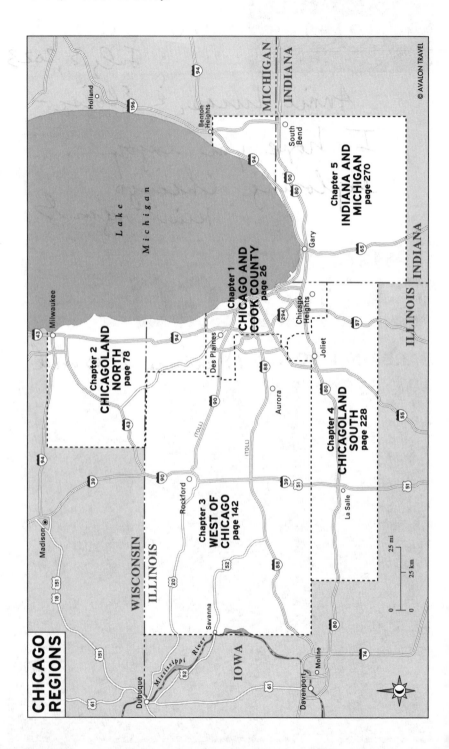

CHICAGO REGIONS

© AVALON TRAVEL

Chapter 1
CHICAGO AND COOK COUNTY
page 26

Chapter 2
CHICAGOLAND NORTH
page 78

Chapter 3
WEST OF CHICAGO
page 142

Chapter 4
CHICAGOLAND SOUTH
page 228

Chapter 5
INDIANA AND MICHIGAN
page 270

Contents

How to Use This Book

ABOUT THE MAPS

This book is divided into chapters based on regions that are within close reach of the city; an overview map of these regions precedes the table of contents. Each chapter begins with a region map that shows the locations and numbers of the trails listed in that chapter.

Each trail profile is also accompanied by a detailed trail map that shows the hike route.

Map Symbols

– – – – –·	Featured Trail	(80)	Interstate Freeway	○	City/Town
– – – – –·	Other Trail	(101)	U.S. Highway	✕✕	Airfield/Airport
▨▨▨▨▨	Expressway	(21)	State Highway	⌁	Golf Course
▨▨▨▨	Primary Road	66	County Highway	▲	Mountain
▨▨▨▨	Secondary Road	★	Point of Interest	♠	Park
▫▫▫▫▫	Unpaved Road	🅿	Parking Area	⬚	Sand
··············	Ferry	🆃	Trailhead	⬚	Swamp
—·—·—·	National Border	▲	Campground	✛	Unique Natural Feature
—··—	State Border	▪	Other Location	⬋	Waterfall

ABOUT THE TRAIL PROFILES

Each profile includes a narrative description of the trail's setting and terrain. This description also typically includes mile-by-mile hiking directions, as well as information about the trail's highlights and unique attributes.

The trails marked by the **BEST** 🅒 symbol are highlighted in the author's Best Hikes list.

Options

If alternative routes are available, this section is used to provide information on side trips or note how to shorten or lengthen the hike.

Directions

This section provides detailed driving directions to the trailhead from the city center or from the intersection of major highways. When public transportation is available, instructions will be noted here.

Information and Contact

This section provides information on fees, facilities, and access restrictions for the trail. It also includes the name of the land management agency or organization that oversees the trail, as well as an address, phone number, and website if available.

ABOUT THE ICONS

The icons in this book are designed to provide at-a-glance information on special features for each trail.

🄝 The trail climbs to a high overlook with wide views.

▪ The trail offers an opportunity for wildlife watching.

◼ The trail offers an opportunity for bird-watching

▦ The trail features wildflower displays in spring.

◣ The trail visits a beach.

▨ The trail travels to a waterfall.

◙ The trail visits a historic site.

▨ The trail is open to snowshoers in winter.

▨ Dogs are allowed.

▥ The trail is appropriate for children.

♿ The trail is wheelchair accessible.

▦ The trailhead can be accessed via public transportation.

ABOUT THE DIFFICULTY RATING

Each profile includes a difficulty rating; the ratings are defined below. Remember that the level of difficulty for any trail can change considerably due to weather or trail conditions. Always phone ahead to check current trail and weather conditions.

Easy: Easy hikes are 5 miles or less round-trip and are nearly level. They are generally suitable for families with small children and hikers seeking a mellow stroll.

Easy/Moderate: Easy/Moderate hikes are 4-10 miles round-trip and have some elevation gain. They are generally suitable for families with active children above the age of six and hikers who are reasonably fit.

Moderate: Moderate hikes are 5-12 miles round-trip and have varied elevation gain. They are generally suitable for adults and children who are fit.

Strenuous: Strenuous hikes are 5-17 miles round-trip and have considerable elevation gain. They are suitable very fit hikers who are seeking a workout.

INTRODUCTION

Author's Note

Exploring the Chicago region by trail is a surprising enterprise. I know it surprised me. After returning to the Chicago area after a long absence, I picked up my outdoor exploration where I'd left off. I found myself staring out over the quiet grasslands and marsh of Goose Lake Prairie one blustery November day. I had the trails to myself, which I love. A weathered boardwalk snaked its way through the sedge and into the quiet pool of water. Walking along the trails I could imagine the bloom of wildflowers in the spring and summer, the chatter of songbirds, and the shocking contrast of butterflies against the many shades of green. I knew I'd be back.

At first glance the terrain seemed invariant. However, one must look a little closer to begin to understand the subtle beauty that lies here. Northern Illinois, southeast Wisconsin, and nearby northwest Indiana and southwest Michigan were all shaped by the glacial ice that covered this land for thousands of years. Although the land was ravaged by this phenomenon, the resulting landscape is full of geologic features that are both unique and intriguing. The Chicago region has preserves, parks, natural areas, and nature preserves in predictable and unlikely locations—and miles of trails just waiting to be explored.

As I began exploring Chicago's trails, I starting asking everyone around me where they liked to hike. I talked with folks at forest preserves, state parks, conservation groups, and outdoor stores. I sat with hunters, kayakers, and campers to find out where they explored. And I began to log trail miles—hundreds of them. I walked through new and old prairie restoration projects and was amazed at the beauty I saw. I encountered white-tailed deer peering nervously through the forest, muskrats hastily ducking into marsh water, and an occasional red fox. I saw countless colorful butterflies, moths with intriguingly patterned wings, and iridescent dragonflies. And then there were the birds—the opportunities for good bird-watching are nearly limitless along these trails. I saw wild turkeys with poults, elegant barred owls, and distinctive red-headed woodpeckers. I eventually took to hiking with my binoculars at the ready.

I enjoy hiking year-round and perhaps you will too. Winter had me strapping on snowshoes in local forest preserves, or along the shore of a frozen lake. In spring I stepped through slippery muck to witness the first wildflowers pushing through the warming forest floor. The mottled leaves of trout lilies and haze of green buds in the forest always signal that a change of season is indeed coming. One day I realized it was summer—riotous wildflowers bloomed in the prairie, forests were abuzz with wildlife, and more trails clamored for my attention.

The hikes in *Take a Hike Chicago* are an eclectic mix and reflect my love for just about any trail experience. I can find joy along a noisy urban trail almost as easily as I can in a remote nature preserve. I discovered there are many places in the Chicago region where one can get out, walk along a trail through a natural area, and remember how we are renewed when we reconnect to nature. It doesn't take long. I hope you use this book to begin some exploring and renewal of your own. Find your own pocket of greenspace and care for it. Get out, take a hike, and bring along your family and friends. I hope you will… again and again.

Barbara I. Bond

Best Hikes

◖ Best for Bird-Watching

Crabtree Nature Center Trails, Chicago and Cook County, page 28.

Camp Logan Trails, Chicagoland North, page 114.

Rollins Savanna Trails, Chicagoland North, page 125.

Nelson Lake Loop, West of Chicago, page 195.

Lake Renwick-Budde Lake Loop, West of Chicago, page 221.

Prairie View Loop, Chicagoland South, page 251.

Dune Blowout-Woodland Loop, Indiana and Michigan, page 293.

◖ Best for Children

Black Oak-White Oak Nature Trails, Chicago and Cook County, page 61.

Lake Katherine Trails, Chicago and Cook County, page 67.

Prairie Ridge-Deer Path-Tamarack View, Chicagoland North, page 121.

Dells Trails, Chicagoland South, page 239.

Twin Oaks-Bunker Field Trails, Chicagoland South, page 264.

West Beach Trails, Indiana and Michigan, page 281.

◖ Best for Geologic Wonders

Ridge Run-Sag Trail Loop, Chicago and Cook County, page 52.

Ice Age Trail: Carlin to Bald Bluff, Chicagoland North, page 83.

Sentinel and Sunset Trails, West of Chicago, page 164.

Lemont Quarry Loop, Chicagoland South, page 230.

West Overlooks and Canyons, Chicagoland South, page 242.

East Canyons, Chicagoland South, page 245.

Mount Baldy, Indiana and Michigan, page 278.

◖ Best for History Buffs

Muir Blue Trail, Chicagoland North, page 90.

Ryerson Woods, Chicagoland North, page 135.

Logger's Trail, West of Chicago, page 174.

I&M Canal Trail: Iron Mile, Chicagoland South, page 233.

Hiking Tips

HIKING ESSENTIALS

There are some things you always want to have along when out on the trail. These things are commonly called the 10 Essentials. Even for hikes on local preserve trails, it's nice to be prepared. You can put together your own small bag of 10 essentials and throw it in your daypack whenever you head out on the trail.

Clothing and Gear

COMFORT AND SAFETY

Dressing for Chicagoland weather can be a challenge for hikers. In the winter one must manage the cold and wind, and summertime brings high heat and humidity. Proper clothing choices can make the difference between a rewarding outdoor experience and a disaster. Wearing synthetic or wool clothing is preferable to cotton, which loses its insulating ability when wet and dries slowly. Good outerwear of waterproof/breathable material is available in lightweight styles for hiking. In the winter you will need a wind/rain jacket and pants, insulated layer, hat and gloves, and eye protection for windy or extremely cold conditions. Layering in winter is essential; you want to have the flexibility to adjust your clothing quickly and easily. In the warmer months light colors and long sleeves protect you from the sun, as will a hat with a brim.

10 ESSENTIALS

The 10 Essentials have been around since the 1930s, when The Mountaineers climbing club pioneered the concept. Whether or not you carry the basic 10 essentials on your hike can make the difference between an exciting outdoor adventure and an epic disaster. Store these items in a zippered plastic bag or pouch so that you have them ready every time you hit the trail. The only things you will need to switch out between hikes are your extra clothing choices, extra food and water, and the map. Remember to check your headlamp and flashlight batteries at the start of each hiking season. Even though many of the hikes profiled are frontcountry hikes, it doesn't hurt to be prepared.

- Compass
- Extra clothing
- Fire starter
- First-aid kit
- Food and water
- Headlamp or flashlight (with fresh batteries)
- Knife
- Map
- Matches
- Sunglasses
- Sunscreen

SHOES AND SOCKS

Sturdy, well broken-in shoes or lightweight hiking boots will help keep you comfortable and safe on Chicagoland trails. Ensure your shoes fit properly and wear wool-blend or synthetic socks to keep your feet dry, and to help prevent blisters.

For some, adding thin liner socks will also help. If you regularly hike in winter, look for waterproof boots with enough room for a heavier sock, and take along gaiters. Gaiters will help keep your feet warm and dry, and keep snow, mud, or water out of your boots. It's often wet and muddy on these trails; shoes with non-slip soles will keep you on your feet. Additionally, light traction devices can keep you upright when the trail is icy. If you are hiking around a lot of water, consider wearing hiking sandals. These provide good traction even when wet, and give you the option of hiking through water without having to slosh around in water-soaked shoes.

Hiking Gear

You can spend a lot of time trying to figure out what "gear" to take hiking. The good news is that you really don't need more than a daypack in which to fit your 10 essentials, including clothing, food, and water. The bad news is that there are lots of products that can add to your outdoor enjoyment. Lightweight hiking poles continue to grow in popularity. These sectional poles can be a great help on rocky, wet ground or when descending a steep trail. Carrying a headlamp, which allows you to keep your hands free, instead of a flashlight can be more versatile if you find yourself heading back to the trailhead in the dark. When hiking with your children, make sure they have a daypack that fits properly and have older children put together their own bag of 10 essentials. Kids love having their own gear and it will help make them enthusiastic hikers.

Food and Water

Hydration Basics

Staying well hydrated while hiking is important, particularly during the hot and humid Midwest summer. Even when you are just heading out for a "short" hike, bring water. There are many systems for carrying water on the trail—pick one that you like and use it! When carrying water bottles, keep them in an easy-to-reach location. A backpack hydration reservoir with a hose (also known as a water bladder) can make drinking water easier. For extreme heat or long days on the trail, consider supplementing your water supply with an endurance or electrolyte formula—however, water is still the best choice for most circumstances. Local sporting goods or running stores will have a good supply of these supplements. The amount of water to carry will depend on many factors. It's best to overestimate the amount you need unless you know you can resupply along the trail. If you plan to use water from natural sources, always treat the water before you drink it. Lightweight water filters as well as chemical treatment supplies are available from camping or sporting goods stores.

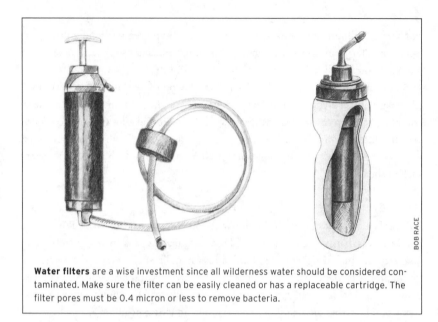

BOB RACE

Water filters are a wise investment since all wilderness water should be considered contaminated. Make sure the filter can be easily cleaned or has a replaceable cartridge. The filter pores must be 0.4 micron or less to remove bacteria.

It is possible to become overhydrated. Severe hyponatremia (low salt content in the body) can cause dizziness and confusion. During periods of extreme heat, either eat snacks that contain salt and potassium or supplement your water with an electrolyte solution or sports drink.

Energy Balance in the Outdoors

Hiking uses a lot of energy, so a little planning will enhance your enjoyment while on the trail. Carry adequate food for the distance you are hiking, taking into consideration the terrain and length of time you will be out exploring. Snacks come in all shapes and sizes—sometimes there is nothing like a good old peanut butter and jelly sandwich while out on the trail. Carry food that you will want to eat, and take along a little extra in case you want to extend your outing.

Navigational Tools

Staying on route along popular trails is usually a simple matter. Sometimes though, even well-established trail conditions necessitate a little extra skill and/ or preparation.

Maps and Compasses

Always carry a map of the area where you are hiking. In some cases a topographic map will come in handy, however most of the hikes in this book have site or trail maps that work just fine. Carry a compass when you are out, and be sure you know how to use it.

Sometimes getting to the trailhead is the most difficult part of the day. Carry the road maps you need for your specific destination. For navigating secondary roads use the official state road map or an atlas. The Delorme Atlas and Gazetteer is a very good state road atlas and they are widely available for the region. Vehicle GPS systems may not be accurate, so having a road map is a good backup.

Rock cairns indicate a turn in the trail.

© SABRINA YOUNG

GPS Systems

If you have a Global Positioning Satellite receiver (GPS) and understand how to use it, bring it along. It can be a great tool for navigation, particularly if you want to do any off-trail exploring or if you find a trail washed out. Today's GPS devices have many features that can be useful on long hikes in new territory; you can track your mileage, elevation gain, and time on the trail, and you can even create a breadcrumb trail to follow. You may also download your hike GPS data to your computer for future outings.

Remember to check the map datum and set your GPS to the same datum as your map. The datum is usually listed in the legend. GPS records your location as a waypoint, which is displayed using latitude/longitude or Universal Transverse Mercator (UTM). You can choose how to display coordinates on your GPS. For outdoor navigation, Universal Transverse Mercator (UTM) is widely used and outdoor maps often have UTM coordinate tick marks along the margins. The UTM coordinates for a location provide you with the zone, easting, and northing. This information will allow you to estimate your location on a map. The GPS coordinates in this book all use the NAD27 datum and are in the UTM system.

Trail Blazes and Rock Cairns

Blazes are color markings along a trail that can help you stay on route. They can be painted on a tree, fencepost, or signpost, or might be a wood or plastic symbol typically placed about six feet high. Some forests have carved blazes on trees; these look like upside-down exclamation points. Some parks or forest preserves use their own unique system of blazes or symbols to signify whether you are hiking to or from a major landmark such as a visitors center. Blazes can be useful when trails are overgrown, obscured by snow, or have been washed out by flooding.

Another navigation aid is a rock cairn, consisting of a small pile of rocks indicating a turn in the trail. If you come upon rock cairns, please don't disturb them. Sometimes hikers affix plastic tape to mark a route in the snow; this is called flagging. Note that flagging is a temporary aid, if you use flagging to mark a route remember to remove the tape when you hike back to the trailhead.

How to Stay Found

Even with navigational aids and well-marked trails, sometimes it is possible to wander off the trail. When you hike a lot, you may occasionally get lost or disoriented. If you do get lost, try not to panic—this is when your map and compass come into play. If you are in a safe location, stop. Take a look around at the area's physical features and use your compass to find yourself on the map. If you have a GPS with a good signal, take a reading and use that information to find yourself on the map.

Safety and First-Aid

First-Aid Kit

A basic first-aid kit is just that—basic. In a marked stuff sack or plastic bag, carry some bandages of various sizes, a roll of gauze or gauze pads, antiseptic wipes, antibiotic cream, and tape. Carry some moleskin and small scissors for padding blisters. You may also want to carry a 24-hour supply of any personal medication you need. Add a bandana or elastic bandage and some pain relievers to round out your kit.

What To Do in an Emergency

Accidents do happen in the outdoors, so it is useful to make sure someone in your party has had first-aid training and carries a kit. If faced with an accident, first calmly assess the situation, and then decide on an action plan. If there is an accident due to natural phenomenon such as a lightning strike, get yourself and everyone else out of danger if you can. Call for help if you are faced with a life-threatening situation and determine if you need to send someone to the trailhead to get help. If there are injuries, keep the injured hiker warm, dry, and hydrated (unless their injury contraindicates food and/or water). Remember the ABCs of first-aid basics: check the Airway, stop any Bleeding, and check for Circulation (heartbeat, pulse).

WEATHER

Chicagoland weather can be extremely variable. By learning what to expect from the weather you can make sure you never have to stay home because of "bad weather." Weather reports are widely available on the radio, television, and via the Internet. Check with the National Weather Service or land managers for the specific location you plan to visit.

In the Chicago area, severe weather can develop quickly. Thunderstorms, followed by flash floods, are a real danger. Tornadoes may develop at any time of the year, although they are most prevalent in the spring. Keep an eye on the sky when storms are developing, and try to take shelter ahead of time.

Temperature variations are part of the outdoor experience. Excessive heat is a reality during summer months; be aware of the heat index. If you are hiking in the open, protect yourself by wearing light-colored clothing, a hat, and sunglasses. Slow down if necessary and stay hydrated. Winter hiking has its own beauty and challenges. Hypothermia may be a factor when it is cold, or wet and windy. Hikers are most susceptible to hypothermia in wet and windy conditions, or when there is a wind chill. The National Weather Service posts the wind chill in the current conditions table when there is danger from freezing temperatures and winter winds. Understanding the weather in the area in which you hike will ensure that you are safe and comfortable all year long.

LEAVE NO TRACE

Leave No Trace (LNT) is a nonprofit educational organization that has worked with land management agencies to promote the responsible use and stewardship of our public lands. Educating yourself, your children and friends, and your hiking party members about outdoor stewardship can be the best way to protect our natural areas. Because so much hiking takes place in parks, preserves, or on urban trails far from the wilderness, LNT has developed a specific program for "frontcountry".

The LNT frontcountry principles are:
- Know before you go.
- Stick to trails and camp overnight right.
- Trash our trash and pick up poop.
- Leave it as you find it.
- Be careful with fire.
- Keep wildlife wild.
- Share our trails and manage your pet.

See the Leave No Trace website (www.lnt.org) for more information on how you can get involved.

ON THE TRAIL

Hiking is an aerobic activity, particularly when hiking along the rolling terrain of Southeast Wisconsin or the Lake Michigan dunes. Walking in your neighborhood, riding your bike, or taking part in other aerobic activities will help prepare you for the trails. If you plan on doing longer hikes along more rugged terrain, are inexperienced, or could use some conditioning, do a little pre-trip planning. Get out for regular walks with friends or join a local group for an organized walk. You'll want to be fit enough to see the sights and have fun while you're out on the trail.

Trail Etiquette

Practicing some trail etiquette basics will contribute to your enjoyment of the outdoors:
• Treat all trail users with respect and courtesy.
• Hike single file on narrow trails, yield to faster hikers.
• Downhill hikers yield to uphill hikers.
• Obey trail closures, restrictions, and posted signs.
• Practice low-impact hiking.
• Stay on the trail, do not create shortcuts or cut switchbacks.
• Yield to horses and riders on shared trails.

HIKING WITH CHILDREN

Introducing children to the outdoors at a young age is a gift they will never forget. Some basic considerations can make it a lot more fun for everyone:
• Make sure your children stay on the trail.
• Teach them not to kick rocks off the trail or throw sticks or other objects.
• Kids can be slow on the trail, so yield to faster hikers early and often.
• Teach children about low-impact hiking by encouraging them not to pick wildflowers, feed wildlife, or litter.

HIKING WITH PETS

Many hikers enjoy hitting the trails with their canine companions. If you do, too, follow these simple guidelines to keep your pet safe and make sure everyone has an enjoyable outing:
• Respect the rules; many nature preserves do not allow dogs.
• Keep your dog on a leash; some areas specify a 6- or 8-foot leash length.
• Make sure your dog is fit enough for the hike you are doing.
• Let your dog carry his or her own provisions.
• Keep your dog fed and hydrated.
• Pick up your dog's waste (and let him carry it out in his pack).
• Check them thoroughly afterwards for ticks, foxtails, burrs, or injuries.
• If hiking with a group, check to make sure pets are welcome ahead of time.

HIKING GEAR CHECKLIST

This basic list will be enough to get you started. It's not necessary to take all this stuff on your hikes; you can personalize or modify your gear for specific preferences, weather conditions, or locale. Adjust your equipment to match your destination. If you are in your local forest preserve or on the lakefront, you may not need the same gear as when you are hiking all day along the Ice Age Trail in southeast Wisconsin.

What to Carry
• Backpack
• Camera
• Emergency blanket
• Foot-care kit
• Insect repellent
• Instant hand warmers (great for winter outings)
• Insulated sit pad
• 10 essentials
• Toilet paper and zippered plastic bags
• Trekking poles

What to Wear
• Fleece jacket
• Fleece or wool cap
• Fleece pants
• Gaiters (nice for winter hikes or hikes with water crossings)
• Gloves (two pairs for long or winter hikes)
• Hat with brim
• Lightweight balaclava (versatile)
• Lightweight pants or shorts
• Long underwear
• Short-sleeved shirt or lightweight long-sleeved shirt
• Sock liners, if desired
• Sturdy boots for longer hikes, lightweight trail shoes for shorter trips
• Waterproof/breathable hooded jacket and pants
• Wool or wool-blend socks

Optional Gear
• Bandana
• Binoculars
• Cell phone or personal locator device
• Lens cleaner or anti-fog solution for glasses or goggles
• Two-way radios

CONSERVATION AND PRESERVATION

Conservation is the responsibility of all outdoor enthusiasts. Although hiking takes place on trails, these are still sensitive environments that require protection. Hikers can become advocates for the preservation of our public lands. Learn more about the places you visit, and practice low-impact techniques. Get involved in local preservation efforts. You can participate in a community work party, express your views at public meetings or by writing letters, and volunteer with conservation organizations.

Wildlife

Hikers share the land with a wide array of wildlife. Be aware of the wildlife in the places you visit. Many Chicago-area hikes take place in natural areas that deer, wild turkeys, and a variety of small mammals call home. Garter snakes, frogs, and several species of turtle also inhabit preserves and parks. Most snakes in the area are not venomous. If you do encounter a snake, it is most likely going to try and get away from you. In areas with known venomous snakes, don't put your hands or feet where you can't see them. Be respectful of wildlife; you are hiking in their home.

Plants and Insects

Poison ivy thrives in many natural areas where you will be hiking. Poison ivy may be a small plant, a large shrub, or a long vine climbing a tree trunk. Remember the old adage—leaves of three, let it be. Poison sumac grows along some wet areas. Stinging nettle inhabits the forest floor in some places. Learn what these plants look like, and try to avoid them. If you do encounter poison ivy, washing with a specialty product like Fels-Naptha or Tecnu Extreme can be helpful.

If you spend any time outdoors in the Midwest, you will have to learn to deal with some irritating insects. You are likely to encounter ticks in many areas. Wearing long sleeves and slippery pants of light-colored fabric can make it easier to see and get rid of ticks. When back at the trailhead after hiking in a tick-infested area, take a moment to check yourself and other hiking partners for these little critters. Check your pants pockets too. It will save you some the excitement of finding them on your clothing on the way home. Mosquitoes are unavoidable in the summer. A mosquito headnet can be helpful in particularly bad areas. Wasps may also be present in some areas, along with biting flies. Carry and use insect repellent to prevent bites. Long sleeves and/or pants may be a deterrent, although mosquitoes do bite through thin fabric. If anyone in your party has sensitivity to bites or stings, make sure they are carrying any necessary medication and that you know where it is and how to use it.

CHICAGO AND COOK COUNTY

BEST HIKES

You might be surprised to learn that amidst the

950 square miles of urban Cook County, there are quiet places to escape to. After all, more than five million residents live here amidst a complicated web of highways and municipalities. Fortunately, the Forest Preserve District maintains nearly 70,000 acres of land – much of it undeveloped and perfect for hiking. Add countless city parks, nature preserves, arboretums, and botanic gardens, and you have a lot of opportunities for outdoor enjoyment.

Chicago and Cook County occupy an area that was created over tens of thousands of years of geologic turmoil. The most recent episode was the Wisconsin Glacial period, when the advance and retreat of glacial ice altered the landscape. Depressions called kettles formed, sinuous eskers remained, and a thick coat of rich soil covered the land. Wetlands, ponds, lakes, and rolling terrain are the glacier's legacy. Glacial Lake Chicago once covered much of the city. When the water began to drain, outlets ran along what is now the Des Plaines River and southward through the Cal-Sag Valley. Eventually Lake Michigan formed. Sandy ridges, rocky moraines, and beaches were left behind. Pockets of forest, oak savanna, and prairie eventually grew to cover the land, punctuated occasionally by wetland or marsh. Nearer to Lake Michigan the sandy soils favored black oak and a shrub layer that persists today in preserves along the shore. Further west, a fire-dependent ecosystem of prairie and oak savanna thrives; some of that prairie is now being restored.

We can see this geologic past by hiking the trails. Northwest Cook County has large oak and hickory forests that are reminiscent of those early woods. Crabtree Forest Preserve has rolling terrain and trails that wind past huge bur oak, restored prairie, and kettle ponds. Wildlife thrives here, as it did long ago, including hundreds of bird species, painted turtles, and white-tailed deer.

To get a feel for the variation along Lake Michigan, one only has to walk the Chicago Lakefront Trail. The shore trail wanders through beaches, patches of woods, and prairie restoration. There may not be black bear here any longer, but a rich collection of bird species and small mammals thrive in the lakefront parks and preserves. Walk through Northerly Island, just south of downtown Chicago. The prairie restoration is thriving – wildflowers bloom throughout the summer, grassland birds have returned, and closer to the lakeshore cottonwoods grow in the sandy soil.

South of the city is the largest section of forest preserve in the county. The combined acreage of the Palos and Sag Valley Regions total nearly 17,000 acres. The triangle of land between the Des Plaines River and the Cal-Sag Valley was once known as Mount Forest Island. Today this hilly, forested preserve is a haven for a diverse collection of wildlife and a magnet for trail lovers who can walk, run, or bike its miles of terrain. The history of the area is also recorded here. Hikers can walk to the site of Argonne Laboratory's first nuclear reactor, or visit the Little Red Schoolhouse Nature Center. Trails include long rolling loops and short nature trails past sloughs and through mixed oak woods.

Just across the valley is the Sag Valley Region, which is home to some of the most unique geologic features in the area. Swallow Cliff rises 90 feet above its surroundings, and the trails cut across deep ravines in this thickly wooded preserve. Cap Sauer's Holdings, an Illinois Nature Preserve, is the largest roadless greenspace in the area. Here intrepid hikers may visit both the Visitation Esker and Prairie by following a footpath through the quiet preserve. Sagawau is home to a modern environmental education center and an 1100-foot-long dolomite canyon. It's easy to spend hours exploring the trails of Sag Valley.

If you want to hike urban trails, rugged trails, or just want to walk along a short nature center trail and enjoy the quiet of an urban oasis, the preserves and parks of Chicago and Cook County have a lot to offer.

TRAIL NAME	LEVEL	DISTANCE	TIME	ELEVATION	FEATURES	PAGE
1 Crabtree Nature Center Trails	Easy	4.5 mi rt	2-2.5 hr	negligible		28
2 East-West Preserve Trails	Moderate	9.8 mi rt	5 hr	240 ft		31
3 Des Plaines River Trail	Strenuous	13.0 mi rt	7 hr	negligible		34
4 Chicago Botanic Garden Loop	Moderate	9.1 mi rt	4.5 hr	negligible		37
5 Lakefront Trail: Navy Pier to Foster Street Beach	Strenuous	17.0 mi rt	8.5 hr	negligible		40
6 Chicago Riverwalk	Easy	4.2 mi rt	2.5 hr	negligible		43
7 Lakefront Trail: Navy Pier to 31st Street Beach	Moderate	11.5 mi rt	5-6 hr	negligible		46
8 Waterfall Glen Red Trail	Moderate	11.7 mi rt	6 hr	385 ft		49
9 Ridge Run-Sag Trail Loop	Easy	2.5 mi rt	1.5-2 hr	negligible		52
10 Palos Orange Trail	Moderate	6.3 mi rt	3 hr	395 ft		55
11 Palos Yellow Trail	Moderate	8.5 mi rt	4-4.5 hr	420 ft		58
12 Black Oak-White Oak Nature Trails	Easy	2.5 mi rt	1 hr	negligible		61
13 Sag Valley Yellow Trail	Moderate	8.9 mi rt	4.5 hr	430 ft		64
14 Lake Katherine Trails	Easy	3.75 mi rt	1.5-2 hr	negligible		67
15 Lost Beach-Dogwood Loop	Easy	3.5 mi rt	1.5 hr	negligible		70
16 Sauk Trail Woods Black Trail	Easy	3.5 mi rt	1.5 hr	95 ft		73

1 CRABTREE NATURE CENTER TRAILS

BEST ☾

Crabtree Forest Preserve, Barrington

🦌 🪁 🌲 👫

Level: Easy

Total Distance: 4.5 miles round-trip

Hiking Time: 2–2.5 hours

Elevation Change: negligible

Summary: Hike the trails of the restored prairie and woodland of Crabtree Nature Center for outstanding bird-watching.

The Crabtree Forest Preserve protects 1,200 acres of former fields now managed for restoration and conservation. Crabtree features rolling terrain with patches of prairie, oak-hickory savanna, marshes, ponds, and lakes. More than 10,000 years ago this land was covered with a thick sheet of glacial ice. When the ice retreated it left behind moraines and kettles, resulting in the gently rolling terrain we enjoy today. Crabtree is home to more than 200 species of birds as well as many small animals, including painted turtles, muskrat, red foxes, and white-tailed deer. During migration, Crabtree Lake is known for its huge flocks of birds.

A visit to the nature center is a good way to begin your exploration of the preserve. By walking the nature center trails, you will hike through a rich and varied environment. Begin at the old map at the start of the loop. Hike west past a few oaks and hickory trees, then along the edge of a pond. Check for painted turtles in the pond; I saw several one morning. Keep following the trail as it makes a crooked path through the trees—check out the gigantic bur oak just before an old wooden bench and frog pond. At the T intersection, keep right, passing an education garden and then alternating between prairie and woods. Cast your eyes upward to catch woodpeckers or white-breasted nuthatch. After leaving the trees, walk along the edge of the marsh until reaching a three-way junction; turn north at 1 mile.

The next 1.5 miles follow the Phantom Prairie Trail, which winds along an irregular loop through an extensively restored area. The preserve is removing invasive dogwood and harvesting native seeds. You can see obvious changes in the landscape as you first walk through woods, then amid large tracts of prairie and savanna. Note some burned areas to the north.

Turn right at a trail junction in front of a pond; the trail is signed indicating a left turn back to the nature center. This trail is a short out-and-back that crosses a narrow dike between two wetlands. Look for a small, wood viewing platform, turtles, and lots of frogs. At 2.75 miles, you will reach a first three-way junction; turn back to return to the nature center in about 0.5 mile.

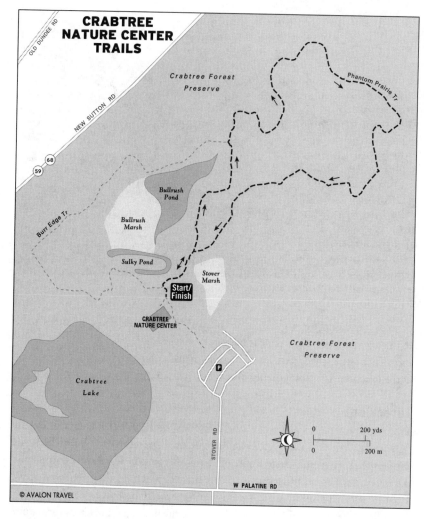

Options

Just southwest of Crabtree is Shoe Factory Woods in the Poplar Creek Forest Preserve. This preserve is home to the paved Poplar Creek Bike Trail and several shorter unpaved trails. The preserve's Brown Trail is a nice loop that goes through some oak savanna, prairie restoration, and a shortcut on the Green Trail passes a pretty lake. The north leg of the Brown Trail travels past the Shoe Factory Woods Nature Preserve, which is home to an unusual short-grass prairie. There is no trail, but it's easy enough to walk north from the trail up the small hill. The Brown Trail begins and ends at the picnic area and trailhead off Sutton Road. From the parking lot, walk east to the huge map. Turn north on the mown grass trail and follow the

a trail sign outside Crabtree Nature Center

posts to stay on the Brown Trail. The Green Trail junction is about 1.5 miles long, marked with a post. The lake has huge oaks on the south side and is a nice picnic spot. Turn left to the Green Trail junction, then continue east on the Brown Trail at the junction. Your total hiking distance is 3.25 miles at Shoe Factory Woods.

Directions

From downtown Chicago and I-290, drive west on I-90 W/I-94, continuing on I-90 for 18.6 miles. Take the Roselle Rd. exit and drive north on N. Roselle Road for 1 mile. Turn west at State Route 62 W/W. Algonquin Road and continue for 3.5 miles. Turn north at Barrington Road, drive for 0.9 mile, then turn west at W. Palatine Road. The entrance is 1 mile west; turn north on Stover Road and drive 0.2 mile to the large parking lot. Walk west on the paved path towards the nature center. A sign and a map are posted ahead of the building. The trails begin to the right of the building. The loops begin at the map north of the nature center.
GPS Coordinates: 16 T 403973mE 4662917mN

Information and Contact

There is no fee. Dogs are not allowed. The preserve is open seasonally; the trails and parking lot are generally open 8 A.M.–5 P.M. daily; hours are shorter November 1 through February 28. Nature center hours vary, but the center is always closed on Fridays. For more information, contact Crabtree Nature Center, 3 Stover Road, Barrington, 847/381-6592, www.fpdcc.com.

2 EAST-WEST PRESERVE TRAILS
Deer Grove Forest Preserve, Palatine

Level: Moderate

Total Distance: 9.8 miles round-trip

Hiking Time: 5 hours

Elevation Change: 240 feet

Summary: Enjoy a hike along the east-side prairie restoration and west-side oak woodlands of Deer Grove.

Traveling west across northern Illinois from Lake Michigan, the terrain undergoes subtle changes. Over 10,000 years ago the advance and retreat of the Wisconsin Glacier forever altered the landscape. Glacial debris remained behind, creating unique landforms including morainal hills. Heading north and west, the topography grows more rolling and there are increasing amounts of greenspace. On the border of Lake and Cook County lies the Deer Grove Preserve, containing a mixture of old fields and recovering oak savanna and prairie with a dense oak woodland. Almost 10 miles of hiking trails, plus miles of unmapped footpaths, make Deer Grove worth a visit.

The preserve is neatly split into two very individual sites, connected by paved and unpaved trails. The east preserve features open wetlands surrounded by old fields and an in-progress savanna and prairie restoration. Hiking along the Brown

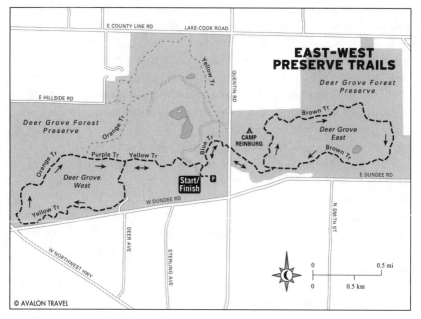

oak woodland

Loop, it's easy imagine how beautiful this area will be as the restoration proceeds. The west side is wilder, the forest denser, crisscrossed with footpaths along the rolling terrain. Quiet woodlands, white-tailed deer, and a completely different experience await hikers who explore the west side's Yellow and Orange Trails.

Begin your hike on the east side; a rainbow of short trails eventually reach the east-side Brown Trail. Start walking into the woods, heading west on the Blue Trail. Turn north on the Yellow Trail, then east on the Tan Trail connector to reach the Brown Trail in 0.9 mile. The next mile weaves in and out of the oak-hickory woods. Bring binoculars for great bird-watching along the trail—you're likely to see goldfinches, sparrows, and wrens. You may even spot a red-bellied woodpecker hammering at a tree trunk. To the north, toward the pond and wetlands, great blue herons and egrets often wade. Turn north at 1.8 miles, passing big cottonwoods and some honey-locust, then hike through open grassland for a while. At 2.5 miles, the trail navigates west into the trees once more before reaching two quick three-way junctions at around 3 miles. Go right, then left, to head southward through big oaks, then a wetland area. Watch for hawks—they seem to like hunting here. When you reach the junction of the Tan and Brown Trails at nearly 3.7 miles, retrace your steps back to the Yellow Trail junction at almost 4.5 miles. Turn west on the Yellow Trail for the second loop in the west-side preserve.

The heavily wooded Yellow Trail ascends toward the west-side entrance in 1.7 miles. Cross Deer Grove West entrance road at 6.2 miles, then follow the trail a short distance and turn north at the post onto the Orange Trail. Here, the trail follows an old roadbed through the deep interior woods of the preserve. This stretch is very quiet, with tall, arched oaks. The trail rolls along a slight descent toward Deer Grove Lake. Before reaching the lake, turn north onto the narrow Purple Trail at 7.75 miles to rejoin the Yellow Trail at 8 miles. Walk east, then south, past more huge oaks along this quiet trail. You will eventually begin to retrace the final bit of trail at 9.4 miles. Reach the trailhead at the end of the short Blue Trail at 9.8 miles.

Options

For a short walk while looking at wildflowers and birds, visit Younghusband Prairie. Grassland birds thrive here and you can bird-watch along the mown-grass path. To get there, from Quentin turn west on Dundee and drive 2.8 miles to Younghusband Prairie on the north side of the road. Baker's Lake Heron Rookery is also just north of here. To visit the rookery, go around to Hillside Avenue just south of the intersection with U.S. 14. Bring binoculars or a spotting scope for the Baker's Lake overlook at 800 East Hillside Avenue.

Directions

From the junction of I-294 and I-90 in Chicago, drive west on I-90 for 24 miles. Take the State Route 53 exit and drive north 7.9 miles. Take the Lake Cook Road W exit and drive west 2 miles. Turn south on N. Quentin Road, then continue 1 mile west and turn into the preserve. Follow the preserve road to its end and park in the lot. The trailhead is on the west side of the parking lot, marked by a blue-blazed post.

GPS Coordinates: 16 T 411933mE 4665554mN

Information and Contact

There is no fee. Dogs are allowed on leash. The park is open sunrise–sunset daily. For more information, contact Deer Grove Forest Preserve, Quentin Road (north of Dundee Road), Palatine, IL 60074, 800/870-3666, www.fpdcc.com.

❸ DES PLAINES RIVER TRAIL

River Trail Nature Center, Northbrook

🏕 🏹 ♿ 🐕

Level: Strenuous

Hiking Time: 7 hours

Total Distance: 13.0 miles round-trip

Elevation Change: negligible

Summary: Retrace the steps of Native Americans and Illinois pioneers on this hike along the Des Plaines River Trail.

The Illinois portion of the Des Plaines River runs 105 miles from the Wisconsin border south to its confluence with the Kankakee. Although the waters are recovering slowly from years of pollution, the area surrounding the river is home to over 40 species of animals, 200 types of birds, and a few dozen species of amphibians and reptiles. Forest preserves have protected some of the land adjacent to the river in both Cook and Lake County. In Cook County, hikers and cyclists cruise along miles of the packed-dirt Des Plaines River Trail, periodically interrupted by picnic areas, canoe launch sites, dams, bridges, and nature centers.

To explore the northern reaches of the trail, begin at the River Trail Nature Center in Northbrook. Here you can learn about the human and natural history of the Des Plaines River and its surroundings. Then walk south from the center's main parking lot onto the Grove Portage Trail. This short interpretive trail refers to a time when the Potawatomi Indians, explorers, and early settlers would portage their canoes here for trade. Keep left at two forks, reaching the Des Plaines River Trail (also called the Bridle Path) in less than 0.5 mile. Turn north onto the wide,

maple and oak forest

packed-dirt trail. The forest canopy is thick, dark, and cool and there are frequently white-tailed deer roaming the woods. At 0.9 mile turn east, passing Allison Woods (note the canoe launch on the left) and then crossing N. Milwaukee Road. Cross the street onto Winkelman Road. The trail continues on the north side of the street, just past some hotels, at about 1.45 miles.

The trail meanders through a maple forest as it heads northward. There is an overpass crossing of Willow Road at about 2.3 miles, which provides a nice sun break from the shaded trail. Cross a footbridge at 3.5 miles, then continue ahead through the trees, passing the picnic groves of Dam #1 at 3.8 miles. Farther north, the trail narrows somewhat, crossing Dam Woods Road at just over 5 miles. The Dundee Road crossing appears after a short distance and the trail then enters Potawatomi Woods as it winds along the river once more. Off to the east is Lake Potawatomi. There is a lot of Native American history in these woods. At one time, there was a "chipping station" north of the lake and south of Lake Cook Road. The woods here are quite overgrown now, however if you search the forest floor you might find chips of rock left over from the thin, sharp flakes that eventually became arrowheads.

Cross Lake Cook Road on the overpass at 6.2 miles. On the north side of the road, the trail enters Lake County—you'll notice some trail signs and a map as the trail proceeds north to the Wisconsin border. This is a good place to take a break and enjoy the river. I continued another 0.3 mile north, crossing a footbridge over a river bend. You might be tempted to explore off trail in this area, just beware of the thick poison ivy. Retrace the path to return to the River Trail Nature Center.

Options

You can enjoy this area without hiking all day. The River Trail Nature Center has three short nature trails, a collection of rescued wildlife, and interpretive displays. Hike the mile-long Green Bay Trail loop, the 0.5-mile Grove Portage Trail, or pick up a trail map and interpretive guide from the nature center.

Directions

From I-90/I-94 in Chicago, take I-94 W to Exit 37A/Dempster St. Drive west on State Route 58 W/Dempster Street for 3.5 miles. Turn right on State Route 21 N/N. Milwaukee Avenue and drive for 4.7 miles. The signed entrance to the preserve will be on the left; drive 0.3 mile to the large parking area at the end of the road.

GPS Coordinates: 16 T 427143mE 4660651mN

Information and Contact

There are no fees. Dogs are not allowed on nature center trails; dogs on leash are allowed on the Des Plaines River Trail. Bicycles are allowed on the Des Plaines River Trail, but not on nature center trails. The preserve is open year-round. The nature center is open 8 A.M.–5 P.M. March 1 until the last Saturday in October; winter hours are 8 A.M.–4 P.M. For more information, contact River Trail Nature Center, 3120 Milwaukee Avenue, Northbrook, 847/824-8360, www.fpdcc.com.

4 CHICAGO BOTANIC GARDEN LOOP   BEST ☾

Skokie Lagoons and Chicago Botanic Garden

Level: Moderate

Hiking Time: 4.5 hours

Total Distance: 9.1 miles round-trip

Elevation Change: negligible

Summary: Walk along the amazing footpaths that wind through the Chicago Botanic Garden.

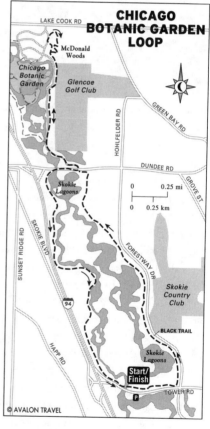

The Chicago Botanic Garden is a quiet, beautiful oasis in far north Cook County. The Chicago Horticultural Society founded the garden with a 300-acre land grant in 1963; the grand opening followed nine years later. Today the 385-acre garden is home to 2.4 million plants and is one of the most visited gardens in the country.

South of the gardens, also in the Skokie River Valley, are the Skokie Lagoons. These interconnected ponds were once wetlands, drained by settlers then remediated in the 1930s by the Civilian Conservation Corp. Now the lagoons are a popular recreation destination and an important natural area and birding hotspot. A visit to the Skokie Lagoons offers options for hiking, kayaking the still waters, or biking one of the bike trails. The trail system has almost 7 miles of mostly paved trails between Willow Road and the gardens. The 4.4-mile paved Black Trail is a great way to combine a tour of lagoons 4–7 with a hike in the Botanic Garden.

Start your hike by heading east on the path from the lot and big meadow north of lagoon 3. Follow the paved Black Trail east then north, on the east side of the lagoons. There are viewpoints of the narrow ponds; the shore is lined with cottonwoods, goldenrod, and some oaks in drier spots. Bird-watchers may see common

© BARBARA I. BOND

the Botanic Garden's serene Japanese Garden

loons, osprey, great egrets, and great blue heron. In the trees, watch and listen for a variety of warblers. At 1.3 miles is a very nice grassy spot with a picnic table; farther along is a narrow footpath that heads westward. Upon reaching Dundee Road, follow the path west to the crosswalk at 2.1 miles. Cross the street and enter the Botanic Garden. Hikers could spend all day along the miles of paths; I am going to suggest one option that explores some of my favorite places. By day's end, you will likely have a favorite garden of your own.

Walk 0.3 mile across Dundee Road to the Dixon Prairie. Cross the bridge and begin your tour of the representative prairies of the region. It is quite a contrast to the woods and water of the lagoons. The grasses of varying heights sway in the breeze and there are lots of sparrows, yellow-headed blackbirds, and goldfinches darting to and fro. Benches placed at regular intervals invite contemplation and relaxation. Walk northward through the prairie, and then turn east toward Evening Island at about 3.1 miles. At this point, your exploration is limited only by your stamina and ability to follow the garden maps/signs. To reach one of the loveliest gardens, continue south across Evening Island, then north and east to the Japanese Garden in about 3.5 miles. Just crossing the island bridge is inspiring—the formal garden unfolds before you with sculpted trees and shrubs, grassy hills, and winding paths. One could spend all day here. Cross back over the bridge and turn east to explore the main island. Stop in at the visitors center and then follow the walking path to the signed McDonald Woods trailhead in about 1.2 miles.

McDonald Woods is a special place—an oak-hickory woodland in a nearly wild state. Two loop trails wind 0.5 mile through the woods, allowing hikers to appreciate the diverse setting. Wildlife such as red-headed woodpeckers, white-tailed deer, and a variety of squirrels and chipmunks all coexist in this restored habitat. After leaving the woods, head south on the walking path for about 0.8 mile along the east side road to the south entrance at Dundee Road. Turn west and then south to follow the Black Trail back to the Tower Woods parking lot. Total mileage will be about 9.1 miles, and may vary depending upon how much exploring you do.

Options

Turn this into a bike-and-hike by riding a bike from Tower Woods up to the Botanic Garden. Lock your bike at any of the east path racks; there is one across from the Dixon Prairie entrance, next to the Plant Resource Building. Walk through the gardens, then pick up your bike for the ride back. For the return trip, ride 4.4 miles on the Black Trail (garden mileage will vary).

Directions

From Chicago, drive north on I-90/I-94, continuing on I-94 for 10.2 miles. Take Exit 33B for Willow Road and drive east 0.5 mile. Turn left on Forestway Drive and go north 0.6 mile. Turn west on Tower Road and park at the lot on the south side of the road in about 0.3 mile. The trail is along the north edge of the lot and is well signed.

Public Transportation: Take Metra's Union Pacific North Line to the Braeside Station and walk west 1 mile along Lake Cook Road (County Line Road) to reach the north garden entrance.

GPS Coordinates: 16 T 436299mE 4662708mN

Information and Contact

There is no fee. Dogs are allowed on the bike path, but not in the gardens. Botanic Garden parking is $20 per vehicle. The park is open 8 A.M.–sunset daily. For more information, contact Skokie Lagoons, Tower Road (west of Forestway Drive), Winnetka, www.chicago-botanic.org; or Chicago Botanic Garden, 1000 Lake Cook Road, Glencoe, 847/835-5440.

5 LAKEFRONT TRAIL: NAVY PIER TO FOSTER STREET BEACH

BEST ◖

Chicago

Level: Strenuous

Total Distance: 17.0 miles round-trip

Hiking Time: 8.5 hours

Elevation Change: negligible

Summary: This urban adventure takes in beaches, parks, bird sanctuaries, and the harbors along the Chicago Lakefront Trail.

The Chicago Lakefront Trail follows the Lake Michigan shoreline from Hollywood Avenue to 71st Street. The 18-mile trail is a true urban destination hike, with opportunities for bird-watching, stargazing, and visiting some of the finest parks in the world. The north trail follows beaches, harbors, and the eastern edge of Lincoln Park, Chicago's largest park at 1,208 acres. Navy Pier, with its adjacent Chicago Children's Museum, is a great place to begin and end your hike.

Start hiking north from Navy Pier, where you'll quickly leave behind the carnival atmosphere. (This part of the path is often busy with bikers, runners, and tourists.) Before reaching Ohio Street Beach, turn and walk northeast along a quiet row of trees in tiny Milton Olive Park. The view of the skyline from the park is stunning. Return west, then north, on the Lakefront Trail, passing in succession Ohio Street, Oak Street, and North Avenue Beaches in nearly 2.25 miles.

© BARBARA I. BOND

Oak Street Beach and the Hancock Building

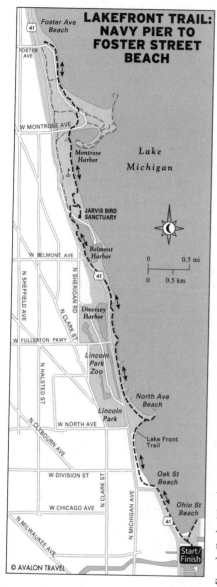

LAKEFRONT TRAIL: NAVY PIER TO FOSTER STREET BEACH

In summer, these sands are packed with people, however they are quiet in fall, when gulls wander the shore. As you approach North Avenue Beach, take a walk along the breakwater that winds northeast and ends abruptly at a tiny point. The views of the city are spectacular from here (but if it's a windy day, I recommend staying on the main path). This is the south end of Lincoln Park, which stretches north to Ardmore Avenue.

Lincoln Park is a narrow and diverse greenspace along the heavily developed lakefront. As Chicago's biggest park, it is home to a zoo, a museum, ponds, lagoons, bird sanctuaries, and more. The Lakefront Trail path traffic thins as the blocks melt away, with the sparkling blue of Lake Michigan to the east and the dynamic cityscape west. There are underpasses west at Fullerton and Diversey; walk across an art deco–style footbridge at the Diversey Harbor outlet at around 4.2 miles. The path begins a wide arc northwest to Belmont Harbor before straightening out. Cottonwoods, honey-locust, and maple trees provide some shade and bird habitat. At around 5.6 miles, just past the active harbor, is the Jarvis Bird Sanctuary. Take a short walk around the fenced area, which is home to thousands of birds. You might see a black squirrel, too. An elevated platform on the east side has a helpful series of bird identification photos.

Keep walking north on the limestone/dirt path, east of and parallel to the Lakefront Trail. (It is nice to hike on a soft surface after the paved Lakefront Trail.) Watch for the Waveland Clock Tower—a striking part of Lincoln Park history—at 6.2 miles or so. Cut east through an arched exterior corridor and along a path toward the lake, then turn left on a gravel road that runs between the golf course and the water. You may see some cormorants on the water here. Continue north another 0.8 mile to the beautiful Montrose Harbor, one of the most popular birding sites in Chicago. Over 300 species of birds have been identified in this area, which is helped in part by the "Magic Hedge," a stretch of shrubs that attracts a high volume of migratory birds.

The grassy mound ahead is Cricket Hill; you may see kite flyers here on a nice fall day. Take a few moments (or more) to walk north and enjoy the beach. Continuing northward, the path works its way through trees, then curves east before reaching Foster Avenue Beach at nearly 8.5 miles. An intersection with the Lakefront Trail is marked by a sign and a few benches. Retrace your steps to return to Navy Pier.

Options

If you want to have a picnic or just hang out at Foster Beach, make this a one-way hike and return by taking CTA bus #146 to Michigan and Illinois Avenues; Navy Pier is just a short walk east. You'll pick up the #146 just a few blocks south of Foster Beach at Argyle and Marine Drive, on the northwest corner.

Directions

From the junction of Lake Shore Drive and I-55, drive north on Lake Shore Drive for 3 miles. Take the Illinois Street exit east for 0.2 mile, turning north on N. Streeter Drive. Parking is available one block west of Navy Pier on either E. Illinois or E. Grand. Navy Pier is located at 600 E. Grand Avenue on Chicago's Near North Side. The Lakefront Trail runs north–south just west of the Navy Pier entrance, between Grand and Illinois.

Public Transportation: There are several public transportation options. From Ogilvie Transportation Center or Union Station, take the #124 bus to Navy Pier. The Chicago Transit Authority has many other bus lines that reach Navy Pier; for options or timetables visit www.transitchicago.com.

GPS Coordinates: 16 T 449298mE 4637706mN

Information and Contact

There is no fee. Dogs are allowed on leash. Lincoln Park is open 6 A.M.–11 P.M. daily. There are public restrooms at the beach houses and water fountains along the trail. For more information, contact the Chicago Park District, 312/742-7529, www.chicagoparkdistrict.com.

6 CHICAGO RIVERWALK

BEST ◖

Chicago River to Navy Pier

Level: Easy

Total Distance: 4.2 miles round-trip

Hiking Time: 2.5 hours

Elevation Change: negligible

Summary: Hike the urban shoreline along the Chicago River and enjoy the diverse offerings of the cityscape.

Only 350 years ago the three branches of the Chicago River were surrounded by a much different landscape. Prairie, wetlands, oak savanna, and sandy dunes all defined an area once subjected to the ravages of glacial ice and water. Once settlers arrived in the area in the 1800s, things rapidly began to change. Beaver and black bear were hunted or driven out and with development and time the environment began to degrade, endangering Lake Michigan's health. Residents took radical action to restore and preserve the river and today the Chicago River flows as both an engineering marvel and an outdoor museum.

Walking along the south bank of the Chicago River, whether along North Wacker Drive or the Riverwalk, is a wonderful way to experience the magnificence of Chicago's architecture and history. The official Chicago Riverwalk runs from Franklin Street to the Riverwalk Gateway. Start your hike farther west, at the confluence near Lake Street. Walking north from Lake Street, one comes upon the wide intersection of the river's branches. Looking east, the Franklin Street Bridge comes into view. As you head east, be sure to check out the bridgehouses—unique structures where the former bridge tenders used to access the lift controls for bridge traffic. Beginning at Franklin are stairs at each corner, until the ramp

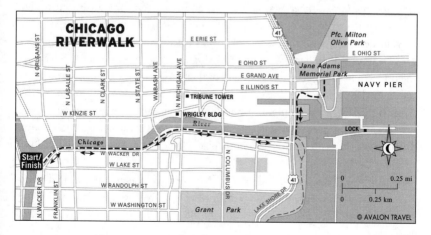

river view west from Wrigley Building and Michigan Avenue

at State Street. The LaSalle Bridge is one of the most impressive, and a historic marker on the northeast corner of LaSalle and Wacker recounts the awful Eastland ship disaster.

After walking three blocks (about 0.6 mile), you'll reach State Street, where you can walk down the steps or ramp to the Vietnam Veterans Memorial Plaza. From here the riverbank path continues without any street crossings all the way to the lake. From this perspective, the soaring skyscrapers of downtown Chicago look even more impressive. Looking east to the Wabash Avenue Bridge it is hard to miss the glistening glass of the 92-story Trump Tower, Chicago's second tallest building. Cross under Wabash Avenue and look west for a great four-bridge view downriver. So much history lies ahead on Michigan Avenue, it could easily be your destination for the day. Markers in the sidewalk remind us that in 1795 Fort Dearborn stood here. Walk up to Michigan Avenue for a detour north across the bridge. First check out the landmark bridgehouse with the historic exterior bas relief. At the north end of the bridge are two buildings. On the west side of the street is the Wrigley Building. Just walking through the doors into the courtyard is like being transported back in time. Across the street is the neo-gothic Tribune Tower, with small mementos of historic places from around the world embedded in the street-level wall.

Return to the Riverwalk and pass the McCormick Bridgehouse and Chicago River Museum, just before walking under Michigan Avenue. Continue east as the tree-lined path becomes noticeably quieter. Bird activity increases as the natural landscape grows. Cross under Lake Shore Drive at around 1.5 miles and enter Ellen Lanyon's Riverwalk Gateway, a beautiful trellised tunnel with murals and artwork. On the east side of the riverwalk gateway, follow the path as it curves southward and you will see a marble marker, which has an award plaque. The award is for the body of work that saved the Chicago River and protected the watershed, including reversing the river flow. Retrace your steps to the Riverwalk Gateway and then follow the path north up a set of stairs to the walkway along Lake Shore Drive. The path heads north, then turns east toward Navy Pier Park. You will reach the front of Navy Pier in 0.4 mile. Explore the parks and museums of Navy Pier, then return the way you came.

Options

Explore more of Chicago and Lake Michigan's shore on the Lake Front Trail. To visit Millennium Park and surrounding sights, walk 1 mile south along the Lakefront Trail to Monroe Drive. At Monroe Drive, continue two blocks west, crossing S. Columbus Drive and into Millennium Park and Lurie Garden. The Art Institute of Chicago is accessible from the park via the stunning Nichols Bridgeway.

Directions

From the intersection of I-290 and I-90/I-94, drive north on I-90/I-94 for 0.6 mile and take Exit 51A for Lake Street. Turn right on W. Lake Street and drive 0.4 mile to N. Wacker Drive. The hike begins on the northeast corner of the street, just south of the Chicago River. Several companies have parking facilities within four or five blocks of the trailhead; an online Chicago parking map is available (www.chicagoparkingmap.com).

Public Transportation: This the best way to reach to the start of this hike. From Ogilvie Transportation Center or Union Station, walk east to N. Wacker and turn north for a few blocks until you reach W. Lake Street. The Chicago Transit Authority (www.transitchicago.com) has up to six stops within several blocks of W. Lake/Wacker.

GPS Coordinates: 16 T 447143mE 4637072mN

Information and Contact

There is no fee. Dogs are allowed on leash, except in the Vietnam Veterans Memorial Plaza. The Chicago Riverwalk is managed by the City of Chicago. Visit Chicago's tourism website for more information (www.explorechicago.org). The Friends of the Chicago River operate the McCormick Bridgehouse and Chicago River Museum (open May 15–Oct. 31). Visit bridgehousemuseum.org for more information, hours, and fees.

7 LAKEFRONT TRAIL: NAVY PIER TO 31ST STREET BEACH

BEST ◖

Chicago

✈ ⛵ 🖼 🚻 🐕 ♿ 🚌

Level: Moderate

Total Distance: 11.5 miles round-trip

Hiking Time: 5-6 hours

Elevation Change: negligible

Summary: This stretch of the Lakefront Trail visits a former island, strolls past historic landmarks, and soaks in views of Chicago's inspiring skyline.

This tour of the south Lakefront Trail allows hikers to pick and choose places to explore—including museums, landmarks, public art, and a bird sanctuary—and will most definitely keep you coming back for new and different experiences on the same path.

Begin by walking south on the Lakefront Trail from Navy Pier, winding around DuSable and Chicago Harbors. In just 1 mile you will reach the north end of Grant Park; detour west at Monroe Drive to visit Millennium Park. Continue south, passing Buckingham Fountain and the never-ending boats of the Chicago Yacht Club. The trail turns east, meeting the Shedd Aquarium in just over 2 miles. The lake views are tremendous from here, as are the views of the city skyline—see if you can pick out the distinctive skyscrapers of Willis Tower, Trump Tower, and the Hancock Building. Head east toward Adler Planetarium; you are walking

the Chicago skyline from Northerly Island

© BARBARA I. BOND

over a land bridge to the peninsula, which was originally an island. (Meigs Field, an airstrip, occupied much of this site until it was dismantled in 2003. Since then, restoration efforts have been underway.) Walk around 12th Street Beach and enter the sanctuary of Northerly Island. The path makes an elongated loop through prairie restoration complete with public art and views of Soldier Field. At 4.4 miles, keep left on the path, following it north around Burnham Harbor to Solidarity Drive, then west to the Museum Campus.

This is a busy area, with the Field Museum and Shedd Aquarium anchoring the cultural offerings, and, of course, Soldier Field just south. If you are not staying to visit the museums, turn south on the continuation of the trail just before crossing Museum Campus Drive. If you are exploring the museums, walk south along the east side of Soldier Field to E. Waldron Drive. Turn east to rejoin the Lakefront Trail.

At around 5.6 miles, you will pass a sled hill on the west and will be approaching hulking McCormick Place. The tranquil McCormick Place Bird Sanctuary lies on the south side of the building at 6.3 miles. Continue past more prairie restoration to reach 31st Street Beach in 7.1 miles. The beach offers good birding and fishing from the pier. There is also a beach house with restrooms and water. Retrace your steps for 4.3 miles on the Lakefront Trail back to Navy Pier.

LAKEFRONT TRAIL: NAVY PIER TO 31ST STREET BEACH

Options

There is so much to do along the Lakefront Trail, you could spend a week exploring just the southern portion. To visit Millennium Park, the Art Institute, or the compact Lurie Garden, retrace your steps north to Monroe Drive. Turn left and head west. Once you cross S. Columbus Drive, follow the path into Lurie Garden then continue west (northwest) for more of Millennium Park. Head back to the trail by crossing the magnificent BP Bridge; the bridge offers great views before dropping you in Daley Bicentennial Plaza. Walk south back to Monroe Drive and retrace your steps east to the Lakefront Trail. Continue north for 1 mile to reach Navy Pier for a total distance of 12.7 miles.

Directions

From the junction of Lake Shore Drive and I-55, drive north on Lake Shore Drive for 3 miles. Take the Illinois Street exit east for 0.2 mile, turningnorth on N. Streeter Drive. Parking is available one block west of Navy Pier on either E. Illinois or E. Grand. Navy Pier is located at 600 E. Grand Avenue on Chicago's Near North Side. The Lakefront Trail runs north–south just west of the Navy Pier entrance, between Grand and Illinois.

Public Transportation: From Ogilvie Transportation Center or Union Station, take the #124 bus to Navy Pier. The Chicago Transit Authority (www.transitchicago.com) has many other bus lines that reach Navy Pier.

GPS Coordinates: 16 T 449298mE 4637706mN

Information and Contact

There is no fee. Dogs are allowed on leash. There are restrooms in the beach houses and water fountains along the trail. Millennium Park is open daily 6 A.M.–11 P.M. For more information, contact the Chicago Park District, 312/742-7529, www. chicagoparkdistrict.com.

8 WATERFALL GLEN RED TRAIL

Waterfall Glen Forest Preserve, Darien

Level: Moderate

Total Distance: 11.7 miles round-trip

Hiking Time: 6 hours

Elevation Change: 385 feet

Summary: This leisurely walk explores the natural and human-made topography of one of the area's longest continuous trails.

Savanna, oak and hickory woodland, and prairie cover Waterfall Glen Forest Preserve, land shaped years ago by the retreating Wisconsin Glacier. Glaciation left behind ridges and kettle holes, which later became ponds and wetlands. Today the preserve covers nearly 2,500 acres of diverse plant and animal habitat—in fact over 75 percent of DuPage Counties' species are found here. There are few places in Chicagoland with the acreage to allow this kind of exploration. For outdoor lovers, it's an easily accessible playground with enough trails to satisfy a wide range of abilities.

Waterfall Glen is one of my favorite places amongst the close-in natural areas. Runners flock to the trails in springtime and it's popular in winter with snowshoers and cross-country skiers. The vast acreage harbors diverse wildlife, including white-tailed deer and a variety of frogs, turtles, and waterfowl. If you're in the

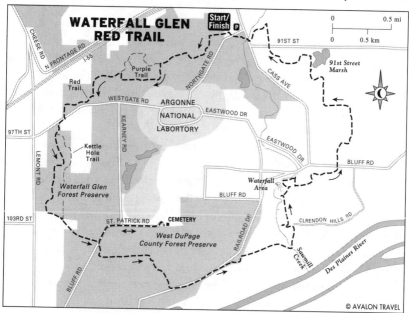

91st Street marsh

woods early in the day, you may spot a barred owl in the upper branches of the trees or perhaps hear the song of the Eastern meadowlark.

The main Red Trail is a wide limestone path that can accommodate bikes and foot traffic. Start on the well-signed main trail, then turn right to head west or counterclockwise. The first mile climbs a little; as you hike, take some time to check out the variety of trees. After about 1 mile, the trail rolls slightly through woodlands and savanna. Watch for cottonwoods in the marshy areas; their leaves produce a lovely rustling sound in the slightest breeze (like their relative, the quaking aspen). I love the mix of bur and black oak, shagbark hickories, and pine plantations in these woodlands. In the 1950s, Argonne Laboratory employees embarked on a huge program of planting pine trees to preserve the rich natural resources surrounding their laboratory.

In 0.44 mile, you'll pass the junction for the Purple Trail; in the spring it's very wet as it goes through Tear-Thumb Marsh. The Red Trail leaves the woods, making a wide arc south past Westgate Road; note the trail marker for the Kettle Hole (brown) Trail at about 2.4 miles. At last visit, I passed a flooded section at 3.4 miles, right at the junction with the south end of the Kettle Hole Trail. The Red Trail goes between two kettle holes, which form a marsh here—there are lots of reeds and cattails. The trail is out in the open for about the next 2.5 miles.

At 3.8 miles, the trail joins Bluff Road for a short distance. Make a 1.5-mile round-trip detour north and east along the gravel road to check out the historic 1849 cemetery at the road's end. Return to the Red Trail and turn left at the interpretive signs for the Poverty Prairie and Savanna. The small, dry prairie isn't as impressive as some tallgrass prairies, yet it still contains important native plants and grasses. Walk through the savanna for about a 0.5 mile as the trail dips southward to the overlook. Here, at nearly 6.2 miles, you can gaze past the I&M Canal and Des Plaines River and imagine what this area might have looked like back in pioneer days.

Take a moment to check out the remnants of the Lincoln Park Nursery on the north side of the trail shortly after passing milepost 5, including a wall and a doorway dating from 1921. Cross Sawmill Creek on a footbridge and turn northward to another human creation—the tiered falls built by the Civilian Conservation Corps more than 80 years ago. After the falls, the trail continues to wind in and out of the woods; look for wood lilies and wild black raspberries, as well as pretty damselflies and dragonflies along the latter part of the trail. The final highlight is the 91st Street marsh at 10.2 mile; check the branches of the trees for great blue heron or great egrets. Follow the Red Trail its final 1.5 miles to return to the start.

Options

For a shorter hike, follow the Red Trail west. At 3.4 miles, you will reach the second Kettle Hole Trail junction. Turn north onto this trail, which may have some standing water in spring. On the east side of the trail are kettle ponds, depressions left by the glacial ice retreat. When you reach the Red Trail again, turn right to return to the start for a 6.5-mile round-trip hike.

Directions

From downtown Chicago, take I-55 S 20.9 miles to Exit 273A for Cass Road. Drive 0.5 mile south and turn west on Northgate Road. Turn north into the Northgate parking lot in about 350 feet. From the parking lot, walk west on a short connector trail to the main loop.

GPS Coordinates: 16 T 419043mE 4619491mN

Information and Contact

There is no fee. Dogs on leash are allowed. The park is open from one hour after sunrise until one hour after sunset. Waterfall Glen has three parking lots; the main lot is on Northgate Road, just west of Cass Road. For more information, contact Forest Preserve District of DuPage County, 3S580 Naperville Road, Wheaton, IL 60189, 630/933-7200, www.dupageforest.com.

🄩 RIDGE RUN–SAG TRAIL LOOP   BEST ☾

Sagawau, Lemont

Level: Easy

Hiking Time: 1.5–2 hours

Total Distance: 2.5 miles round-trip

Elevation Change: negligible

Summary: Visit the only limestone canyon in Cook County and hike amongst its rare plant life.

The Sag Valley Region is one of the true wonders of the Cook County Forest Preserve. The land here, south of the Calumet Saganashkee (Cal-Sag) Channel, was shaped by glaciers more than 10,000 years ago when retreating glacial ice left behind moraines, kettle holes, ravines, and bluffs, creating a wealth of biodiversity in one of the largest preserves in the county. Ponds, marshes, wetlands, woodland, and prairie form a landscape that just begs to be explored. Take a guided hike through the exposed limestone of Sagawau Canyon—or explore three short trails yourself—and learn about the area and its natural history at the stunning Sagawau Environmental Education Center.

Until recently, hikers could only explore the trails of Sagawau on a guided hike. With the 2010 opening of Sagawau Environmental Education Center, the trail system is now accessible for spur-of-the moment activities. The three trails'

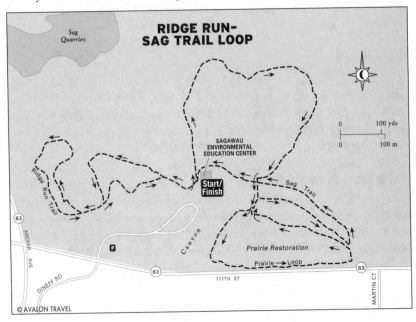

© BARBARA I. BOND

Sagawau Canyon

intertwined loops will give you a flavor for the terrain, flora and fauna, and natural history of the Cal-Sag region. Start with the 0.75-mile Ridge Run Trail, which is really two very short, connected loops. Outside the education center, head west on a mown path, which leads into the woods and to a short loop; keep left at the intersections to continue clockwise. The forest canopy is open and wildflowers such as asters or false Solomon's seal thrive. As you wind through the woods, watch for white-tailed deer. I saw a young buck here early one morning. Return east to the education center and go inside to read the displays or continue hiking the remaining loops.

The combined Sag Trail and Prairie Loop is 1.4 miles. The trail begins behind the education center, in the northwest corner. Follow the 0.5-mile Sag Loop Trail first by walking north along the edge of the trees. The trail curves right into the woods and crosses a wooden footbridge, then two more footbridges, as you work your way around the lowest section of this trail. Circling the huge oaks is a highlight of this trail, particularly as you work your way back on the east end. As you approach a set of intersections, take note of the gigantic old oak trees on the left side of the trail. At 1.3 miles you will reach a four-way trail junction; you'll eventually be returning west on the trail to your left. For now, continue straight and uphill, passing another four-way intersection, and onto the Prairie Loop Trail.

The Prairie Loop Trail begins at a marker stone at 1.3 miles; turn right. It's quite a contrast from the forest to now be walking along prairie grasses and wildflowers. The trail climbs gently as the path goes south, then east along the edge

of the trees, reaching a high point around 1.5 miles. There's an almost impercep-
tible decline as you complete the loop. Time your visit right and this area can be
a sea of purple coneflowers punctuated by orange butterfly milkweed. At 1.64
miles, cross a short boardwalk and keep left at the next two three-way junctions
to complete the Prairie Loop. On the way back to the trailhead, you will pass an
old concrete foundation on the right. Turn right and retrace your steps back into
the woods at around 1.78 miles, turning right again to walk along a joined section
of trail. At 1.95 miles, turn left. In just under 0.25 mile, you will reach a four-way
intersection and then cross a footbridge. If you'd like to try to catch a great blue
heron in action, linger here a moment and gaze upstream. Check out Sagawau
Canyon for a good view of a short cliff band adjacent to a small waterfall. Continue straight on the Sag Trail to return to the start at 2.27 miles.

Options

For an unforgettable hike, visit Sagawau on a weekend and accompany a naturalist
on a free guided tour of the Sagawau Canyon. In less than 0.5 mile, you'll descend
a narrow wooden staircase into the cool, shady dolomite canyon. The hike will be
on bare rock and mostly in the water in order to preserve the fragile plants that
grow here, including five rare species of lichen. Although the canyon is only 1,100
feet long, you'll emerge feeling like you completed a major exploration.

Directions

From the junction of I-294 and I-55, take I-55 S for 2.6 miles. Take Exit 274
for IL 83 S/Kingery Highway and go south for 4.2 miles. Turn left at the light
on 111th Street (also called State Route 83/Cal Sag Road). Turn left again into
the park entrance in 0.1 mile. Park in the main lot and walk up the road to the
main building.
GPS Coordinates: 16 T 422731mE 4615370mN

Information and Contact

There are no fees. Dogs are not allowed. The park is open 9 A.M.–5 P.M. daily.
There is a cross-country skiing program in winter. For more information, contact Sagawau Environmental Learning Center, 12545 West 111th Street, Lemont,
630/257-2045, www.fpdcc.com.

10 PALOS ORANGE TRAIL
Palos Forest Preserve

Level: Moderate

Hiking Time: 3 hours

Total Distance: 6.3 miles round-trip

Elevation Change: 395 feet

Summary: This short and fun hike winds along rolling hills and past the historic site of the original Argonne reactor.

The Palos region is known for its rolling terrain and miles of trails. The Palos Orange Trail upholds that reputation with its many twists and turns across short, steep ravines. Although you are hiking in one of the busiest preserves in Cook County, it feels very remote; you'll hardly see another hiker. Mountain biking is popular, however, so if you do not want to share the trail, go early in the day or wait for a light rain or snowfall.

The Palos Orange Trail begins on the east side of Wolf Road, adjacent to the easternmost parking spots. Cross Wolf Road and turn south at the orange post. You will pass post 13 in about 0.2 mile (this is where you return to the Orange Trail). Note the footpath on the east side of the trail just before it turns west; there are some tall oaks creating a nice canopy with a tangle of smaller ash and walnut, some covered with long, thick vines. Near mile 0.9, pass an old foundation and

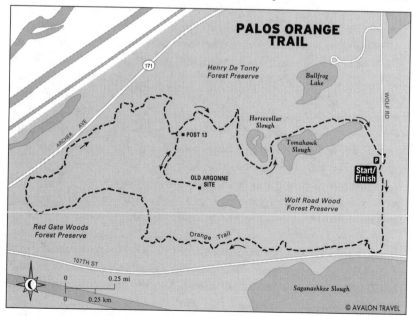

Tomahawk Slough

cross a wooden footbridge. You will pass post 17, marking a short trail heading north. The next 0.7 mile has some ups and downs as it crosses several ravines before reaching the high point around 1.65 miles. Continue west along the rolling terrain, passing two more numbered trail junctions and another footpath.

The trail curves northward toward Archer Avenue around 2.5 miles. The next mile is one of the lowest sections of the trail; start uphill again just before the junction with the Old Preserve Road at 3.7 miles. Turn south to walk the 0.6-mile crumbling blacktop to the site of the original Argonne Labs, home of the world's first nuclear reactor. The lab moved to its present location in the late 1940s; a plaque now marks the old site. Along the way, enjoy the beautiful grassland and savanna; you may see some gray-headed coneflower or black-eyed Susans. An engraved boulder marks the historic site at 4.3 miles.

Retrace your steps and at post 13, turn north to return to the Orange Trail. At 5.1 miles, you'll reach intersection (post) 12 and turn south on a now-wide limestone path. There are some big maples, white oaks, and cottonwoods as you weave around Horsecollar, then Tomahawk Slough. At 5.6 miles, a nice view of Tomahawk Slough opens up just east of the trail. After being in the woods for most of this hike, the sloughs are breathtaking. Pass a gigantic white oak as you walk the last 0.5 mile. At post 19, the trail is joined for a short section with the Brown Trail. When you reach Wolf Road, turn south to return to the parking lots.

Options

For an all-day hike, combine the Orange Trail with the Yellow Trail (see listing in this chapter). Instead of returning to your car, continue across the road to post 18 to reach the Yellow Trail trailhead. The combined hiking distance will be about 14.6 miles.

Directions

From downtown Chicago, take I-55 S for 14.2 miles. Take the exit for U.S. 12/S. La Grange Road and drive south 1.9 miles. Exit onto State Route 171 S/ Archer Avenue and drive 3.1 miles. Make a slight left onto 95th Street for 0.2 mile, then turn right onto Wolf Road. Drive south 0.8 mile on Wolf Road to the last parking lot for Wolf Road Woods; park near the east end of the lot. From the parking area, walk east across Wolf Road and turn right onto the Orange Trail, heading south.

GPS Coordinates: 16 T 425548mE 4617083mN

Information and Contact

There is no fee. Dogs on leash are allowed. The park is open sunrise–sunset daily. Maps are available for download from Chicago Area Mountain Bikers (cambr. org/SMF/index.php?topic=359.0). Call to request the "Explorer's Packet" from the Cook County Forest Preserve District, which contains all the regional maps; Palos is Region 6. The map is sufficient for driving to the trailheads and keeping track of your location on any major trail. Footpaths, marked by reddish-orange posts, are not listed, although some show up on Google maps. For more information, contact Wolf Road Woods, Wolf Road/95th Street, Willow Springs, 800/870-3666, www.fpdcc.com.

11 PALOS YELLOW TRAIL
Palos Preserve, Willow Springs

Level: Moderate   **Total Distance:** 8.5 miles round-trip

Hiking Time: 4-4.5 hours   **Elevation Change:** 420 feet

Summary: Enjoy the wooded, rolling terrain of this premier nature preserve.

The triangle of land between the Des Plaines River and the Cal-Sag Valley was formed during the Wisconsin period of glaciation and was at the west border of ancient Lake Chicago. This highland was historically called Mount Forest Island and continues to contribute rich biodiversity to the region. The Palos Forest Preserve contains two nature preserves with lakes, forests, sloughs, and more than 25 miles of trails. It is one of the few places in this heavily populated region where hikers can get out on the trail for hours with little interference from the outside world.

The Palos Yellow Trail is a wonderful introduction to this preserve. Hiking it will take you through oak and hickory woods, past countless sloughs and ponds, and around the Cranberry Slough Nature Preserve. Highlights include a quaking bog and wildlife such as beaver and muskrat. You may see snakes or frogs near

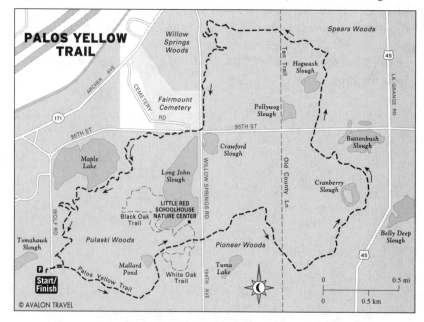

north of Saganashkee Slough

Cranberry Slough, and be sure to listen for the tapping of red-bellied or downy woodpeckers in the woods.

The Yellow Trail winds through beautiful oak and hickory woods for most of its 8.5 miles. There are some oak openings, a patch or two of prairie, and, of course, wetlands and sloughs—but this is a heavily forested preserve. The Yellow Trail begins at post 1 and heads east into the trees, rolling toward the junction with the Little Red Schoolhouse Nature Center trails at 1.39 miles. Cross Willow Springs Road and continue eastward, past the Old Country Lane at 2 miles. The trail begins an arc around Cranberry Slough and at around 2.9 miles there are some nice views of the open water to the west; you may hear some frogs along here. You are now traveling north and the trail features some oak openings. Cross 95th Avenue at 3.7 miles. The trail begins turning westward and at 4.5 miles the most rugged section begins.

The trail heads west for about a mile, beginning a series of hairpin curves as it winds around deep ravines and creek beds south to the 95th Street/S. Willow Springs Road intersection at 6.15 miles. Head south, then west, following 95th Street west a short distance. Return to the woods at mile 6.3. The trail will be obvious; as you re-enter the woods, a huge shagbark hickory seems to stand sentinel. Continue into the dense black oak, hickory, and maple woods.

The trail descends past Maple Lake with nice views across an opening at nearly 7 miles. The trail then heads west for a short distance, zigzags over a rolling section, and finishes south and uphill at starting post 1 in 8.4 miles. Turn west and walk the remaining 0.1 mile on the Tan Trail to return to the start.

Options
Turn this into an all-day hike by combining the Yellow Trail with the Palos Orange Trail. Instead of returning to your car, turn south off the Tan Trail and onto the Orange Trail for a total distance of about 14.6 miles.

Directions
From downtown Chicago, take I-55 S for 14.2 miles. Take the exit for U.S. 12/S. La Grange Road and drive south 1.9 miles. Exit onto State Route 171 S/Archer Avenue and drive 3.1 miles. Make a slight left onto 95th Street for 0.2 mile, then turn right onto Wolf Road. Drive south 0.8 mile on Wolf Road to the last lot for Wolf Road Woods; park near the east end of the lot. From the parking area, walk east across Wolf Road onto the trail marked with a tan post. Continue a short distance east to a post number 1 with a yellow arrow. This is the trailhead for the Yellow Trail loop.
GPS Coordinates: 16 T 425548mE 4617083mN

Information and Contact
There is no fee. Dogs on leash are allowed. The park is open sunrise–sunset daily. Maps are available for download from Chicago Area Mountain Bikers (cambr. org/SMF/index.php?topic=359.0). Call to request the "Explorer's Packet" from the Cook County Forest Preserve District, which contains all the regional maps; Palos is Region 6. The map is sufficient for driving to the trailheads and keeping track of your location on any major trail. Footpaths, marked by reddish-orange posts, are not listed although some show up on Google maps. For more information, contact Wolf Road Woods, Wolf Road/95th Street, Willow Springs, 800/870-3666, www.fpdcc.com.

12 BLACK OAK–WHITE OAK NATURE TRAILS

BEST ◖

Little Red Schoolhouse Nature Center, Palos Preserve

🦌 ✈️ 🧭 👫

Level: Easy

Total Distance: 2.5 miles round-trip

Hiking Time: 1 hour

Elevation Change: negligible

Summary: A wonderful introduction to the unique flora and fauna of the Palos region.

The Palos region is home to the Little Red Schoolhouse Nature Center. Palos, a nearly 7,000-acre wedge of land, is bounded on the northwest by the Des Plaines River, Chicago Sanitary and Ship Canal, and I&M Canal; and on the south by the Calumet Sag Channel. Glacial retreat left behind the highlands of the Valparaiso moraine and scattered ice that resulted in the ponds, lakes, and sloughs that dot the landscape today. As early as 1886, area farmers sent their children to the tiny one-room schoolhouse. After the building was moved in 1932, times changed and the schoolhouse was closed. The Forest Preserve purchased the schoolhouse and moved it to its current location in 1952. In 1955, the Preserve opened the restored schoolhouse as a nature center. The Little Red Schoolhouse is iconic for generations of area residents who have come here to learn about nature, wildlife,

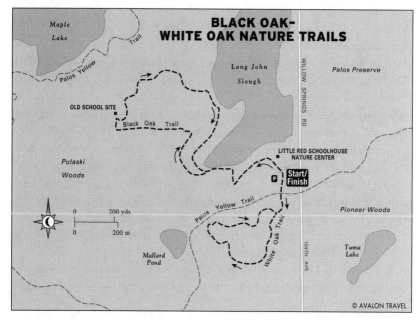

BLACK OAK–
WHITE OAK NATURE TRAILS

© BARBARA I. BOND

Long John Slough

and the human history of the region. Today, the Little Red Schoolhouse Nature Center educates around 500,000 visitors annually. A 17,000-square-foot education center opened in July 2010, and will be the focal point for programs for years to come. Exploring the nature trails around the center provides hikers of all ages an opportunity to learn more about the natural history of the area.

Two beautiful nature trail loops start adjacent to the center. The Black Oak Trail leaves the nature center to head along the south shore of Long John Slough. Bird blinds are set up for waterfowl viewing and there can be a lot to see. Watch for the occasional sandhill crane in spring and a host of great blue heron. In the evening, you may even catch the black-crowned night-heron. As the trail curves south away from the slough, turn right and cross an open area. At the main forest loop, go clockwise (of course, you can go either direction). The trail travels west into an oak and hickory forest. Although this land has been restored, the woods still feel wild and natural. Leaves and woodland plants cover the forest floor and the air is filled with birdsong. I've spotted a rose-breasted grosbeak, nuthatch, and several woodpeckers, as well as butterflies in early summer. Note the deer exclosure at 1.2 miles, a fenced site to keep out the white-tailed deer. The local naturalists are studying the growth inside the enclosure to learn more about the impact of the deer's grazing habits.

Follow the trail past the old school site as it snakes its way north, then turns east toward Long John Slough. In 1 mile, you will reach the west shore of the slough. Walk south a short distance before returning to the beginning of the loop and retracing your steps back to the nature center.

The White Oak Trail is just 1 mile long and has its trailhead south of the nature center. From the trailhead, walk south and in less than 0.2 mile you will reach the start of the loop section of trail. Enjoy hiking among the oak forest, noting the light-gray bark and rounded leaves of the state tree—white oak. It's a contrast to the very dark bark of the older black oaks with their pointy leaves.

Options

The Little Red Schoolhouse Nature Center is centrally located in the Palos region with access to the Palos Yellow Trail (see listing in this chapter), an irregular oval loop about 7 miles long. The Yellow Trail follows a rolling path around numerous sloughs and through the Pioneer Woods and restored savanna of Spears Woods. The forest preserve trails are well marked, with color-coded posts at major intersections, inviting hikers to further explore. To connect to the Yellow Trail, follow the White Oak Trail a short distance and turn east at the trail junction to start the loop.

Directions

From downtown Chicago, take I-55 S for 14.2 miles. Take the exit for U.S. 12/S. La Grange Road and drive south 3.9 miles. Turn west on 95th Street for 1.2 miles, then turn south on 104th Avenue/S. Willow Springs Road. The nature center entrance will be on the west side of the road in 0.3 mile. From the parking lot, walk north to the nature center. The trailheads are signed and are located adjacent to the nature center.

GPS Coordinates: 16 T 427014mE 4617571mN

Information and Contact

There are no fees. Dogs are not allowed. The park is open seasonally; summer hours are 8 A.M.–5 P.M. daily. The nature center is open year-round. There is an online map of the region with all color-coded trails, picnic areas, restrooms, and parking areas. For more information, contact Little Red Schoolhouse Nature Center, 9800 Willow Springs Road, Willow Springs, 708/839-6897, www.fpdcc.com.

13 SAG VALLEY YELLOW TRAIL

Sag Valley Preserve, Palos Park

Level: Moderate

Hiking Time: 4.5 hours

Total Distance: 8.9 miles round-trip

Elevation Change: 430 feet

Summary: Hike the rolling Sag Valley Yellow Trail to see old-growth trees and a historic toboggan run built into Swallow Cliff.

The Sag Valley Region has more than 8,500 acres spread over the rugged terrain south of the Calumet Sag Channel. Here you will find 90-foot cliffs, deep ravines, and mature woods with unique geologic features. The 1,520-acre Cap Sauer's Holdings is one of the largest roadless areas in this region and it is bisected by an esker—a thin ribbon of glacial rock deposited 10,000 years ago. Called the Visitation Esker, it is considered one of the finest examples of this glacial feature in northeastern Illinois.

If you are accustomed to the nearly flat terrain covering much of Chicagoland, Sag Valley trails will surprise and delight you. These trails, with the deep quiet of the woods, somehow feel wilder than other natural areas in the region. Forest blooms include trillium, may apples, solomon's seal, and other shade-loving wildflowers. Hikers have nearly endless opportunities for bird-watching; in fact over 300 bird species have been seen here. Sag Valley is also home to red fox, gray squirrel, and white-tailed deer.

Begin this hike by walking south from the Swallow Cliff Woods parking lot to climb up the 125 steps of North Swallow Cliff. After catching your breath, walk

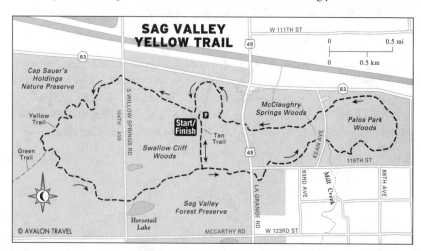

the deep, quiet woods along the Sag Valley Yellow Trail

through an old toboggan slide and check out the views north across the Cal-Sag Valley. From the top of the stairs, turn left then right on a short connector trail that leads 0.4 mile south to a trail junction with the Yellow Trail. Turn east onto the Yellow Trail and weave in and out of the trees for the next mile, crossing upper La Grange Road to Forty Acres Woods then zigzagging across the south end of McClaughry Springs Woods. At 1.6 miles, a footbridge leads across Mill Creek and the trail winds through quiet Palos Park Woods and curves west. Huge oaks attract a variety of birds; watch for the distinctive red-headed woodpecker. At 3.4 miles, cross Mill Creek once more and head west through maple woods along the base of the cliffs. At 4.3 miles, you will reach Swallow Cliff Woods. Follow the Yellow Trail as it loops around the lot, continuing west in about 0.5 mile.

Enjoy the maple, basswood, and hickory forest as the trail rolls along the base of the cliffs. At 5.5 miles, climb across a ravine as the trail turns southward. In the next mile or so you will find yourself in the quiet zone along the Cap Sauer's Preserve. Cross a footbridge, then pass a junction with the Green Trail at around 6.7 miles.

Continue southeast along the Yellow Trail, popping out of the woods at around 7.5 miles as the trail levels off for a mile. Enjoy the huge black oaks before descending to an intersection with the Tan/Brown Trail at nearly 8.5 miles. Turn northward to retrace your steps to the top of the toboggan and Swallow Cliff. As you hit the top of the steps at nearly 8.9 miles, descend to the bottom again to return to the start of the hike.

Options

You can split this hike into a short loop using the Tan Trail. From the North Swallow Cliff trailhead, choose either the east or west loop. The east loop is about 4.3 miles with 235 feet of elevation change; the west loop is about 4.5 miles with 200 feet of elevation change.

You can also check out the Esker Trail, which goes through the middle of the Cap Sauer's Holdings Nature Preserve and is surrounded in local mystique. From the prairie restoration sign along Calumet Sag Road, follow the windy and somewhat overgrown 1.25-mile trail as it climbs onto—then along—the narrow Visitation Esker. This is one of the most remote places in Cook County—take a moment and savor the quiet. The south end of the Esker Trail ends at the Green Trail. Turn left to continue eastward on the Green Trail, then head north on the Yellow Trail to the trailhead at Teasons Woods. Alternatively, go north on 104th Avenue just prior to Teasons Woods, then west along 111th Street (Calumet Sag Road) to return to your car.

Directions

From downtown Chicago, take I-55 S for 14.8 miles. Take Exit 279A for La Grange Road and drive south 6.4 miles. Turn west on IL-83/Calumet Sag Road and drive 0.3 mile to the entrance to Swallow Cliff Woods–North, on the south side of the road. Park and walk south to the base of the steps.

Public Transportation: Take Metra's SouthWest Service from Chicago's Union Station to the Palos Park stop. To pick up the W. 119th Street trail junction in 2.3 miles, walk northeast on 82nd Street. Turn left on W. 121st Street then right onto IL-7N before turning left again on S. Timberland Drive. Turn left onto W. 119th Street and walk 1.3 miles west to catch the trail on the north side of the street.
GPS Coordinates: 16 T 428264mE 4614711mN

Information and Contact

There is no fee. Dogs on leash are allowed, except in the nature preserve. The park is open sunrise–sunset daily. For more information, contact North Swallow Cliff Woods, Calumet Sag Road (0.4 mile west of La Grange Road), Palos Park, 800/870-3666, www.fpdcc.com.

14 LAKE KATHERINE TRAILS BEST ◖

Lake Katherine Nature Center and Botanic Gardens, Palos Heights

Level: Easy

Hiking Time: 1.5-2 hours

Total Distance: 3.75 miles round-trip

Elevation Change: negligible

Summary: Hike along lakeside and old canoepath trails to soak in the riches of the preserve's scenic beauty.

Nestled in south-suburban Palos Heights is place of surprising natural beauty and calm. It wasn't always so for this 20-acre wedge of land south of the Calumet-Saganaskee Channel. Decades ago it was a local dumping ground and generally neglected. In the 1980s, a Palos Heights mayor had a vision for the future of this site—one that was about environmental stewardship and outdoor education. Thus began a multi-decade transition to the preserve that exists today. The Lake Katherine Nature Center and Botanic Gardens provide a quiet setting for outdoor recreation and education.

Start your hike north across the bridge, heading toward the clubhouse and learning center. The wide and inviting path is well graded as it works north past the buildings, curving west to follow the lakeshore. Note the dugout canoe to the left near the shore; on the right are the Herb and Butterfly Gardens. A walk along the short paths around these pretty little gardens is a pleasant diversion, particularly in summer when butterflies are active. Watch for question mark, monarch, tiger swallowtail, red admiral, and great spangled fritillary. As the trail works west, glance to the right to catch a glimpse of the Cal-Sag Channel. You will quickly

© BARBARA I. BOND

lake view from the clubhouse

reach a short spur trail that goes to the canal overlook; walk the short path north to the edge of the water. The views across the channel take in a boat launch and dock, while the rest of the shore is thick with trees and shrubs.

Return to the main path, heading west to a Y intersection. (A left turn here offers a diversion along the lakeshore for a short, open section.) In 0.5 mile you will reach a short loop at the west end of the lake, which includes the Children's Forest and Birder's Trail. At a three-way intersection, continue ahead and follow a short loop path, making two left turns until you reach a footbridge. Cross the bridge and continue back towards the lake and main path. Along the way, enjoy the multitude of trees in this tiny forest. Volunteers have been working to turn this into a native plant restoration area. Turn left at the Lake Katherine Trail and walk a few yards to the Palos School House Arch. This bit of historic architecture was salvaged from the 1941 Palos School and moved here to preserve a bit of city history.

Return to the main path, enjoying the variety of trees as you head east back to the clubhouse. The remaining 0.5 mile features multiple spots with benches for lake views and quiet reflection. Quaking aspens, maples, and conifers mark this pleasant path (some of the trees have identification tags and offer a great educational opportunity for kids). At 1.3 miles, you'll pass the bridge where you began this hike—continue east. The wood-chip path passes the pretty waterfall gardens and the entry gate to the conifer garden. Turn left on the paved path for a short distance, then right along the channel towards the eastern preserve. Cross under

Harlem Avenue at 1.6 miles to enter the remote Eastern Preserve. As you emerge from the underpass, the manicured preserve fades and the trail enters a more overgrown natural area. This is the Old Canoepath Trail. For the next mile you'll be hiking along the channel; there are lots of butterflies and cicadas, and the trail is muddy and rougher than the lakeshore path. Keep left at any trail junctions and as you near the end of the trail, look for a fire ring and some benches. Just off the trail's end is an overlook and bench.

The path makes a shallow turn south, then west, onto the Overlook Trail. This 1-mile path climbs slightly, leading to a gazebo at mile 2.7; the gazebo provides a great viewpoint. The path narrows more past the gazebo, passing through a burned area as it heads steeply downhill to a footbridge across the creek. At 3.2 miles, make a quick right then a left. This returns you to the footpath heading west back to the preserve. At 3.5 miles, cross back under Harlem Avenue. Just before the underpass, check out the views north of the spillway and channel—it's a pretty sight. When you reach the prairie restoration and farm implements, take a moment to enjoy the garden paths. When done, it's just a scant 0.2 mile or so back to the start.

Options

Shorten this hike to spend more time in the pretty gardens. Start and end at the clubhouse, walking the lakeshore loop for a 1-mile hike. Then spend the rest of the day enjoying the lovely gardens.

Directions

From downtown Chicago, take I-55 S for 24.5 miles to the exit for U.S. 45/La Grange Road S. Drive south on U.S. 45/La Grange Road for 6.4 miles to the State Route 83 exit. Turn right at the light and drive 3 miles east to Lake Katherine Drive/S. 75th Avenue. Turn east at the T and continue 0.2 mile to the preserve. Park on the north or south side of the dead-end road.
GPS Coordinates: 16 T 433350mE 4613985mN

Information and Contact

There are no fees, however there is a donation box outside the clubhouse. Dogs on leash are allowed. The park is open sunrise–sunset daily. For more information, contact Lake Katherine Nature Preserve, 7402 W. Lake Katherine Drive, Palos Heights, 708/361-1873, www.lakekatherine.org.

15 LOST BEACH-DOGWOOD LOOP
Sand Ridge Nature Center, South Holland

Level: Easy

Total Distance: 3.5 miles round-trip

Hiking Time: 1.5 hours

Elevation Change: negligible

Summary: Sand Ridge Nature Center offers hikers a glimpse of a landscape altered by glacial Lake Chicago.

Shabbona Woods Forest Preserve is home to the Sand Ridge Nature Center. Over 10,000 years ago, melting ice created Lake Chicago, which flowed over much of Cook County. When the waters receded eastward, a low, sandy ridge was left behind. Native Americans used the ridge as a travel path, and pioneers built their cabins on the slight rise to keep them out of the swampy surroundings. Today the slightly elevated ground provides habitat for a variety of unique plant life. The 235-acre Sand Ridge Nature Center includes cabins and other pioneer buildings that introduce visitors to this settlement history. Many trees have nameplates so that explorers young and old can become more familiar with native woods. In spring, the woodlands erupt in wildflowers.

From the nature center, walk north past the gardens and pioneer settlement. After passing a sign for the Redwing Trail, turn northeast onto the short loop. The black oak woods contain many mature trees, and ferns line the trail, as do a thick understory layer of shrubs. Catch views of pretty Redwing Pond through the trees—you might spot some ducks, heron, or egrets on the water. (A belted kingfisher flew by when I last walked this trail.) At the boardwalk, turn north onto Lost Beach Trail. Willows, cottonwoods, maple, and swamp oak populate these wetlands, as do lots of brown frogs. In fall, colorful orange and yellow leaves litter the water's surface. Go through a gate and cross a section of grassland filled with lots of prairie sunflowers. Turn right in about 0.9 mile and onto the loop.

This 1-mile loop winds along an ancient sandy ridge and through a diverse collection of catalpa, shagbark hickory, aspens, and honey-locust trees. There are tons of birds—at least three species of woodpecker—and bright-yellow sulphur

A boardwalk sign signals the Lost Beach Trail.

mushrooms growing on the deadwood. Finish the loop, returning to the Redwing Trail junction at 2.2 miles, and keep right. Go south to pass through the settlement on the way to the Pines and Dogwood Trails. Follow the signed Pines Trail, turning southeast at 2.4 miles. As you walk past this patch of prairie, you may see goldfinches and common yellowthroat flying about. The east half of the loop travels through the trees; keep left at the trail junction to continue south along the Dogwood Trail at 2.5 miles.

A boardwalk crosses the wetlands along the east side of the loop and an observation platform offers views west across the water. After the boardwalk ends, the trail continues east, then south, through tall black oaks. There is a lot of deadfall in these woods, some of it covered in mushrooms or ferns. At 3 miles, look for an opening with prairie flowers and grasses. Watch for blue jays or northern flickers as the trail curves north, passing a bench, then another open area. At 3.4 miles turn left, passing through the gate, and finish up the remainder of the hike on the Pines Trail. Return to the nature center at nearly 3.6 miles.

Options

Visit the Sauk Trail Woods Black Trail to hike the 3.5-mile lake loop (see listing in this chapter). This long trail winds through black and bur oak, hickory, and black cherry woods, along deep ravines and across a creek.

Directions

From the junction of I-55 and I-94 in Chicago, drive 19.1 miles on I-94 E. Take Exit 73B and merge onto U.S. 6 E/159th St./E. 162nd Street. Follow U.S. 6 E./159th Street east for 1.1 miles. Turn north on Paxton Avenue and drive 0.4 mile to the preserve entrance on the east side of the road. Walk east to the Nature Center from the parking lot.

GPS Coordinates: 16 T 452727mE 4605930mN

Information and Contact

There is no fee. Dogs are not allowed. The parking lot and trails are open 8 A.M.–5 P.M. Monday–Friday and 8 A.M.–5:30 P.M. Saturday–Sunday March–October. For more information, contact Sand Ridge Nature Center, 15891 Paxton Avenue, South Holland, 708/868-0606, www.fpdcc.com.

16 SAUK TRAIL WOODS BLACK TRAIL

Sauk Trail Woods, Chicago Heights

Level: Easy

Hiking Time: 1.5 hours

Total Distance: 3.5 miles round-trip

Elevation Change: 95 feet

Summary: Take a peaceful walk through the dense woods around Sauk Trail Lake.

Sauk Trail originally was a deep, narrow footpath Native Americans used to travel across Illinois through Indiana and Southern Michigan. In time, the path became a route for explorers and traders. By the time settlers arrived on horseback, the path had become a road, one that is still in use today. Sauk Trail Road runs through this small wooded preserve. The watershed is part of the Thorn Creek sub-basin of southeast Cook County, and is a valuable natural resource in this heavily developed

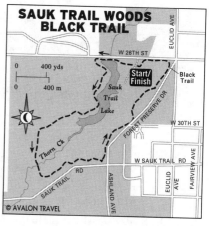

urban region. Thorn Creek runs northeast through the preserve to the confluence with Little Calumet River. Songbirds, small animals, black and white oak, deep ravines, and the blue water of Sauk Trail Lake make this small preserve a good place to enjoy nature while walking the quiet path.

The Black Trail crosses the park entrance road. From the path, walk west into the woods towards the tall black oaks. The trail descends across an earthen dam at the north end of Sauk Trail Lake, then gently ascends as the path curves south. A thick canopy of black cherry, black and white oak, and hickory shades the trail while cicadas and frogs pepper the air with their song. As the trail curves 1 mile along the western lakeshore and across the rolling terrain, an impressive collection of huge oak trees appear at 1.2 miles, just before a power line right-of-way.

At 1.4 miles is the junction with the Tan Trail. Continue south and downhill to the bridge crossing of Thorn Creek in 0.2 mile. The trail levels out here, turning north, and is lined with trees bearing thick vines clinging to their trunks. Zip up your jacket for this windy section, as the trail passes ravine after ravine along the north side. Milepost 3 appears at 2.2 miles and the trail passes between two huge bur oaks before exiting the woods to cross the road at Sauk Trail Woods South.

Sauk Trail Lake

The trail passes under power lines and along some grasses before continuing into the woods at 2.7 miles.

Near the finish, you'll pass some more deep ravines before turning west to reach the parking lot at 3.5 miles.

Options

Just north of Sauk Trail Woods is the Sand Ridge Nature Center (see listing for Lost Beach-Dogwood Loop in this chapter). The nature center has exhibits, three short loop trails, gardens, and a settlement re-creation. To reach Sand Ridge Nature Center, drive east on W. 26th Street for 1.2 miles and turn north on Chicago Road. Drive one mile, turning right at U.S. 30 E/E 14th St. Follow U.S. 30 for 3.3 miles. Merge onto State Route 394 north at the Chicago ramp and drive for 1.9 miles. Take Exit 73B and merge onto U.S. 6E/159th St./E 162nd St. Drive 0.9 mile east on U.S. 6 E/159th Street. Turn north on Paxton Avenue; the preserve road will be on the east side of the street in 0.3 mile.

Directions

From Chicago, take I-94 E. Exit toward State Route 394 S and drive south for 5 miles. At the split, keep right on SR 394 S, just before the Illinois Tollway junction. Exit onto U.S. 30 W/14th Street and drive west for 3.5 miles. Turn south at Chicago Road, drive for 1 mile, then turn west on W. 26th Street. Drive 0.6 mile before turning south into the Sauk Trail Woods North parking lot.
GPS Coordinates: 16 T 445654mE 4593188mN

Information and Contact

There is no fee. Dogs on leash are allowed. The preserve is open sunrise–sunset daily. Restrooms, water, and a picnic shelter are available at the north lot and along the trail at other picnic groves. For more information, contact Sauk Trail Woods, W. 26th Street (west of Euclid Avenue), Chicago Heights, 800/870-3666, www.fpdcc.com.

CHICAGOLAND NORTH

© BARBARA I. BOND

BEST HIKES

North of Chicago, and extending into southeast

Wisconsin, is a swatch of land where sandhill cranes nest, hundreds of bird species thrive, and a diverse collection of natural landscapes create an outdoor playland. In Wisconsin, enthusiastic hikers can visit state forests and recreation areas with miles of trails. The pine plantations, oak-hickory forest, and rolling terrain of the Kettle Moraine State Forest's Southern Unit invite hiking, mountain biking, and cross-country skiing. Like much of the Chicago region, this year-round destination was shaped by glaciation. Over 10,000 years ago, after years of advance and retreat, the Lake Michigan Lobe of the Wisconsin Glacier made its final retreat. What remained are the features that we appreciate today — small hills called kames, moraines, and kettles.

The Ice Age Trail follows these formations and wanders through Kettle Moraine for about 100 miles. This trail offers an opportunity for long hikes along some more rugged sections of the forest, and also serves as a great example of the result of cooperation between managing agencies and a dedicated group of volunteers. Further south is the Richard Bong State Recreation Area, a more recently conserved area in Wisconsin. Full of wetlands, prairie, oak forest, and oak savanna, the 4,515 acres have a well-developed trail system. Hikers can experience the unique ecology of the area, evident in the abundant birds, butterflies, and wildflowers along the trails.

The northeast corner of Illinois, along Lake Michigan, is where ancient Lake Chicago receded, leaving sand dunes and wetlands. Illinois Beach State Park has two separate and distinct units, each with several types of habitat and rich natural diversity. The south unit has dune and swale topography, and a trail along the Dead River and across sand prairie. The park is home to the only sand ridge left along the Illinois shore and is an important birding site with a nationally recognized hawk-count program. It's quite a contrast to walk along the marsh-like river, then cross the dunes to the expanse of open water that is the Lake Michigan shore.

Lake County has wetlands, ponds, rolling terrain, and lakes – lots of lakes! The Lake County Forest Preserve system has a long history of acquisition, resulting in a rich collection of popular and diverse parks. At Van Patten Woods Forest Preserve, you can hike amongst soaring old oaks and see sandhill cranes. The beautiful flowers along the shore of the preserve's Sterling Lake belie its past as an old gravel pit. Lake County is also home to the Ryerson Conservation Area, another premier natural site and home to a rare forest of northern flatwoods – one of the few remaining in the state.

To the west, Chain O' Lakes State Park abuts three lakes and is connected via the Fox River to a "chain" of seven lakes. The park and adjacent conservation area provide over 5,000 acres of plant, animal, and bird habitat to hundreds of species. The rolling terrain has plenty of oak savanna and grassland, which provides hikers with beautiful views from along the trail, and you may see white-tailed deer, fox, beaver, or badger.

Nearby Volo Bog State Natural Area contains a "quaking" bog, tamarack forest, and wetlands. Thousands of years ago, Volo Bog was a 50-acre lake, slowly being filled in by vegetation. Only a small portion of open water remains, and it is shrinking annually as the surrounding plant life continues its march inwards. The 1,000 acres of land that constitute the state natural area include two nature preserves, an interpretive center, and several miles of trails. Volo provides an unusual hiking experience along a series of boardwalks through the bog succession zones, where one can view oddities like the carnivorous pitcher plant.

Hiking the diverse collection of trails in the lands north of Chicago means that one may never want for variety. Between the rugged Ice Age Trail, the trails of Kettle Moraine, and the nearby preserve trails of Lake County, there is a lot of exploring to be done.

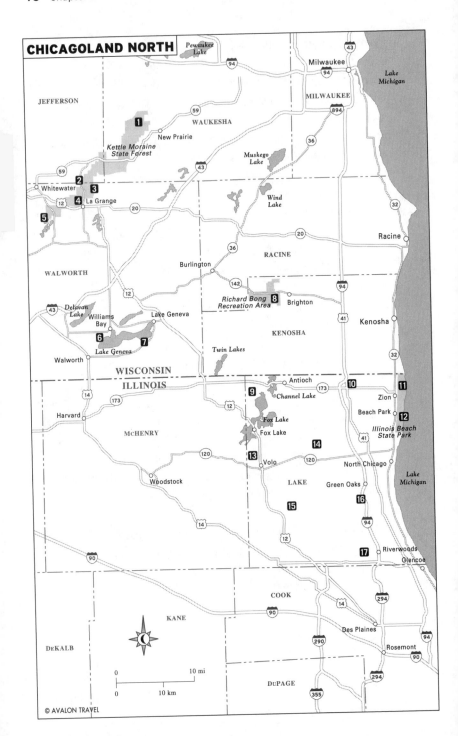

CHICAGOLAND NORTH

© AVALON TRAVEL

TRAIL NAME	LEVEL	DISTANCE	TIME	ELEVATION	FEATURES	PAGE
1 Scuppernong Green Trail	Moderate	5.4 mi rt	3 hr	270 ft		80
2 Ice Age Trail: Carlin to Bald Bluff	Strenuous	14.1 mi rt	7-8 hr	1,450 ft		83
3 Nordic Blue Trail	Moderate	9.0 mi rt	4.5-5 hr	535 ft		86
4 Muir Blue Trail	Moderate	12.0 mi rt	6-7 hr	640 ft		90
5 Ice Age Trail: Lake La Grange to Rice Lake	Strenuous	13.5 mi rt	6.5-7 hr	1,040 ft		94
6 Geneva Lake Shore Path: Lake Geneva to Fontana	Moderate	10.4 mi one-way	5-6 hr	negligible		97
7 Geneva Lake Shore Path: Fontana to Lake Geneva	Moderate	11.0 mi one-way	5-6 hr	negligible		100
8 Wolf Lake Trail	Easy	4.5 mi rt	2 hr	125 ft		103
9 Badger-Goldfinch Trail Loop	Easy	3.4 mi rt	1.5 hr	negligible		106
10 Des Plaines River Trail	Easy/moderate	5.2 mi rt	2.5 hr	negligible		110
11 Camp Logan Trails	Easy/moderate	5.7 mi rt	3 hr	negligible		114
12 Dead River-Dunes Loop	Easy	3.5 mi rt	1.5 hr	negligible		118
13 Prairie Ridge: Deer Path-Tamarack View	Easy	5.5 mi rt	2.5-3 hr	negligible		121
14 Rollins Savanna Trails	Easy/moderate	5.7 mi rt	2.5-3 hr	negligible		125
15 Millennium-Fort Hill Trails	Easy/moderate	6.1 mi rt	3 hr	160 ft		128
16 Old School Forest Preserve Trails	Easy	5.6 mi rt	2.5-3 hr	negligible		132
17 Ryerson Woods	Easy	5.0 mi rt	2-2.5 hr	negligible		135

1 SCUPPERNONG GREEN TRAIL

Kettle Moraine State Forest, Southern Unit, Wisconsin

Level: Moderate

Hiking Time: 3 hours

Total Distance: 5.4 miles round-trip

Elevation Change: 270 feet

Summary: Hike through tall mixed pines and white and bur oak forest to a lovely viewpoint.

Kettle Moraine State Forest (Southern Unit) has over 20,000 acres of dense woods, oak savanna, prairie, and wetlands. The rolling terrain is a hint of the glacial past of the area. Over 10,000 years ago, after thousands of years of advance and retreat, the Lake Michigan Lobe of the Wisconsin Glacier left for good. In its wake there remained ribbons of gravelly rock called eskers, hilly moraines, and kettle depressions. Today outdoors enthusiasts of all kinds flock to the trails of KMSF for hiking, mountain biking, and cross-country skiing. The forest has dedicated trail systems for hiking and numerous other mixed-use trails. Long and short, rugged and tame, hilly and flat, Kettle Moraine has a trail for you.

In the northern part of the unit is the Scuppernong Trail system. The hiking and ski trail has miles of trails that wind through large pine plantations, and some oak and hickory woods interspersed with oak savanna. The Scuppernong Trails also offer several access points to the Ice Age National Scenic Trail. In

mixed oak and hickory woods along Scuppernong Green Trail

© BARBARA I. BOND

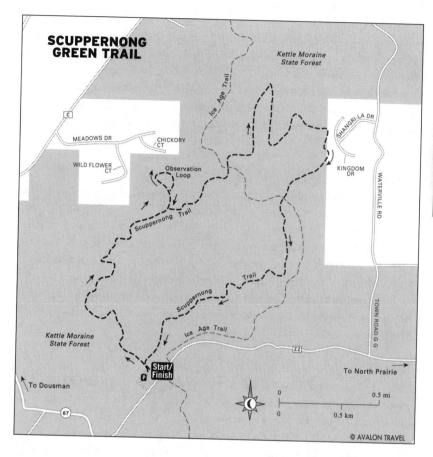

SCUPPERNONG
GREEN TRAIL

Kettle Moraine
State Forest

Ice Age Trail

MEADOWS DR

CHICKORY
CT

WILD FLOWER
CT

Observation
Loop

Scuppernong Trail

SHANGRI-LA DR

KINGDOM
DR

WATERVILLE RD

Scuppernong

Trail

Kettle Moraine
State Forest

Ice Age Trail

TOWN ROAD G G

ZZ

To North Prairie

Start/
Finish
P

To Dousman

67

0   0.5 mi

0   0.5 km

© AVALON TRAVEL

contrast to trails further south, this section of the KMSF has trails that wind through less hilly terrain. Walk northwest from the trailhead, past a quick trail junction, to head clockwise on the green loop. The trail passes through pine and hardwood forest of black and white oak, bur oak, and some eastern juniper. The trail climbs a bit for about 0.4 mile, then passes through gently rolling terrain. Approaching 1.4 miles there is a spur trail north, from a signed junction for the Observation Loop. Turn left and walk through the pretty cedar, oak, and hickory woods to a viewpoint and bench on the west side of the loop. There are some pretty stands of aspens and if it is early enough, perhaps some wildflowers. It is overgrown, though.

Returning to the main northward trail, you skirt the edge of some pines, then make a hairpin loop through yet more pines. Ascend along a rocky section beginning at 3.3 miles, passing a nice stand of quaking aspens. The trail begins a mile-long descent through the trees, which now include some black cherry, passing the junction with the Ice Age Trail at nearly 3.9 miles. You may see some chickadees or woodpeckers in the woods, and there are mossy nurse logs in places. Watch too for white-tailed deer and wild turkeys. I was hiking near sunset and the woods were definitely more active as dusk approached. A spur trail on the south side at 4.6 miles goes to the Mackie Shelter, just west of the Ice Age Trail. Continue southwest and downhill through mostly pine woods to the junction right before the trailhead; turn left at 5.2 miles to reach the parking lot.

Options

If you are in the mood to learn more about the human history and culture of the area, why not explore some of the nature trails? There are two nearby trails worth exploring. The Scuppernong Springs Nature Trail is a 1.5-mile interpretive loop. Highlights are the remains of a marl plant, hotel, sawmill, and of course, the springs. Further south is the Paradise Springs Nature Trail, a 0.5-mile fully accessible trail. The Paradise Springs Hotel was removed 40 years ago, however there are remnants of the "high life" remaining, in addition an old spring house. All the forest nature trails have brochures at the trailhead. Drive south on Kettle Moraine Scenic Drive for both signed trails.

Directions

From the junction of I-90 and I-294 in Rosemont, drive north on I-294 for 12.6 miles, continuing north on I-94 29.5 miles. Take Exit 344 for State Route 50 W and drive 23.7 miles. Take the ramp for U.S. 12 W and drive 10.6 miles, continuing on U.S. 12 W/State Route 67 N for 7.2 miles. Continue on State Route 67 for 12 miles. Turn east on County Road ZZ and park in the lot on the north side of the road in 0.4 mile. The trailhead is clearly marked and is at the north/northwest side of the lot.

GPS Coordinates: 16 T 380747mE 4755034mN

Information and Contact

There is no fee. Dogs allowed on eight-foot leash. There is excellent camping at the Pinewoods Campground in the northern part of the forest. At the intersection of U.S. 12 and County Road H is the LaGrange General Store, where you can buy good sandwiches and trail food. There is water and restrooms at the trailhead. Visit www.dnr.state.wi.us/org/land/parks/specific/kms/ for map downloads. Kettle Moraine State Forest, Southern Unit, S91 W39091 Highway 59, Eagle, WI 53119, 262/594-6200.

2 ICE AGE TRAIL: CARLIN TO BALD BLUFF

Kettle Moraine State Forest, Wisconsin

BEST (

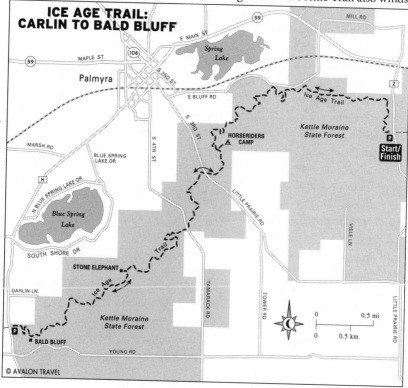

Level: Strenuous

Total Distance: 14.1 miles round-trip

Hiking Time: 7-8 hours

Elevation Change: 1,450 feet

Summary: Come hike this rugged, rolling section of the Ice Age National Scenic Trail for good views, big trees, and geologic wonders.

Kettle Moraine State Forest is home to diverse wildlife, dense oak forest, and the glacial features left behind 10,000 years ago when the Wisconsin Glacier finally retreated for good. The forest is known for its namesake features: dozens of lakes and ponds, and the rise and fall of moraines, some of which rise several hundred feet above the surrounding landscape. Trails crisscross the popular forest and offer hikers a nearly endless choice of hiking length, difficulty, and destination.

That is good news for hikers, since the Ice Age National Scenic Trail also winds

spur trail to the Stone Elephant

through the forest along its 1,200-mile path. Hiking this trail offers glimpses of geologic eras of the past as the path crosses moraines, passes kettles and erratics, and snakes along eskers. Expect a workout both physical and mental as you learn about the unique glacier features that make this trail so outstanding.

The Carlin–Bald Bluff section of trail travels through the Southern Unit of this forest, winding its way through bur and black oak woods, oak savanna, and past marshes and kettle ponds. Follow the short connector trail from the trailhead through some pine trees to the Ice Age National Scenic Trail junction, marked by a yellow blaze. For the next 3 miles, the trail steadily climbs, then drops west through the bur and black oak forest. Right after the trail turns west, look on the north side of the trail—you should see a tree that has partially grown around a large flattish boulder. Note milepost 14 on a tree at 0.6 mile. (You will see these periodically along the trail.) As you climb through the big trees, check out the tangle of black raspberry and wild grape alongside the trail. Pretty maples and ash grow here also, and you will walk through several pine plantations too. The trail drops to a low point around 2.5 miles. There are several kettle ponds along the trail here; if you are quiet, you can catch a glimpse of ducks on the water. (I flushed either a grouse or pheasant in the woods here.) Begin a somewhat steep ascent before passing through the Horseriders Campground at almost 3.1 miles. Walk straight ahead to catch the trail, which is marked by a post.

Enjoy the views from the narrow ridgetop around 3.4 miles—you earned them! The trail rolls along to cross the road, then descends to another road crossing at almost 4.3 miles. You are now in the Oak Opening State Natural Area, a mix of forest and savanna. Watch and listen for woodpeckers—there always seem to be a few hammering away. At 5.39 miles is the signed spur to the Stone Elephant, a huge glacial erratic with a colorful history. Descend the spur for a short distance west to check out the gray boulder. Back on the rolling trail, continue through the woods and across the Orange Trail to begin climbing at around 6.5 miles. Watch for wild turkeys around the bluff. Make the final steepish climb to the top of Bald Bluff, cresting the hill at nearly 7 miles. (Toward the end of the 19th century, Native Americans used Bald Bluff as a signal hill by building huge fires atop the mound.) The views are great and there are a couple of benches on the open hilltop. A mix of prairie flowers bloom on the bluff all summer, and the view highlights the nature of the terrain. Continue descending to the trailhead at County Road H. The trail continuation south is signed; you are now following the Bald Bluff interpretive trail. If you descend to the trailhead at nearly 7.2 miles, you can pick up a map that explains the history of the area. Return the way you came.

Options

For a shorter hike in Kettle Moraine State Forest, visit the Nordic Trailhead. Several hikes of different length begin from this popular trailhead—the Nordic Blue Trail, at 9 miles, is a favorite (see listing in this chapter).

Directions

From the junction of I-90 and I-294 in Rosemont, drive north on I-294 for 12.6 miles, then continue north on I-94 for 29.5 miles. Take Exit 344 for State Route 50 W and drive 23.7 miles. Take the ramp for U.S. 12 W and drive 10.6 miles, continuing onto U.S. 12 W/State Route 67 N for 7.2 miles. Continue on State Route 67 for 3.2 miles and turn left at Little Prairie Road/Palmyra Road. Drive north, continuing onto County Road Z for 1 mile to the parking lot on the west side of the road. The trailhead is at the northwest corner of the lot.
GPS Coordinates: 16 T 373886mE 4747386mN

Information and Contact

There is no fee. Dogs allowed on an eight-foot leash. Water and restrooms are available at the trailhead. The Ice Age Trail Alliance (www.iceagetrail.org) has an atlas and a collection of maps. There is excellent camping at the Pinewoods Campground in the northern part of the forest. The LaGrange General Store has good sandwiches and trail food; it is located at the intersection of U.S. 12 and County Road H.

For more information, contact Kettle Moraine State Forest, Southern Unit, S91 W39091, Highway 59, Eagle, WI, 53119, 262/594-6200, www.dnr.state.wi.us.

3 NORDIC BLUE TRAIL

Kettle Moraine State Forest, Southern Unit, Wisconsin

Level: Moderate

Hiking Time: 4.5–5 hours

Total Distance: 9.0 miles round-trip

Elevation Change: 535 feet

Summary: Lovers of trees will enjoy this hike through old oaks and large plantations of red pine along the Nordic Blue Trail.

The Southern Unit of Kettle Moraine State Forest is an Ice Age museum of sorts. The geologic tale of glacial advance and retreat is told on the rolling landscape, marked as it is with kettle ponds, rocky moraines, and sinuous eskers. The Lake Michigan Lobe of the Wisconsin Glacier scoured this land over 10,000 years ago, leaving behind rugged terrain that begs to be explored. Hikers get to enjoy over 54 miles of hiking trails in the Southern Unit. The Nordic trail system is one of several dedicated trail systems that allows only hiking. The dense woods, oak savanna, prairie, and wetlands provide diverse animal and plant habitat, indeed over 137 species of birds nest within the forest boundaries. Look for woodpeckers, warblers, and hawks around the meadows. The rolling trails of the Nordic System offer hikers of all abilities the chance to stretch their legs and enjoy a beautiful natural environment.

© BARBARA I. BOND

The rolling hillsides are dotted with oaks.

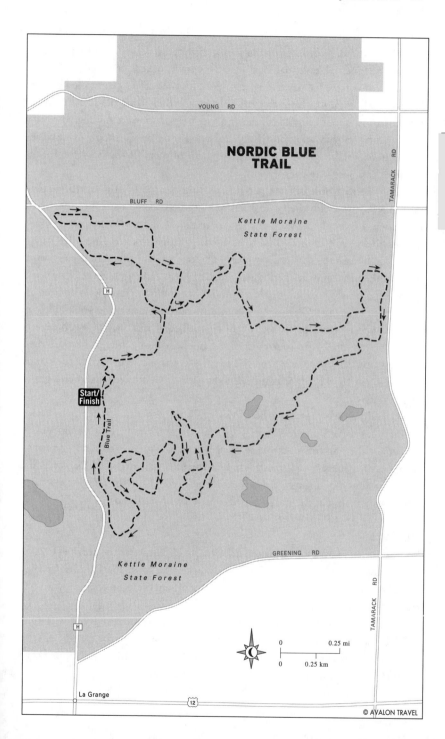

The Nordic Blue Trail is a rolling loop through oak woodland, open fields and prairie, and oak savanna. There are large tracts of red pine, and depressions and kettle ponds with frogs and salamanders. It's the perfect place to spend a day hiking. Walking north from the trailhead on the Blue Trail, note that there are mileposts just about every half mile and the intersections are numbered so that you can find your location on the map. The trail has only a couple of sustained flat sections, this clockwise loop ends along one of them. If you want to hike the flat part first, just hike counterclockwise.

Along the first mile of trail, you'll hike from tall oaks to the startling openness of a narrow field, then transition to a needle-covered path through a pine plantation. I love shifting from one kind of terrain to the next, watching the open grasses give way to the scattered trees of oak savanna along rolling hills. At 1.5 miles, you'll reach the northwest corner of the trail, which turns abruptly eastward, still in the forest. Benches periodically invite you to contemplate the beauty and quiet. After nearly a half mile of level ground, the rolling terrain again dominates, and the views change. On the way to the northeastern pine woods, you follow the trail up and down the pretty oak openings with some nice views from the crests across the treetops. Turn south just past 4 miles, still in a pine plantation, then jog west up a slight incline, then back south to pass between two kettle ponds around 5.5 miles. There are some nice light brown and orange mushrooms growing on tree trunks.

The trail, mown-grass now, heads downhill past some snags then uphill once again. Some aspens provide a splash of contrast, and you will hit a small grassy area where the trail turns sharply south at N9 and 6.6 miles. You'll now return to the pines once more for another 1.5 miles, while the trail levels off. Maples, and a couple of short, open, grassy fields provide some relief from the pine. At 8.5 miles is a short downhill as the trail proceeds north to the trailhead.

Options

Want to learn more about the human history and culture of the area? The Paradise Springs Nature Trail is a 0.5-mile fully accessible trail. The Paradise Springs Hotel was removed 40 years ago, however remnants remain including an old spring house.

The Scuppernong Springs Nature Trail is a 1.5-mile interpretive loop. Highlights include the remains of a marl plant, hotel, sawmill, and the springs. All the nature trails have brochures at the trailhead. Follow Kettle Moraine Scenic Drive (County Road H) north to reach both signed trailheads.

Directions

From the junction of I-90 and I-294 in Rosemont, drive north on I-294 for 12.6 miles, continuing north on I-94 for 29.5 miles. Take Exit 344 for State Route 50 W and drive for 23.7 miles. Take the ramp for U.S. 12 W and drive 10.6 miles, continuing onto U.S. 12 W/State Route 67 N for another 9.3 miles. Turn north on County Road H and drive for 1.5 miles. The trailhead is on the west side of the road, in the southwest corner of the parking lot.
GPS Coordinates: 16 T 369146mE 4742019mN

Information and Contact

There is no fee. Dogs allowed on an eight-foot leash. There are restrooms, a large trail map, an information kiosk, and vending machines at the trailhead. The park has snowshoeing in winter and excellent camping at the Pinewoods Campground in the northern part of the forest. The LaGrange General Store, at the intersection of U.S. 12 and County Road H, has good sandwiches and trail food.

For more information, contact Kettle Moraine State Forest, Southern Unit S91 W39091, Highway 59, Eagle, WI, 53119, 262/594-6200, www.dnr.state.wi.us.

4 MUIR BLUE TRAIL

BEST ◖

Kettle Moraine State Forest, Wisconsin

Level: Moderate

Total Distance: 12.0 miles round-trip

Hiking Time: 6-7 hours

Elevation Change: 640 feet

Summary: Hilly, windy Muir Blue Loop leads hikers past two historic sites.

Kettle Moraine State Forest occupies a unique strip of land formed by the retreat of the Wisconsin Glacier over 10,000 years ago. The forest is full of moraines, eskers, and kettle holes—all left behind when the massive ice sheet moved down into Illinois and then receded. Years later, after black and bur oak forest, prairie, and oak savanna spread across this land, outdoors enthusiasts get to enjoy miles of trails amidst a beautiful natural setting. Kettle Moraine State Forest is home to hundreds of species of birds—eastern meadowlark, bobolink, and various sparrows—small mammals, and a diverse plant community. The Muir Trails are in the south half of the forest, providing hikers, cross-country skiers, and mountain bikers with an undulating trail system that will take you past ponds, across grassland, and through dense forest. The two historic sites accessible from the Muir Trails provide visitors with a bit of perspective on life as a settler 150 years

© BARBARA I. BOND

the restored Oleson Cabin

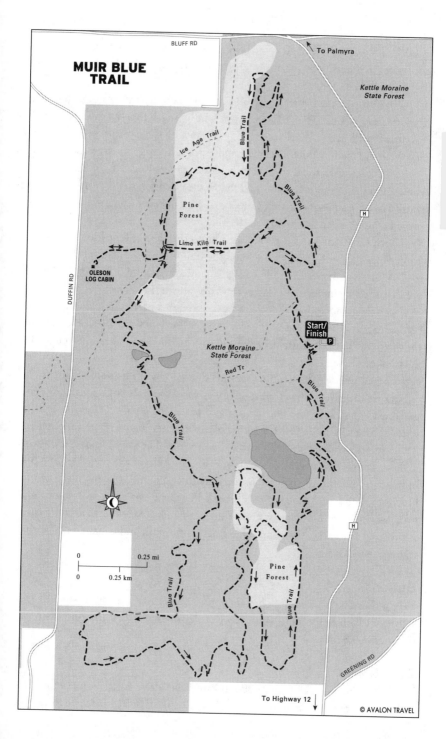

MUIR BLUE TRAIL

BLUFF RD

To Palmyra

Kettle Moraine State Forest

Blue Trail

Ice Age Trail

Pine Forest

Blue Trail

Lime Kiln Trail

DUFFIN RD

OLESON LOG CABIN

Kettle Moraine State Forest

Start/Finish P

Red Tr

Blue Trail

Blue Trail

0   0.25 mi

0   0.25 km

Blue Trail

Blue Trail

Pine Forest

H

H

Blue Trail

GREENING RD

To Highway 12

© AVALON TRAVEL

ago. Although the Blue Trail is my favorite, the Muir system has lots of options available, so hikers with various interests and experience levels can enjoy a day on the trails here.

Walk west past the big trail map and turn north into the black oak and shagbark hickory woods. The trail is narrow, windy, and rolling as you head north towards Bluff Road. The tall oak canopy fills in with some maple around 1 mile; keep your eye out for white-tailed deer and gray squirrel. Ignore the trail junctions until you reach the extension in the northeast corner around 1.7 miles. Here, if you were going ultra-long, you would follow the extension to the Nordic Trails. I walked north a bit to check it out, there were a lot of beautiful ferns but I quickly turned around. Keep left to stay on the blue trail as it makes a couple of hairpins then begins working south towards the spur to the pioneer lime kiln.

As you walk south through the pines the trail nearly levels out for 0.5 mile or so. Pick up the Lime Kiln Trail at a signed junction around 3.2 miles, and head uphill east on an increasingly narrow and overgrown trail. The final bit has a lot of blackberry vines; you will have to push through a particularly dense section before reaching the remains of the old, boulder-lined kiln at 3.7 miles. Return to the main trail to head south just a short distance before heading west through old fields to the Oleson Cabin, an 1840s pioneer cabin that was restored in 1991. The cabin has immense oaks standing sentinel nearby, it is a fine spot for a break.

Back on the narrow Blue trail at 4.9 miles, head south through a meadow peppered with goldenrod and blazing star and past some ponds. The trail begins a series of ascents and descents, benches placed strategically between miles 6 and 7.8 or so give you a chance to break if you want. The very windy trail again makes a couple of hairpins, reaching the largest of the kettle ponds around 9.1 miles, once more in the pines. Continue south and uphill, turning north at the hillcrest around 10.2 mile. You will pass a huge white oak as you descent for a mile, working around the east end of the big pond. Keep an eye out for garter snakes and frogs near the pond. One final push uphill and you are back at the trailhead at 12 miles.

Options
Take a shortcut at 6.1 miles onto the Green Trail eastward. By cutting off the southwest loop of the Blue Trail, you can shave some miles, bringing the total distance to 9.8 miles.

Directions
From the junction of I-90 and I-294 in Rosemont, drive north on I-294 for 12.6 miles, continuing north on I-94 for 29.5 miles. Take Exit 344 for State Route 50

W and drive for 23.7 miles. Take the ramp for U.S. 12 W and drive 10.6 miles, continuing onto U.S. 12 W/State Route 67 N for another 9.3 miles. Turn north on County Road H and drive for 1.5 miles. The trailhead is on the west side of the road, in the southwest corner of the parking lot.

GPS Coordinates: 16 T 368953mE 4741872mN

Information and Contact

There is no fee. Dogs allowed on an eight-foot leash. There are restrooms, a large trail map, an information kiosk, and vending machines at the trailhead. The park has snowshoeing in winter and excellent camping at the Pinewoods Campground in the northern part of the forest. The LaGrange General Store has good sandwiches and trail food; it is located at the intersection of U.S. 12 and County Road H.

For more information, contact Kettle Moraine State Forest, Southern Unit, S91 W39091, Highway 59, Eagle, WI, 53119, 262/594-6200, www.dnr.state.wi.us.

5 ICE AGE TRAIL:
LAKE LA GRANGE TO RICE LAKE
Kettle Moraine State Forest, Wisconsin

Level: Strenuous

Hiking Time: 6.5-7 hours

Total Distance: 13.5 miles round-trip

Elevation Change: 1,040 feet

Summary: Visit two lakes along this fun and challenging loop in the southern tip of Kettle Moraine State Forest.

The Ice Age National Scenic Trail winds through Kettle Moraine State Forest along a 1,200-mile path, taking in kettles and erratics, moraines, and other geologic wonders. The La Grange trailhead takes hikers through the southernmost section of this forest. A variety of birds populate the area, including cedar waxwing, hawks, and waterfowl on the lake.

Begin by walking north from the trailhead on the orange-blazed Moraine Ridge Trail, an equestrian trail that allows hikers to create loop hikes with the Ice Age

A hiking club explores the Ice Age Trail.

National Scenic Trail. Follow the wide trail for 1.7 miles through mostly oak-hickory woods with some maples, catalpa, and wild grape mixed in. After passing milepost 3, keep right at the two three-way junctions as the trail winds around to pass milepost 4 after cresting the first hill. Now heading north, at 1.7 miles turn west on a narrow connector trail that leads onto the yellow-blazed Ice Age National Scenic Trail. A three-way junction appears at 2.2 miles; continue north and into a crossing of a restored prairie with little and big bluestem in summer. The trail turns south along the west side of Lake La Grange; after crossing an old wood footbridge and some climbing, reach U.S. 12 and the trailhead at 4 miles.

Walk south across the highway and around the gate to continue following the Ice Age National Scenic Trail. The terrain rolls for the next 3 miles. You will see some black cherry and occasional stands of aspen in the mixed oak forest; there are red pines near 5.6 miles. After passing a bench with western views, the trail eventually climbs to a great viewpoint at 7.5 miles. After a short downhill, ignore the spur trail at 6.7 miles and continue south, then west, after the road crossing to meet Clover Valley Road. Turn left on Clover Valley Road to reach Kettle Moraine Drive. Turn north and at 8.8 miles follow the north shore of Rice Lake around to a picnic area at the tip of the small peninsula. Here you can enjoy a well-deserved break.

When you are ready to pick up the trail again, walk north along State Park Road until reaching the Rice Lake Nature Trail (blue blazes). Follow Rice Lake Nature Trail north and west around a marshy pond. At 9.7 miles, the trail rejoins the Ice Age National Scenic Trail as it heads north for almost 1.4 miles. Keep right at 11.1 miles on the orange-blazed horse trail and follow the old roadbed north to the trailhead at 13.5 miles.

Options
To enjoy some rugged sections of trail, good views, and a lakeside picnic, do this as a one-way hike along the Ice Age National Scenic Trail. Hike from the U.S. 12 trailhead to Rice Lake and the tip of the peninsula where the covered picnic tables are. The total distance is 5.8 miles.

Directions
From the junction of I-90 and I-294 in Rosemont, drive north on I-294 for 12.6 miles, then continue north on I-94 for 29.5 miles. Take Exit 344 for State Route 50 W and drive 23.7 miles. Take the ramp for U.S. 12 W and drive 10.6 miles, continuing onto U.S. 12 W/State Route 67 N for another 12.1 miles. The trailhead is on the north side of the road, adjacent to a large information kiosk with maps.
GPS Coordinates: 16 T 364858mE 4740222mN

Information and Contact
There is no fee. Dogs allowed on an eight-foot leash. Water and restrooms are available at the trailhead. The Ice Age Trail Alliance (www.iceagetrail.org) has an atlas and a collection of maps. There is excellent camping at the Pinewoods Campground in the northern part of the forest. The LaGrange General Store, located at the intersection of U.S. 12 and County Road H, has good sandwiches and trail food.

For more information, contact Kettle Moraine State Forest, Southern Unit, S91 W39091, Highway 59, Eagle, WI, 53119, 262/594-6200, www.dnr.state.wi.us.

6 GENEVA LAKE SHORE PATH: LAKE GENEVA TO FONTANA

BEST [

Lake Geneva, Wisconsin

Level: Moderate

Total Distance: 10.4 miles one-way

Hiking Time: 5-6 hours

Elevation Change: negligible

Summary: The popular Geneva Lake Shore Path travels through intimate gardens, park-like yards, and along some of the most exclusive waterfront in the area.

Geneva Lake's 8.6 square miles sit in the gently rolling landscape of southeastern Wisconsin. The lake occupies a valley that was left behind when the last glaciers retreated. Before leaving the area in 1831, the chief of a Native American tribe negotiated a treaty guaranteeing public access to the lakeshore path in perpetuity. We enjoy that legacy today, with 21 miles of footpath through a diverse array of yards, public property, and historic sites. Since the development of Maple Lawn along the north shore in 1870, Lake Geneva has been the summer retreat of choice for generations of wealthy urbanites.

The most popular starting point is at Library Park, just west of the public beach in Lake Geneva. A building here offers public restrooms, something in short supply along the trail. At the start of the path, note a sign detailing the rules of the

Geneva Lake Shore Path sign and footbridge

© BARBARA I. BOND

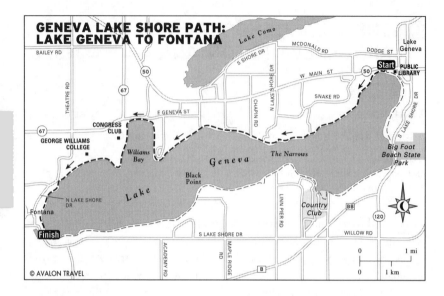

GENEVA LAKE SHORE PATH:
LAKE GENEVA TO FONTANA

Lake Shore Path—you will see these throughout your walk. Walk west from Library Park to begin.

The narrow path is inviting as it winds towards a weathered wooden fence that skirts a huge cottonwood and a tangle of shrubs. Blooming day lilies contrast with the sparkling blue water of the lake. Then, on the north, there are the houses—get used to the weird feeling of walking through someone's backyard. After 2.3 miles, the views across the lake will take your breath away. Soon, you're walking past "The Narrows"—the place where the north and south lakeshores are pinched together. Climb up some steps and a stone ramp then quickly hike downhill and across a bridge. You will cross Chapin Road at 3.5 miles.

Pass the pretty white vacation homes of the Elgin Club before entering a park-like area at 4.25 miles. Cottonwoods line the trail, as do stately oaks, sugar maples, and aspens. Around 5.6 miles, climb some steps and walk above the lake. Williams Bay lies ahead; at 6.5 miles, begin passing by the park at the north end of the bay. There are public restrooms at 6.9 miles.

A mixture of sights lie along the next 3 miles to Fontana. After passing some apartments and Gage Marine, reach the 1882 Congress Club at 7.6 miles. The Congress Club, with its imposing white clubhouse, was built in 1882 as a Chicago summer retreat. For a short distance the path follows a narrow wooden walkway, passing older homes, before changing into a shady dirt path along a wild tangle of trees. At 8.7 miles, pass through a concrete gate at the beautiful campus of George Williams College. Aurora University's George William College was originally a

YMCA facility. Today, the college is known for its many education, community outreach, and elderhostel programs.

At around 9 miles, continue along a wooden boardwalk through a thick grove of trees. After passing a sign for the Embree House (a 1902 Prairie-style home), hike up a wooden walkway and then some steps. You will enter Fontana at about 10 miles. Continue south along Lake Street towards the beach. The intersection of Lake Street and S. Lakeshore Drive is at 10.4 miles and the end of your adventure.

Options

Hike the entire Lake Shore Path in a day by continuing on from Fontana and along the south shore of the lake. You will reach Big Foot Park at around 19.2 miles (there are restrooms here). Continue north along the road, then turn left back onto the well-signed path to the library where you began the hike. The total hiking distance will be about 21.4 miles.

Directions

From Chicago, drive west on I-90, exiting onto State Route 53 N. Drive for 7.9 miles and exit onto Lake Cook Road W., driving west for 0.7 mile. Turn right and drive northwest on U.S. 12 W/N. Rand Road for 28.6 miles, continuing on U.S. 12 W for 3.4 miles. Just after the Wisconsin state line, take the ramp for U.S. 12 W to continue for 8.8 miles. Take Exit 330A for Lake Geneva, and drive west on State Route 50 W/County Road 120 for 1.5 miles. In town, State Route 50 W becomes Main Street; Library Park is bordered by Wrigley Drive and Main Street. Parking is available in the neighborhood north of Main Street. Walk to Library Park to begin the counterclockwise hike.
GPS Coordinates: 16 T 382041mE 4716242mN

Information and Contact

There is no fee. Dogs on leash are allowed. Reservations (262/248-6206) are required for the boat back to Lake Geneva from Fontana. Public restrooms are available in Lake Geneva, Williams Bay, and Fontana. The Geneva Lake Shore Path is public, however all property is private. Some homeowners have benches, water fountains, or guest books along the path. Please respect any notices and stay on the path. A free visitor's map is available from various shops and hotels in Lake Geneva. For more information, contact the Lake Geneva Area Convention and Visitors Bureau, 201 Wrigley Drive, Lake Geneva, WI 53147, www.lakegenevawi.com, 800/345-1020. The Chamber of Commerce (www.lakegenevawi.com) also has guides and maps available.

7 GENEVA LAKE SHORE PATH: FONTANA TO LAKE GENEVA   BEST ☾

Lake Geneva, Wisconsin

Level: Moderate

Total Distance: 11.0 miles one-way

Hiking Time: 5-6 hours

Elevation Change: negligible

Summary: The southern section of the Geneva Lake Shore Path passes historic mansions, modern homes, and unique natural areas.

Lake Geneva has been the summer retreat of Chicago's well-to-do residents, since the late 1800s when development began along the north shore. The southern section of the Geneva Lake Shore Path travels across wooden footbridges, past old iron fences, and zigzags around unusual homes. Walking the southern Lake Shore Path allows hikers to experience the other side of the lake lifestyle.

The starting point of this southern section of the path is the village of Fontana, on the lake's west side. Begin walking south along the Lake Shore Path, which parallels South Lake Shore Drive for a short distance. The path travels east through a black wrought-iron gate before climbing uphill to a paved section above the lake. At 0.6 mile, pass the Indian Hills subdivision and cross a wooden bridge. Lovely trees line the shore as you walk through the Harvard Club, established in 1875 as a summer residence for families from Harvard, Illinois. It continues to be one of the prettiest lakefront properties along the shore. After winding a mile up and

westward on the path

down some steps and across a grassy yard, pass the Lake Geneva Club, with a gazebo on the lakeshore, at about 2.3 miles.

Spend the next few miles gazing in awe at the amazing mix of historic and modern homes. This section of the path hops up and down steps, passes through an old rusty iron gate, and follows a winding path across a bridge and through a small wooded area.

At 3.8 miles, the path curves around Black Point; the three-story mansion, hidden behind huge fir and pines trees, was built in 1888 and is open for seasonal tours. Around 6.2 miles, enter the Lake Geneva Country Club and walk under the building along the well-marked path as it continues around the golf course. Follow the signs the next 0.5 mile. After walking through the neighborhood, follow Burr Oak Drive to Hillside Road, which you will take north towards the dock. Just before reaching the dock, turn right and back onto the path (unsigned) at 7.2 miles.

You'll walk across wood planks, boardwalks, and bridges before returning to the path along the water. At 8.6 miles, walk down to the road; Big Foot Beach State Park is across the road, with restrooms and drinking water. Follow signs to veer back towards the lake at 9.2 miles. The path continues to be a mix of stone, dirt, or brick and the houses along it are equally eclectic. At 10 miles, begin crossing a large expanse of grass; the well-known Stone Manor sits regally atop a small rise to the east. The landmark 18,000-square-foot home was built in 1901 and was the largest on the lakeshore; it now houses a half-dozen condominiums. A whimsical fence painted with encouraging phrases guides you as you continue walking north into town, then west through the busy waterfront area. Stop for photos at the fountain in front of the Riviera Ballroom; from there it is a very short walk back to Library Park.

Options
Spend all day along the lake by hiking both the north and south sections of the Lake Shore Path. From Library Park, follow the 10.4-mile northern section from Lake Geneva to Fontana (see listing in this chapter) for a total distance of 21.4 miles.

Directions
From Chicago, take I-90/I-94 west/northwest for 51 miles. Take the U.S. 20 exit for Hampshire/Marengo and turn northwest on U.S. 20, continuing for 8.9 miles. Turn right at State Route 23/S. State Street for 10.6 mile, turning left at U.S. 14/S. Division Street and continuing on U.S. 14 N 9.4 miles (entering Wisconsin). Turn east on Kenosha Street for 0.5 mile, then north on Valley View Drive. Drive 1.5 miles, turn right on Fontana Boulevard and drive east 0.3 mile. Fontana merges onto S. Lake Shore Drive, Lake Street is the next street south. Begin hiking here, adjacent to the public beach. There is a parking lot just west of the road.
GPS Coordinates: 16 T 370887mE 4711595mN

Information and Contact
There is no fee. Dogs on leash are allowed. Reservations (262/248-6206) are required for the boat back to Lake Geneva from Fontana. Public restrooms are available in Lake Geneva, Williams Bay, and Fontana. The Geneva Lake Shore Path is public, however all property is private. Some homeowners have benches, water fountains, or guest books along the path. Please respect any notices and stay on the path. A free visitor's map is available from various shops and hotels in Lake Geneva. The Chamber of Commerce (www.lakegenevawi.com) also has guides and maps available.

Tours of Black Point Mansion (http://blackpointmansion.com) are available through the Lake Geneva Cruise Line (www.cruiselakegeneva.com/bptours.php), via Motor Coach, or through field groups. For reservations, contact Black Point Historic House and Gardens, 262/248-1888, (email) blackpoint1888@att.net, http://blackpointmansion.com.

For more information, contact the Lake Geneva Area Convention and Visitors Bureau, 201 Wrigley Drive, Lake Geneva, WI 53147, www.lakegenevawi.com, 800/345-1020.

8 WOLF LAKE TRAIL

Richard Bong State Recreation Area, Wisconsin

BEST [

Level: Easy

Total Distance: 4.5 miles round-trip

Hiking Time: 2 hours

Elevation Change: 125 feet

Summary: Hike past wetlands and through the woods and prairie surrounding Wolf Lake.

Richard Bong State Recreation Area is part of the Lower Fox River–Illinois Watershed of southeastern Wisconsin. Shaped by glacial retreat over 10,000 years ago, the gently rolling land is dominated by wetlands, prairie, oak forest, and oak savanna. Richard Bong State Recreation Area is Wisconsin's first parcel designated as a recreation area. The 4,515-acre area is still recovering from abuse suffered during

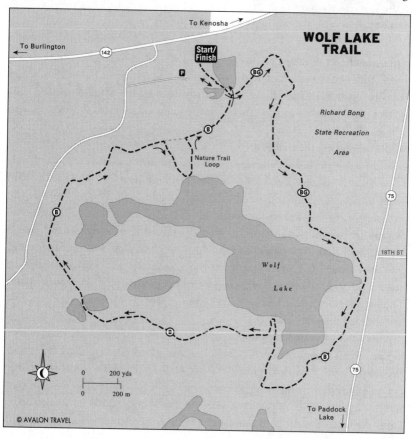

© BARBARA I. BOND

This wooden viewing platform is great for bird-watching.

a period of heavy development in the 1950s (it was slated to become a military air base). Today conservation practices are in place and slowly the natural landscape is being restored. Richard Bong State Recreation Area has a well-developed trail system that allows visitors to experience the unique ecology of the area. Hikers will see abundant birds and butterflies, as well as beautiful woodland and prairie wildflowers along the trails.

Walk across the boardwalk between two ponds surrounded by cattails. Watch for waterfowl on the water. Cross the park road and turn left to follow the blue posts, which will guide you along this nearly 4-mile loop. The trail follows the road northeast, then curves southward towards Wolf Lake. The grassland wildflowers are stunning in summer, particularly the rattlesnake master and prairie blazing star. Prairie gives way to oak and hickory savanna and the lake comes into view around 0.8 mile. Shortly the trail crosses the dam, then curves south around the lake. You may see beaver-gnawed trees as you pass close to the water. The Blue Trail parallels the Horse Trail in spots, at 1.3 miles, keep right and follow the trail back into the trees.

After winding around the southeast tip of Wolf Lake past aspens and some eastern juniper, you'll emerge in savanna. Walk near the water's edge around 2 miles, and take in the northward view across the water. Orchard Pond is south of the trail at 2.4 miles. Keep an eye out for egrets and great blue heron on the lake, too. The trail remains in the open now, passing a couple of more ponds and some cottonwoods. Cross the road approaching 3 miles, passing the campground on the east and ball fields on the west, then cross the road again before reaching the Visitors Center Nature Trail at 3.5 miles. Take a detour, turn south, and walk the loop by heading south. The wooden viewing platform on the lake is the highlight, and serves as a great bird-watching spot. You might hear muskrat under the wood deck and or see waterfowl or waders on the water, including a white swan. Walk past some huge bur oak, pines, and red cedar as you complete the short loop. Return to the Blue Trail where you started and continue eastward. Walk through the prairie grasses and wildflowers 0.3 mile to the trail junction at 4.3 miles and turn north. Watch for sparrows, bobolink, and butterflies along here, including red-spotted purple on the coneflowers. Cross the boardwalk and you are back at the trailhead parking lot.

Options

Extend this hike by heading north to the Red Trail. Pockets of woodland and wetlands create a great bird habitat here—watch for bluebirds, great blue heron, and egrets. Frogs, crickets, and rustling leaves on the wind are the only sounds along this quiet trail. Follow the red posts from the trailhead to reach the north trails for a total combined distance of 12 miles.

Directions

From the junction of I-294 N and I-94 W, drive north on I-94 W for 32.8 miles. Take Exit 340 for State Route 142 and drive west on State Route 142/Burlington Road for 9.2 miles. After crossing State Route 75, turn south into the recreation area and drive 0.2 mile to the trailhead parking lot just east of the visitors center. A map and sign with colored arrows for either the north or south trail system is at the northeast corner. Begin the Blue/Wolf Lake Trail by walking to the boardwalk in the southeast corner of the lot.

To hike the Red Trail, park at the trailhead north of County Road BB/7th Street. Exit the park and drive east on State Route/Burlington Road. Turn north on State Route 75 and drive 1.1 miles to 7th Street. Turn west and drive 0.8 mile to the Lot A trailhead on the north side of the road. Park in the west lot; the trail heads east from the northeast corner of the lot at a red post.

GPS Coordinates: 16 T 407797mE 4720590mN

Information and Contact

Admission fees vary; call to confirm. Dogs on leash are allowed, except on the nature trails. The park is open 6 A.M.–11 P.M. daily. Water and restrooms are available along the lake trail. For more information, contact Richard Bong State Recreation Area, 26313 Burlington Road, Kansasville, WI 53139, 262/878-5600, www.dnr.wi.gov.

9 BADGER-GOLDFINCH TRAIL LOOP

Chain O' Lakes State Park, Spring Grove

Level: Easy

Hiking Time: 1.5 hours

Total Distance: 3.4 miles round-trip

Elevation Change: negligible

Summary: Grab your binoculars for excellent birding along the gentle slopes of Chain O' Lakes State Park.

Chain O' Lakes State Park lies just south of the Wisconsin state line and is part of the Northeastern Morainal Division of Illinois. The land is a rolling mix of marshes, peat bogs, and wetlands, all the result of glacial scouring and deposit more than 10,000 years ago. Upland forest enhances the park's ecological diversity and makes it an excellent habitat for sandhill cranes. Chain O' Lakes covers nearly 2,800 acres and is adjacent to another 10,000 acres of conservation area. Great blue heron, egrets, terns, and a host of small mammals call the park home. Grassland bird species, wildflowers, and an 80-acre nature preserve make this a worthy destination for any outdoor adventurer seeking a peaceful locale.

Hiking on the Badger and Goldfinch Trails is a great way to experience nearly all of the ecosystems of Chain O' Lakes. This short double loop descends past savanna and grasslands, curving along a bend of the Fox River before visiting oak-hickory woodlands and a small prairie restoration. That's a lot in just under 3.5 miles! To begin, walk south on the Badger Trail, a wide limestone path. A covered shelter almost immediately offers a chance to pause and take in the expansive, rolling grassland and savanna. The Fox River appears as a sliver of blue in the distance. The trail winds southward, past little bluestem, Indian grass, and a smattering of wildflowers. In 0.5 mile is the southwest tip of the loop where a connector trail leads south to the Sunset Trail and Catfish Cove Picnic Area. For now, continue ahead as the trail curves north around a small hill on the left. There are scattered oaks to the east and a covered bench up ahead that is great for bird-watching. Check these small grassy hills for sandhill cranes—I recently saw a pair making their way towards the trees. The trail briefly enters the trees before emerging again at just under 1 mile.

Pass westward through open grassland, turn north at a three-way intersection around mile 1.3. This is the start of the Goldfinch Trail, which briefly heads north through the trees before reaching the loop. At the loop, turn east in front of a prairie area with a small, fenced deer exclosure. (Naturalists can gauge the effect of white-tailed deer grazing on the native flora.) This beautiful prairie is

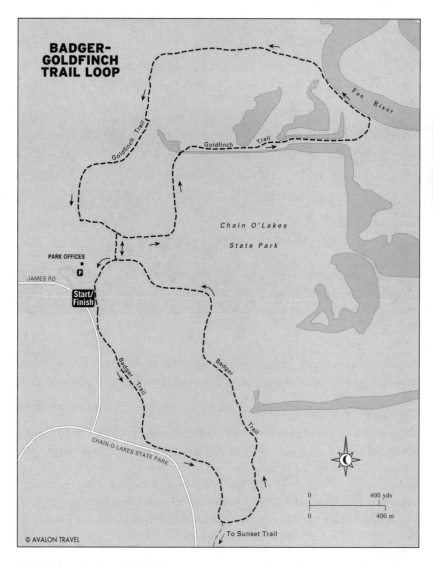

full of flowers; look for black- and brown-eyed Susans, hoary vervain, purple coneflower, and cardinal flower.

Zigzag toward the Fox River, reaching the shore after passing a low-lying area north of the trail. At 2 miles, the trail curves lazily north then northwest along the river—be sure to soak in the views. The large flat leaves of American lotus dot the water and sedge, cattails, and grasses line the shore. The trail climbs gently away from the river and alternates between the woods and open grassland over the next mile. As you head south, pass the prairie, ignore the spur on the right; it only leads

© BARBARA I. BOND

grasslands and savanna along the Badger Trail

to the park offices. In 3.2 miles reach the start of the loop, turn south, and then quickly turn right to finish the Badger Loop and return to the trailhead.

Options

Want to double your hiking mileage? At the connector trail at 0.5 mile, turn south and make a quick right to follow the Sunset Trail for a mile through open grasslands. At the southern tip of the loop, continue on or turn right to hike an additional 0.7 mile to the Catfish Cove parking area where you can explore nature trails and Grass Lake. Retrace your steps 0.7 mile to the loop, turning east and then north for the 1.1 miles back to the Badger Trail connector. Follow the rest of the hike as described for a total distance of 6.9 miles.

Directions

From the junction of I-90 W and I-294 N, drive north on I-294 for 3.3 miles. Exit onto U.S. 14 W/Dempster Street and drive 0.4 mile, turning right at Rand Road. Drive northwest for 24 miles, continuing onto State Route 59 N/U.S. 12 W for another 11.6 miles. Turn right on Johnsburg/N Wilmont Road and drive 1.8 miles. The signed park entrance is the east side of the road. Drive 1.4 miles on the park road and turn north at James Road to park in the large lot on the east side of the road. The park offices are just north of the lot. The trail begins at the southeast corner of the lot; walk onto the limestone path a few yards and turn south.

Alternatively, from I-94 N take the exit for State Route 173/Rosecrans Rd. Drive west on State Route 173 W for 15 miles to Johnsburg/N Wilmot Rd. Turn south and drive 1.5 miles to the park entrance on the east side of the road. Continue as described.

GPS Coordinates: 16 T 402210mE 4701965mN

Information and Contact

There is no fee. Dogs on leash are allowed. The park is open 6 A.M.–9 P.M. daily April 1–October 31 and 8 A.M.–sunset daily the rest of the year (Nov. 1–mid-Dec.). For more information, contact Chain O' Lakes State Park, 8916 Wilmont Road, Spring Grove, 847/587-5512, www.dnr.state.il.us.

10 DES PLAINES RIVER TRAIL

Van Patten Woods Forest Preserve, Lake County Forest Preserves, Wadsworth

🦌 🛶 ✈️ 🌷 🚶 🐕 👫

Level: Easy/moderate

Total Distance: 5.2 miles round-trip

Hiking Time: 2.5 hours

Elevation Change: negligible

Summary: Bring your camera for a hike around picturesque Sterling Lake and through the oak forest of Van Patten Woods.

In 1961 the Lake County Forest Preserve District acquired the first parcel of land that would become Van Patten Woods Forest Preserve. Today this beautifully restored site enjoys status as a premier recreation and natural area. An old gravel pit was transformed into the sparkling blue water of Sterling Lake, which is now surrounded by restored, flower-laden shores. To the east of the lake runs the Des Plaines River. In the spring and summer a multitude of flowers add to Van Patten's beauty and attract scores of butterflies. The native woods of the east preserve provide a shady respite from the sun and provide important habitat for birds and wildlife, as does the floodplain adjacent to the Des Plaines River. Preserve trails and the Des Plaines River Trail can be combined in any number of ways to give hikers plenty to enjoy.

Begin hiking south along the Blue trail, which follows the lakeshore for the next 0.5 mile. There are a few trees along the west-side trail, which mostly passes through prairie grasses, and flowers including golden Alexanders and asters. You pass a bench at the south tip of the lake, it's a great spot to look northward across the lake. At a three-way intersection keep left to head north as you continue onto the Des Plaines River Trail and head into the trees. Make a right at the sign and cross the bridge to reach the east-side woodland trails.

After the bridge, you can go north or south on the 1.6 mile Yellow Loop trail. What a contrast the native oak forest is—the mature trees create a dense green canopy and it's cool and shady. There are huge mature oaks, smaller wild black cherry trees with their "burnt chip" bark, and maples here. Watch for woodpeckers, chickadees, and warblers here—you might hear them before you see them flitting from branch to branch. You'll pass a grove of planted pine trees, an odd contrast to the maples. Watch too for a catalpa tree with its giant leaves. Ignore three trail junctions from 1.3–1.6 miles, they lead to picnic or parking areas. From the northern point at 1.9 miles, head south to the bridge, then turn west to reach the Des Plaines River Trail.

Now head north along the Des Plaines River Trail, which follows a narrow band

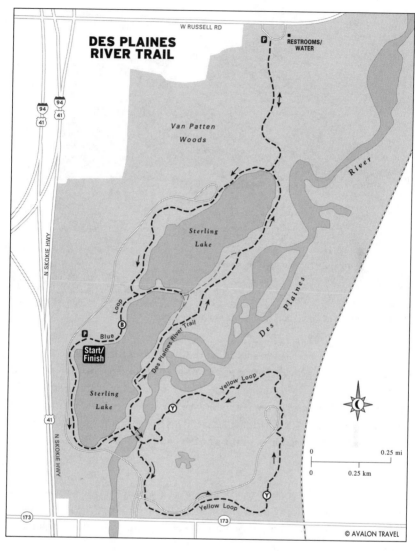

DES PLAINES RIVER TRAIL

W RUSSELL RD

RESTROOMS/
WATER

Van Patten
Woods

Sterling
Lake

Loop

Blue

Start/
Finish

Des Plaines River Trail

Sterling
Lake

Yellow Loop

Yellow Loop

Des Plaines

River

N SKOKIE HWY

N SKOKIE HWY

0   0.25 mi

0   0.25 km

© AVALON TRAVEL

of land between the lake and river. In early summer you're likely to be swarmed by mosquitoes while you are near the river. You'll pass another bench and viewpoint along the lakeshore. At mile 2.7 is a junction with the lakeshore path, keep right on the Des Plaines River Trail, which remains in the trees another 0.3 mile. The next 0.3 will take you north around the lake and continue north, leading away from the water towards a small grove of huge oaks in the middle of an old field which is slowly being taken back by native plants and flowers. I saw a sandhill crane under one of the trees; they are relatively common up here.

This small grove of huge oaks marks the north preserve.

Continue to the northern trailhead for the Des Plaines River Trail at 3.8 miles. Here you can take a break, have a picnic in the shade of more mature oaks, and then return south to the lakeshore path. At 4.2 miles you reach the northern tip of the lake and the three-way junction with the lakeshore path. Turn right to continue. At 4.9 miles is a path between the north and south lake with a pretty footbridge. Continue 0.3 mile to the starting point.

Options

To extend your hike about a mile you can walk a path that goes through the woods and meadow north of the Yellow loop. Turn north onto the path at about 1.7 miles. Total mileage with the addition is about 6 miles. In summer this area may have heavy mosquitoes.

Directions

From the junction of I-90 W and I-294 N, drive north on I-294 N 12.3 miles, then continue on I-94 W 22 miles. Take the IL-173/Rosecrans Road exit and turn right. In 0.8 mile turn left on U.S. 41/Skokie Highway for 0.3 mile and take the first right into the preserve. Turn left on the preserve road for about 0.2 mile and park in the large lot north of the small boat dock. The Blue trail is along the south edge of the lot.

GPS Coordinates: 16 T 422368mE 4702539mN

Information and Contact

There is no fee. Dogs on leash are allowed. Drinking water, restrooms, and picnic areas are available on the west side of Sterling Lake, at the Des Plaines River Trail lot off Russell Road, and at locations near the east preserve trails. Preserve hours are 6:30 A.M.–sunset daily. For more information, contact Van Patten Woods, State Route 173, Wadsworth, IL, 847/367-6640, www.lcfpd.org.

11 CAMP LOGAN TRAILS   BEST 🄲
Illinois Beach State Park, North Unit, Zion

🏞 🌼 🏊 ⚛ 👁 ♿

Level: Easy/moderate   **Total Distance:** 5.7 miles round-trip

Hiking Time: 3 hours   **Elevation Change:** negligible

Summary: Explore restored prairie and the Lake Michigan shore in the North Unit of Illinois Beach State Park.

Illinois Beach State Park sprawls 4,160 acres over two sites, including 6.5 miles of Lake Michigan shoreline. Thousands of years ago, this landscape was forever changed when ancient Lake Chicago receded, leaving sand dunes and wetlands behind. The mild yet distinctive topography resulted in a variety of habitats and rich natural diversity—it is the only remaining sand ridge left along the Illinois shore. The North Unit of Illinois Beach State Park is widely known for birding, in particular, it has an innovative hawk tracking program.

The park's North Unit was once home to an Illinois National Guard rifle range, built in 1892. Most of the buildings were removed or dismantled in the 1970s;

looking south along the Lake Michigan shore

© BARBARA I. BOND

however, the North Unit is still called Camp Logan by locals. (There is also a Camp Logan multi-use trail.) The 1,925-acre North Unit is now home to a small nature preserve filled with rare plants and birds, including the Henslow's sparrow and American bittern. The trails are quiet as they wind through the preserve, across prairie and oak savanna, and along the dunes to the lakeshore.

From the trailhead, start hiking south; you will pass a trail sign as you curve around Sand Pond. The pond and adjacent nature preserve are filled with lots

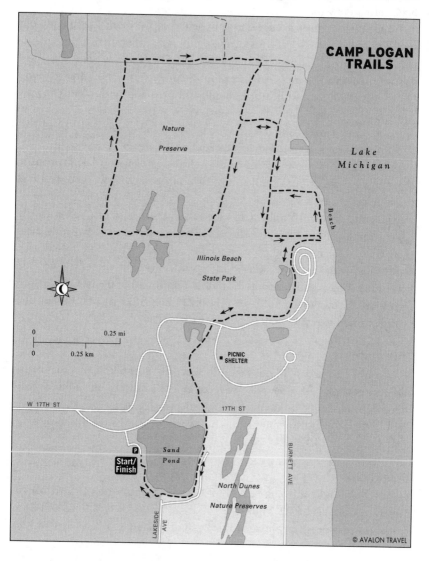

of bird activity—I saw an osprey and belted kingfisher almost immediately—and there are tall cottonwoods around the lake. In about 0.5 mile, cross 17th Street and enter the prairie. Flowers bloom through summer; in late summer, watch for deep purple gentian, milkweed, goldenrod, yarrow, and blazing star. This is also another bird-watching area; there is a lot of hawk activity late in the day or in fall. Just east is the first picnic area, a popular bird-watching spot. The trail winds east to the main beach trail junction at 1.3 miles; look for a big information sign.

Turn left (north), then left again to walk west along the Camp Logan multi-use trail. The trail skirts a row of trees for a short distance; the north side is full of cattails and sunflowers. Turn north for 0.4 mile to reach a three-way junction. Turn west, then south at 1.9 miles to begin a loop around the wetland. After traveling in oak woodland for a while, the ground gets wetter and cottonwoods appear. There is a lot of water along the southern section of this trail, as well as cattails, sedge, and sunflowers. Watch for great blue heron and egrets—they seemed to like it here. Turn north at 2.6 miles and continue along the marshy trail.

Pass an old rusty gate and fence on the right; yarrow and sunflowers populate the overgrown weeds. At 3.1 miles, turn right just past the fence, and walk east through lots of sunflowers along the open grassy path. Turn right at the three-way junction around 3.5 miles. Cross a creek and then turn east before shortly turning south again at 3.8 miles. The sound of waves lets you know that the lakeshore is close. To get there, turn left at 4 miles and walk to the shore. Spend some time exploring the beach, walking south towards a few cottonwoods, a pier, and breakwater. When ready, pick up the trail just northwest of the trees. Hike west for a short distance to 4.4 miles, pass the big Illinois Beach State Park sign, and continue ahead to retrace your steps back to Sand Pond.

Options

Visit nearby Van Patten Woods Forest Preserve for more hiking in a completely different environment. The preserve features a mix of trails, including a wonderful 5.2-mile loop hike around Sterling Lake (see listing for Des Plaines River Trail in this chapter). Combining this hike with the Van Patten hike brings the total distance to 10.9 miles.

Directions

From downtown Chicago, drive north I-94 and take the exit for U.S. 41/Skokie Highway; continue for 22.2 miles. Turn east at W. Wadsworth Road and drive 5.8 miles. Turn north on Sheridan Road and drive 2.4 miles. Turn east on 17th

Street for 0.7 mile and turn right on the park road to reach the Sand Pond lot. The trailhead is at the south end of the lot. There is a fishing pier and restroom.
GPS Coordinates: 16 T 433452mE 4701223mN

Information and Contact

There is no fee. Dogs are not allowed on the beach or in the nature preserve. The park is open sunrise–8 P.M. from Memorial Day through Labor Day; seasonal hours apply the rest of the year. Restrooms are available at the trailhead; drinking water and restrooms are available at other picnic areas along the trail. For more information, contact Illinois Beach State Park, South Unit, 1 Lake Front Drive, Zion, IL 60099, 847/662-4811, www.dnr.illinois.gov. For information about Van Patten Woods Forest Preserve, contact Lake County Forest Preserves, 2000 N. Milwaukee Avenue, Libertyville, IL 60048, 847/367-6640, http://www.lcfpd.org/preserves.

12 DEAD RIVER-DUNES LOOP

Illinois Beach State Park, South Unit, Zion

Level: Easy

Hiking Time: 1.5 hours

Total Distance: 3.5 miles round-trip

Elevation Change: negligible

Summary: The unique habitats of Illinois's first nature preserve await on this easy path.

The swale and dune topography of Illinois Beach State Park's South Unit was shaped by the receding water of ancient Lake Chicago. The landscape encompasses several natural communities, each with its own distinctive birds, animals, and plants. A well-developed trail system takes hikers on a journey along the marshes around the Dead River and across sand prairie, black oak woods, savanna, and ponds.

The Dead River resembles wetlands—the small meandering waters are landlocked most of the year. In the spring, when the water builds up, it breaks through a sandy ridge near the lake to flow into the larger body of water. From the map at the trailhead, follow the Dead River Trail south into the black oak woodland. The wood-chip trail cuts through thick wild grape that seems to have overtaken the forest floor as it winds up tree trunks. The woods are alive with birds early in the day—once you reach the river, you may see resident and migratory waterfowl

view southeast across Dead River

© BARBARA I. BOND

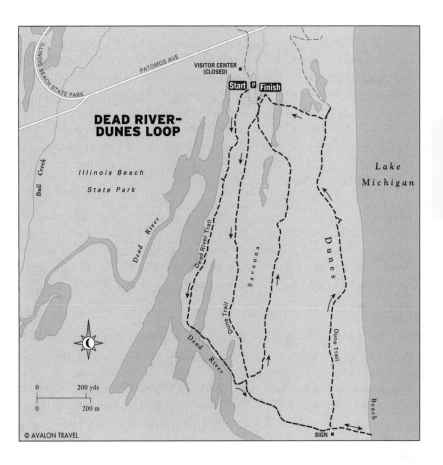

and waders. Walk along the still river for about 0.3 mile, enjoying the pretty sun-flowers, gentian, and sedges along the bank.

Soon the trail begins curving eastward, reaching a trail junction near 0.8 mile. Turn south on the Dune Trail, heading east towards the lakeshore. Hiking east, the terrain changes from savanna to sandy foredune as you approach the beach. Pass a sign marking the southeast corner of the trail, and continue a short distance to the lakeshore. (As you walk south toward the river, take care not to walk into the closed zone beyond the south bank.) The calm summertime waters are quite a contrast to the roaring energy of spring. (If visiting in spring, use extreme caution approaching the bank, as the sand can be quite unstable.) Gaze upriver, noting how the cottonwoods look out of place amidst the dune grasses.

Return to the Dune Trail and walk north along the sandy transition zone; you may spy some cinquefoil among the grasses and goldenrod. At 1.9 miles, the trail curves westward back towards the woods. After crossing a wood boardwalk, walk to the parking lot and turn south at the sign to continue on the Dune Trail, which now heads south in the black oak woods. Gray and thirteen-striped squirrels and woodpeckers keep you company along the trail; watch for the fresh hoofprints of white-tailed deer crossing the path in places. At 2.8 miles, you'll reach a trail junction and turn east. (If you look ahead before turning you will see the junction with the Dead River Trail.) Continue east, then north, as the woods thin to savanna while more grape claims the groundcover. You are now on the continuation of the Dead River Loop. At 3.3 miles, the trail curves northwest to return to the trailhead at 3.5 miles.

Options
Extend this hike by following a gravel path to the park office, where there are spotting scopes set on a pleasant deck overlooking Lake Michigan. Walk west to the former nature center (now closed indefinitely) to pick up the trail again, then follow it for 0.4 mile to the park office for a total hiking distance of 4.3 miles.

Directions
From downtown Chicago, take I-94 to U.S. 41/Skokie Highway and continue for 22.2 miles. Turn east at W. Wadsworth Road and drive for 6.2 miles. Just after crossing the railroad tracks, turn right onto the park road. Drive 0.7 mile south, then continue west on Patomos Avenue/Old Beach Road. Turn south in 0.4 mile, following signs for the nature center and trailhead. Drive into the large lot and park. The trailhead is in the southwest corner of the lot, marked by a Dead River Trail map.
GPS Coordinates: 16 T 433510mE 4696686mN

Information and Contact
There is no fee. Dogs are not allowed. The park is open sunrise–8 P.M. from Memorial Day through Labor Day; seasonal hours apply the rest of the year. Restrooms and water are available at the park office. For more information, contact Illinois Beach State Park, South Unit, 1 Lake Front Drive, Zion, IL 60099, 847/662-4811, www.dnr.illinois.gov.

13 PRAIRIE RIDGE-
DEER PATH-TAMARACK VIEW   BEST 🌙
Volo Bog State Natural Area, Ingleside

🦌 🪁 🌲 🥾 👫

Level: Easy

Hiking Time: 2.5-3 hours

Total Distance: 5.5 miles round-trip

Elevation Change: negligible

Summary: Walk among bog oddities and view a host of wildlife along Volo Bog's trails.

Volo Bog State Natural Area is the site of Illinois's only quaking bog and is an artifact of the region's glacial past. Over 6,000 years ago, Volo Bog was a 50-acre lake slowly being filled in with vegetation. Today, a tiny section of open water remains and it shrinks annually as plant life continues to move inward. Dedication and foresight 50 years ago began the process of protecting this valuable landscape. Today, after land acquisition and restoration efforts, over 1,000 acres of land constitute the state natural area, which includes two nature preserves, an interpretive center, and several miles of trails. Known as a prime spot for bird-watching, Volo Bog continues to be a unique part of the state's natural resources.

Tamarack stands around the open water of Volo Bog.

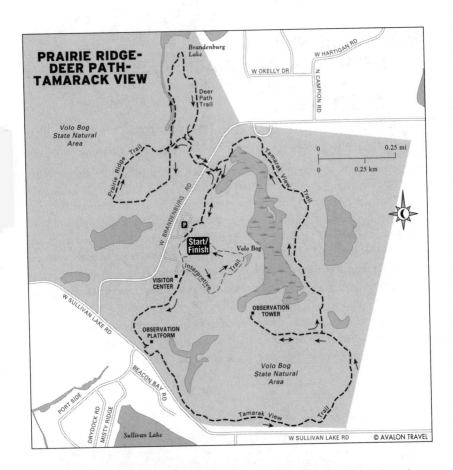

Three main types of wetlands are found in the glaciated terrain of northern Illinois, forming in the kettles left behind as the ice melted. These depressions hold water. Volo Bog is more like a fen since it receives a little run-off from the surrounding land. Succession is changing Volo; in time, no open water will remain. Today you can experience this succession from two viewpoints—one is the overall picture of the landscape from the perimeter of the Tamarack View Trail. You also can walk through the succession zones by strolling along the boardwalk of the interpretive trail. There you can easily track the change in plant life as the floating walkway passes from marsh to the small open-water center.

Volo Bog State Natural Area is divided in two by Brandenburg Road. Think of this as a two-part hike. To first hike the northwest trails walk east to the path and follow it northerly past the restrooms to the trailhead sign. Continue in the oak and hickory woods a few tenths of a mile and follow the signs to the Deerpath Trail Loop, across Brandenburg Road. Cross the road, return to the trail and continue on the mown path. I thought the 2 miles of trails here, adjacent to Pistakee Bog Nature Preserve, were lovely—quiet, with an abundance of butterflies and dragonflies in midsummer. I saw a white-tailed deer along the Prairie Ridge Loop. The restored prairie has woodland along its edge, perfect habitat for deer and a variety of grassland and woodland birds. You may see chickadees, sparrows, and woodpeckers. Turn left at all the trail junctions to complete the trails. At about 2.1 miles you will cross back over the road to the Tamarack View Trail, then the visitors center, at about 2.5 miles. Begin part two by walking south on the path. At post 1, after checking out the Interpretive Trail, walk downhill to the trailhead sign.

The Tamarack View Trail makes an irregular loop around the marsh and bog of Volo, while passing through the diverse habitats. Beginning in the black, white, and bur oak woods walk south on the packed-dirt trail. Walking 0.4 mile brings you to a nice observation platform, with views east across some open water and marshland. Wood ducks, egrets, and great blue heron can be seen here. Continue on the trail as it curves northward at 1.16 miles. Look for sunflowers, brown-eyed Susans, and blazing star along the grassland. Turn left at 1.5 miles, at the sign for the Observation Tower, one of my favorite spots. Even without binoculars you'll see dozens of birds on the marshes. Egrets, sandhill cranes, a swan or two, and various ducks may be seen depending upon the season. Return to the trail, turn northward and continue. There are nice views west across the marsh for a couple of tenths, and a bird blind at 2.85 miles, followed by a bench. Enjoy the views of the marsh.

The trail begins a gradual turn south at 3.1 miles, walking past some pine trees as you near the end of the trail. At 3.4 miles you'll walk off the trail at the picnic area.

Options

For an in-depth look at the bog, hike the interpretive trail 0.5 mile along boardwalks and wooden viewing platforms. (Note: Poison sumac grows along the boardwalk; play it safe and avoid touching any plants.) Enjoy the pretty needles of the tamarack trees and watch for green heron on the marsh; as you return past the small pond, look for painted turtles. All sorts of unique plants grow here—including the carnivorous pitcher plant—and in spring there are lots of blooms.

Directions

From the junction of I-90 W and I-294 N, drive north on I-294 for 3.3 miles. Exit onto U.S. 14 W/Dempster Street for 0.4 mile and turn right and drive northwest on Rand Road 23.9 miles. Continue on State Route 59 N/U.S. 12 W for 4.3 miles, turn left (west) on W. Sullivan Lake Road. In 1.4 miles, turn right and drive north on W. Brandenburg Road. The parking lot for Volo Bog is on the east side of the road in 0.4 mile. There is a trailhead east of the lot, past the restrooms and picnic area, or walk south past the visitors center for the other.

GPS Coordinates: 16 T 402130mE 4689376mN

Information and Contact

There is no fee. Dogs on leash are allowed except on the Interpretive Trail. The park is open sunrise–sunset daily; visitors center hours vary (call ahead to confirm). Trail guides for the Tamarack View and Interpretive Trails are available at the Visitor Center. For more information, contact Volo Bog State Natural Area, 28478 W. Brandenburg Road, Ingleside, IL, 815/344-1312, www.dnr.state.il.us.

14 ROLLINS SAVANNA TRAILS   BEST ◖

Rollins Savanna Forest Preserve, Lake County, Grayslake

Level: Easy/moderate

Total Distance: 5.7 miles round-trip

Hiking Time: 2.5-3 hours

Elevation Change: negligible

Summary: Walk restored prairie, wetlands, and oak savanna while enjoying one of Chicagoland's best birding spots.

Less than 25 years ago, Rollins Savanna was a mix of old fields and former ranchland interspersed with remaining prairie and oak savanna. Lake County began buying up the property in the late 1980s and since then has undertaken a monumental restoration project. Outdoors enthusiasts definitely are the beneficiaries; today a visit to Rollins Savanna includes miles of trails through thriving habitat.

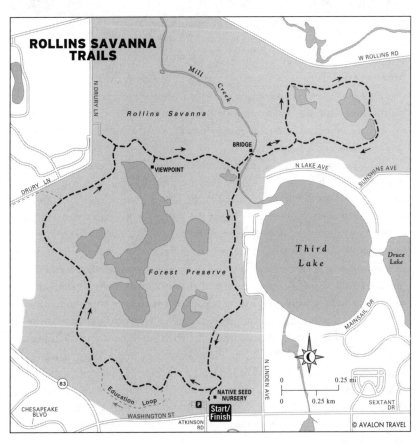

looking south from the observation area at Rollins Savanna

The old Picket Fence Farm is also home to a native seed nursery which includes 10 acres of seed beds. As with many sites in Lake County, the retreating glacial ice over 10,000 years left a landscape dotted with wetlands, ponds, and marshes. Visit Rollins Savanna for a walk through lush prairie and thriving wetlands and see why the National Audubon Society named it one of America's most important bird sites in 2005.

Take a moment to look at the information signs at the main entrance. From there, walk north to the main loop and turn west. Immediately you can enjoy unrestricted views across the grassland north, it is an impressive sight. Follow the wide trail as it winds northward for nearly two miles. You will pass the entrance/exit to the short Education Loop. This 0.5-mile trail uses boardwalks to explore some ponds and wetlands just west of the main trail. By now, you probably have already seen dozens of goldfinches and sparrows. Check the ponds along the east side of the trail for ducks and perhaps an egret. At nearly 2 miles there is a trail junction with a spur northwest to the Drury Lane lot, where there is a restroom.

The restored prairie blooms throughout summer. Depending upon your timing you may see blazing star, compass plant, or coneflowers blooming. Walking east now, you may detour south at 2.3 miles to a viewpoint overlooking the large pond in the center of the main trail. The binoculars are helpful for identifying birds like blue-winged teals. The oak savanna, with some huge bur oak, is a nice break on the way to the trail junction at 2.7 miles. Turn left and walk northeast then east across the footbridge to the nearly 1.2 mile loop. This quiet trail winds through a bit of savanna and has great views across some small ponds. I saw a lot of ducks and some egrets on the water, which is surrounded by cattails and goldenrod.

Return to the main trail at 4.6 miles and walk south towards the seed beds in the southeast corner. You will pass through some wetland and parallel the creek a short distance before returning to open grassland. Here you may see yellow-headed blackbirds or marsh wrens. At about 5.6 miles the trail begins curving west past the seedbeds and a bench. The main entrance is ahead 0.1 mile.

Options

For a shorter hike with a lot of natural beauty and bird-watching opportunities, just hike the main loop. By skipping the pond loop, the total hiking distance drops to 3.8 miles.

Note: In fall 2011, a new section of trail will open, connecting Rollins Savanna to Fourth Lake, north of the preserve, allowing hikers to walk the gravel trail to a mown-grass loop with a scenic overlook of Fourth Lake.

Directions

From the junction of I-294 and I-94, take I-94 W and drive north for 13.6 miles. Take the exit for State Route 120 W/Belvidere Road and drive west for 4.6 miles. Turn north on U.S. 45 N and drive for 1.5 miles. Turn left on W. Washington Street and drive 1.2 miles to the park entrance on the north side of the street (Atkinson Road/Washington Street).

Public Transportation: Take Metra from Union Station to the Washington Street (Grayslake) stop. Walk east on Washington Street for 1.4 miles to Rollins Savanna.

GPS Coordinates: 16 T 415663mE 4690152mN

Information and Contact

There is no fee. Dogs on leash are allowed. The park is open 6:30 A.M.–sunset daily. The trailhead parking lot has water, restrooms, picnic tables, and maps. For more information, contact Rollins Savanna Forest Preserve, 19876 W. Washington Street, Grayslake, IL, 847/367-6640, www.lcfpd.org.

15 MILLENNIUM-FORT HILL TRAILS

Lakewood Forest Preserve, Wauconda

Level: Easy/moderate

Hiking Time: 3 hours

Total Distance: 6.1 miles round-trip

Elevation Change: 160 feet

Summary: A visit to Lakewood Preserve will be a fun experience for novice and experienced hikers alike.

On the western edge of Lake County sits the 2,715 acres that comprise the Lakewood Forest Preserve. The popular natural and educational area is home to a museum and several recreation sites. Lake County has the wetlands, ponds, lakes, and rolling terrain left behind by the glacial retreat over 10,000 years ago. The further west one travels, the more varied the terrain. This is good news for outdoors enthusiasts. The preserve is also home to a variety of wildlife including white-tailed deer, fox, beaver, and a host of bird species.

The central "museum and recreation core" of Lakewood is well-developed. The core is home to the Discovery Museum, where one can see a woolly mammoth replica and learn about the rich history of the area. The are a number of mown-grass trails in the core section and several fishing lakes. Just walking through this popular area one is likely to come across sandhill cranes. Just south of Ivanhoe Road is a segment of preserve with equestrian trails.

The southeast corner of Lakewood Preserve has gently rolling hills and is dotted with lakes and ponds. Predictably, this is a popular cross-country skiing and sledding area for much of the year. The rest of the time, hikers and bicyclists enjoy the scenic 3.5-mile section of the Millennium Trail. Walk north on the trail downhill to a T intersection with a sign and map. We are going to explore two short segments of the trail from this intersection.

Go east to first head towards the quiet oak savanna and woods. The trail drops steeply, then climbs back through the oak and hickory woods, which is overgrown with black raspberry and wild grape in places. Turn left at the two trail junctions in the first 0.8 mile. Then walk east past Schreiber Lake, which is surrounded by marshland and cattails. The Schreiber Lake woods have a lot of bird activity, even in summer. The trail flattens out in the woods, then drops down to cross the outlet stream between Davis and Owen Lake. This is a good place to have a picnic, cast a line, or just enjoy the goldenrod and white water lilies.

Retrace your steps to the trail junction just past Schreiber Lake and turn left, then right, to walk north on a short loop. The trail descends, then climbs

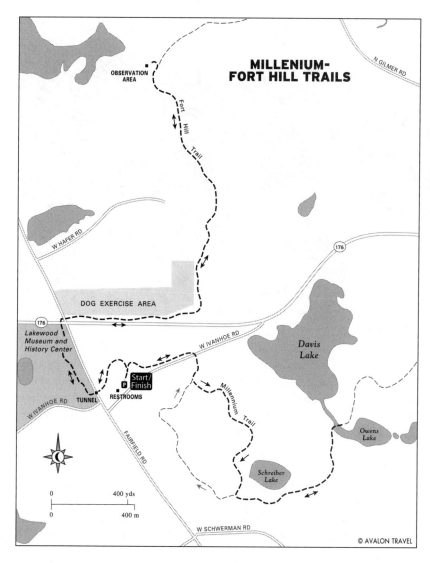

around a restored prairie and oak savanna and is very quiet. At 2.3 miles, turn left once more to retrace your steps to the top of the short hill adjacent to the T junction and trail sign.

Follow the Millennium Trail west, then north, for 0.5 mile to get through the museum core. Go under N. Fairfield in the tunnel, then walk north to cross Wauconda at Fairfield Roads to reach the trail continuation at the northeast corner at 3.1 miles. Over the next 0.7 mile you'll pass what's likely to be the biggest dog park you have ever seen, then the trail climbs slightly through the oak savanna

© BARBARA I. BOND

hikers relaxing along Owen Lake

once more. At 4.1 miles is a bridge over a slender pond; this is a nice place to watch for waterfowl. At 4.4 miles, take the short spur on the left to an overlook. Take some time here to look for ducks, geese, or egrets on the lake. There was a swan on the lake when I was there. A number of short trails allow you to explore the east side of the Fort Hill Trail. Return the way you came.

Options

For a longer outing, drop a car at the Singing Hills Forest Preserve farther north. From Lakewood, the Millennium Trail winds its way north for 6.4 miles, past Broberg Marsh and numerous ponds and marshes. There are restrooms, water, and a picnic shelter at Singing Hills. The total hiking distance is 12.5 miles.

Directions

From the junction of I-90 and I-294, drive north on I-294 for 2.3 miles, then continue on I-94 W for 8.8 miles. Take the Rockland Road/State Route 176 exit and drive west for 10.4 mile. Turn left at County V61/N. Fairfield Road and drive 0.2 mile. Turn east on W. Ivanhoe Road into the parking lot. Walk north to the end of the lot; the trailhead is to the right.

GPS Coordinates: 16 T 409423mE 4679046mN

Information and Contact

There is no fee. Dogs on leash are allowed. The park is open 6:30 A.M.–sunset daily. The trailhead parking lot has water, restrooms, picnic tables, and a bike-trail map. For more information, contact Winter Sports Lot, Lakewood Forest Preserve, Fairfield Road, Wauconda, IL 60084, 847/367-6640, www.lcfpd.org.

Singing Hills Forest Preserve is located off Fish Lake Road (north of Gilmer Road). For more information, contact Lake County Forest Preserve, 2000 N. Milwaukee Avenue, Libertyville, IL 60048, 847/367-6640, www.lcfpd.org.

16 OLD SCHOOL FOREST PRESERVE TRAILS

Old School Forest Preserve, Libertyville

Level: Easy

Hiking Time: 2.5-3 hours

Total Distance: 5.6 miles round-trip

Elevation Change: negligible

Summary: A fitness loop in the woods and a pretty lakeside path make Old School trails worth a visit.

Lake County has embraced the concept of recreation in a natural setting, and the wide range of preserve holdings reflects that belief. The annual Hike Lake County Challenge encourages use of the preserve's trail system, which includes more than 100 miles of forest preserve trails. Popular Old School Forest Preserve encompasses 360 acres of oak woodland with pockets of prairie and has 6 miles of trails, plus a one-way road that bicyclists use for training. The preserve also has a hiking trail/fitness loop featuring a variety of challenging activities in the oak-hickory woodland.

To begin, walk south from the parking area onto the Des Plaines River Trail (DPRT). The limestone trail winds through the oak woodland and openings south for 0.8 mile. In the open areas, wildflowers like sunflowers and tall goldenrod bloom all summer. Watch for goldfinch and sparrows in the open areas, and woodpeckers in the big white oak and hickory trees. Turn north onto the

Des Plaines River Trail-North

© BARBARA I. BOND

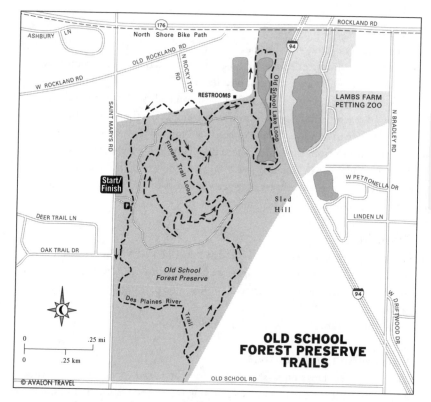

preserve trail at a signed junction at 0.8 mile. This part of the preserve was once home to a log cabin school; see if you can spot the trees that look planted instead of natural.

Walk north through the thinning trees. There are some ponds on either side of the trail. Cross the preserve road and at 1.6 miles you will reach a three-way junction with the DPRT-North. Before continuing on the DPRT, take a detour and walk south, then across a parking lot to the start of the wooded fitness trail. This fun loop is a wonderful challenge for kids or anyone who is up for it. There are all sorts of activities including a wall scaling station! Even if you skip the added exercise, this trek offers a quiet walk amongst the trees. Retrace your steps back to the main trail and resume walking north at 3.2 miles.

After you cross the road, turn east at about 3.7 miles, then north when you reach the Old School Lake loop. As you walk the 0.9-mile loop, you will see large cottonwoods along the shore, some weeping willows, and aspens. The shore is dense with cattails, and lily pads dot the water. Retrace your steps to the junction with the DPRT and turn west into the woods for the final 0.6 mile. Enjoy the huge bur oaks, and end at the trailhead at about 5.7 miles.

Options

You can easily extend your hiking time by using the North Shore Bike Path to reach nearby Middlefork Savanna Forest Preserve. Middlefork Savanna has 4.5 miles of trails and is an important bird habitat. The 670-acre preserve has a rare parcel of tallgrass savanna that supports threatened species like the Blanding's turtle. To reach the bike path from the lake loop, take the spur north around 4 miles. Walk east just over 1 mile to reach Middlefork Savanna. The trail heads west then south from the North Shore Bike Path, midway between the railroad tracks and Waukegan Road. It is 1.8 miles to the woodchip nature path, with boardwalks over sensitive areas. Retrace your steps to Old School to resume hiking for a total distance of 12.3 miles.

Directions

From the junction of I-294 and I-94, drive north on I-94 W for 5.5 miles. Take the Town Line Road exit and drive west for 1.3 miles. At County 19/N. St. Marys Road, turn north and drive 2.1 miles. The parking lot is on the east side of the road.

GPS Coordinates: 16 T 423822mE 4680059mN

Information and Contact

There is no fee. Dogs on leash are allowed. The park is open 6:30 A.M.–sunset daily. The trailhead parking lot has drinking water, and restrooms and water are available at various sites throughout the preserve. For more information, contact Old School Forest Preserve, 28201 St. Marys Road (south of W. Rockland Rd.), Libertyville, IL, 847/367-6640, www.lcfpd.org.

17 RYERSON WOODS

BEST ☾

Ryerson Conservation Area, Lake County Forest Preserves, Riverwoods

Level: Easy

Total Distance: 5.0 miles round-trip

Hiking Time: 2-2.5 hours

Elevation Change: negligible

Summary: A hike at Ryerson Conservation Area includes a rare northern flatwood forest, three historic cabins, and a modern environmental education center.

The Ryerson Conservation Area, also known as Ryerson Woods, has more than 550 acres of woodland. Over half of that acreage is protected by its designation as an Illinois Nature Preserve. Ryerson Woods is unique in that it contains four distinct forest communities. The southern half of the preserve contains wet floodplain, mesic sugar maple, and upland woods remain in their nearly natural state, and the wetlands provide habitat for several bird and waterfowl species. Years ago

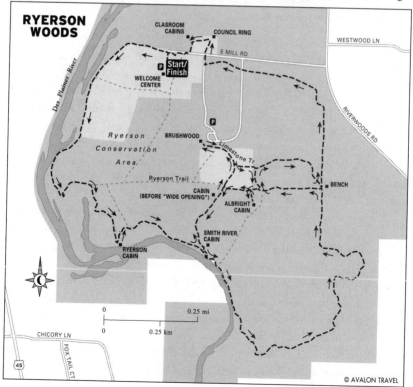

© BARBARA I. BOND

boardwalk along the Des Plaines River

the Ryerson Family lived in the Brushwood house and built cabins on the land for recreation. Later, they began donating the land for conservation and a preserve began to take shape. Today visitors can enjoy 6.5 miles of trails, boardwalks, and bridges while viewing hundreds of plant species, and learn about the human and natural history from the interpretive displays at the Smith River Cabin.

Ryerson Woods has a virtual maze of short interconnected trails that cover most of the property. This hike makes a big loop that covers the various types of woods, and includes a short inner loop for an exploration of the unique features in the center of the conservation area. Walk north from the parking lot to the gated path that takes off west. At first you'll walk west, skirting the trees, towards the meandering Des Plaines River; then turn southward along the edge of a field. The mown trail then enters the dense woods around 0.4 mile. In the warmer months, entering the shady woods provides a nice break from the heat. Green leaves from bur oak and silver maple contrast with the dark, ridged bark of the older trees. The forest floor is rife with shade-loving plants and shrubs. This includes poison ivy, so take care when brushing up against leaves that encroach on the trail. There is a glimpse of the river through the trees, and the rhythmic song of frogs can be heard here. At 0.7 mile or so, you will reach a three-way trail junction; turn right and walk southwards 0.2 mile to the Ryerson Cabin. Just prior to the cabin, keep right at a junction, then continue straight ahead a very short distance south. The cabin sits just north of a river bend. The maples around this area are sometimes huge and you may even see a few trillium on the forest floor.

Returning to the trail, now heading north, walk about 0.1 mile then turn right to continue our loop east. Cross the first of many boardwalks and at the second intersection turn north to visit the Ryerson Trail (accessible), Brushwood House, and prairie restoration in the center of the property. The maples in this part of the woods create an airy canopy and somehow the forest seems less dense. Just before you reach a wide opening is the Smith River Cabin on the east side of the trail. After checking it out, continue north, cross an open area then turn left onto the limestone trail to Brushwood. After a look, return to the limestone path and continue east to the second trail junction and turn south to reach a short spur to the Albright Cabin (not on the official map). Return to the main trail and turn left (west), then left again at 2.1 miles. Head south to reach the river trail at about 2.3 miles, turning left to continue the river/woods loop.

Back on the river trail the trees are the stars—cottonwoods in the wet areas, catalpa with its huge leaves, and more tall maple. Over the next mile you'll cross more boardwalks as the trail wanders south, then eastward, away from the river a short distance. The trail turns north, makes a hairpin turn, then resumes its northward trend. At 3.45 miles you will reach a three-way trail junction with a bench. Turn left and walk west to 3.6 miles, which takes you out of the woods, then turn north. The prairie restoration will be to your left and the woods to your right as you walk a short distance, turning right at another bench to re-enter the trees. As you walk the 0.2 mile back to the main trail, you will pass a stand of conifers that were planted in the early part of the 20th century. At 4 miles you reach the junction with the bench; turn left to resume your northward trek. The eastern forest contains sections of flatwoods, areas where there is a perched water table. This is why boardwalks are needed—the elevated trail allows the water to flow naturally. In turn the ephemeral ponds can form; they are a crucial part of the flatwood ecology. At 4.2 miles the trail turns west to head towards the main visitor area where you began. Continue through the woods and turn right to cross the entrance road at 4.5 miles. This short detour will take you past the Council Ring. There are some stately old oaks near here. Finally, walk south past the classroom cabins. The cabins used to be scattered around the property but were moved to accommodate students. The main visitor buildings are ahead.

Options

If you want to explore the cabins, flatwoods, and Ryerson Trail then park at the Brushwood lot in the center of the property. From here you can walk south on the trail, turn east and walk 0.2 mile to the second trail junction. Turn south and walk 0.3 mile to the river trail and turn left. Over the next mile you will go south, then curve gradually back northward in a wide arc. At the trail junction with the bench, skip the sharp left and take the second left which will take you past the conifers as you return to Brushwood. Follow the trail west to your starting point for about a 2.0-mile hike.

Directions

From the junction of I-90 and I-294 in Rosemont, drive north on I-294 for 12.3 miles, continuing on I-94 W for 0.2 mile. Take the Deerfield Road exit and drive west for 0.5 mile. Turn right on Riverwoods Road and drive northwest for 1.7 miles. Turn west onto the preserve road for 0.4 mile, turn south just before the gate. The hike begins at the gated trail, on the north side of the lot where the road turns.
GPS Coordinates: 16 T 424441mE 4670190mN

Information and Contact

There is no fee. Dogs on leash are allowed. Trails are open 6:30 A.M.–sunset. Call for welcome center hours. For maps visit www.lcfpd.org. Ryerson Woods Welcome Center and Ryerson Conservation Area, 21950 N. Riverwoods Road, Riverwoods, IL, 847/367-6640.

WEST OF CHICAGO

© BARBARA I. BOND

BEST HIKES

Many people probably envision the lands west

of Chicago as a vast plain – monotonous and never-ending. Yet this region encompasses so much more. This area stretches from DuPage County all the way to the Mississippi River and covers several distinct natural divisions that organize the state into communities with similar ecology, geology, and flora and fauna. Get out and explore this territory on foot and you will find abundant wildlife, birds, and unique plant life, as well as a surprising amount of landform diversity (even though much of the land has been heavily impacted by human activity).

DuPage and most of Kane County are in the Northeastern Morainal Division, and have been shaped by the glacial period that left its mark on the northeast corner of Illinois. Frontcountry trails through these parks and preserves work their way through morainal forests, wetlands, and kettle ponds. A day spent on the trails in Moraine Hills State Park allows hikers to experience much of this variety up close. Trails wander through upland forests and along marshy borders of kettle ponds. Higher ground always beckons hikers, and at Blackwell Forest Preserve glacial kames rise up and make a statement.

Farther west, in the Rockford area, adventurers will discover the dramatic Rock River Hill Country, which offers quite a contrast. This division is marked by rivers and streams, which support rich forests, and dry uplands covered with prairie grasses. Along the Rock River are distinctive sandstone formations that provide a unique ecosystem for wildlife, flora, and fauna. Hiking out here is unlike anything else in the Chicagoland area. You are just as likely to be accompanied by wild turkeys as you are other hikers. Lowden-Miller State Forest started off as private land and is now part of the Illinois Department of Natural Resources. Hikers here can enjoy views of the river rock formations as well as glimpses of red-shouldered hawks, red-headed woodpeckers, and white-tailed deer.

The Wisconsin Driftless Division encompasses a unique pocket of far northwestern Illinois. This area has the ravines and valleys associated with lands that escaped the scouring effect of recent glacial activity. The undulating landscape is what makes hiking at Mississippi Palisades State Park such a rewarding experience. The trails are quiet and rolling and multiple layers of dolomite and limestone rock create the bluffs and palisades that form a picturesque and rugged outdoor playground. Butterflies are abundant as are woodland birds like the scarlet tanager, wood thrush, and several wood warblers.

The wonderful diversity of animal and plant species and the sharply contrasting landscapes of this region have lots of attractive features that will entice you to lace up your boots and head outdoors. This variety will keep most hikers busy exploring for a long time.

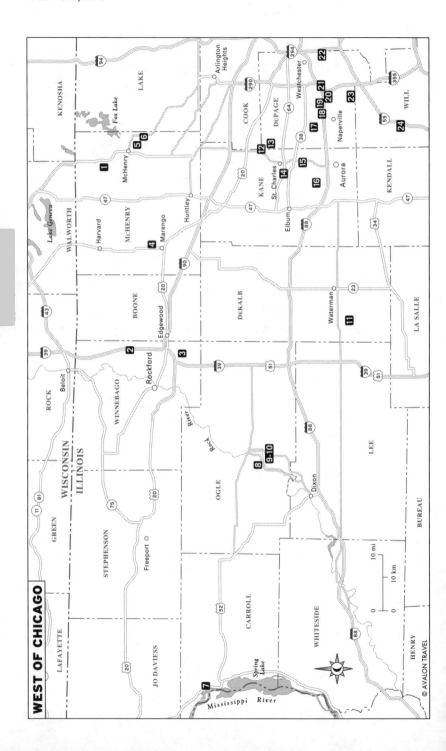

WEST OF CHICAGO

TRAIL NAME	LEVEL	DISTANCE	TIME	ELEVATION	FEATURES	PAGE
1 Deerpath, Marsh, and Coyote Loop	Easy	4.0 mi rt	2 hr	300 ft		144
2 Pierce Lake Trail	Easy/moderate	4.5 mi rt	2–2.5 hr	negligible		148
3 Blackhawk Springs–Oak Ridge Forest Preserve Trails	Moderate	9.6 mi rt	5 hr	260 ft		151
4 Marengo Ridge Trails	Moderate	5.2 mi rt	3 hr	290 ft		154
5 Leatherleaf Bog Loop	Easy	3.2 mi rt	1.5 hr	negligible		158
6 Lake Defiance Loop	Easy	4.2 mi rt	2.5 hr	negligible		161
7 Sentinel and Sunset Trails	Strenuous	3.7 mi rt	2–2.5 hr	870 ft		164
8 Castle Rock North Trails	Easy/moderate	3.6 mi rt	2 hr	380 ft		168
9 Lowden-Miller River Loop	Easy	4.5 mi rt	2–2.5 hr	negligible		171
10 Logger's Trail	Easy	1.5 mi rt	1 hr	negligible		174
11 Shabbona Lake Loop	Moderate	6.2 mi rt	3 hr	negligible		177
12 Blazing Star–Bluestem–Indigo Trails	Easy	4.5 mi rt	2–2.5 hr	260 ft		181
13 Lake and West Trails	Moderate	3.5 mi rt	2 hr	negligible		184
14 Horlock Hill Prairie–Preserve Loop Trail	Easy	3.3 mi rt	1.5 hr	negligible		187
15 Fox River Trail: Geneva to Batavia Loop	Easy/moderate	5.5–5.9 mi rt	2–3 hr	negligible		191
16 Nelson Lake Loop	Easy	4.2 mi rt	2 hr	negligible		195
17 Regional-Bobolink Trail Loop	Easy/moderate	7.0 mi rt	3.5–4 hr	negligible		198
18 Herrick Lake Loop	Easy/moderate	5.7 mi rt	3 hr	negligible		202
19 Danada Regional and Nature Trails	Easy	3.4 mi rt	2 hr	negligible		205
20 West and Schulenberg Prairie Loop	Moderate	4.6 mi rt	2–3 hr	190 ft		208
21 Big Rock Trail Sampler	Easy/moderate	4.3 mi rt	2.5 hr	negligible		211
22 Fullersburg-Graue Mill Loop	Easy	3.0–4.0 mi rt	1.5–2 hr	negligible		214
23 Main-Greene Valley Loop	Easy/moderate	6.4 mi rt	3–3.5 hr	175 ft		218
24 Lake Renwick-Budde Lake Loop	Easy	3.0 mi rt	1.5 hr	negligible		221

■ DEERPATH, MARSH, AND COYOTE LOOP

Glacial Park Conservation Area, McHenry County Conservation District, Ringwood

🏞 🦌 🌸 ❀ 🦌

Level: Easy

Hiking Time: 2 hours

Total Distance: 4.0 miles round-trip

Elevation Change: 300 feet

Summary: Glacial Park has enough terrain for any hiker, including glacial kames, marsh, and prairie grasses and forbs.

The McHenry County Conservation District has created a wonderful opportunity for recreation and education in 3,400-acre Glacial Park. History buffs can enjoy the historic 1854 Powers-Walker homestead. The Wiedrich Education Center is housed in the 1902 Wiedrich Barn. Conservationists will appreciate the prairie restoration and hundreds of acres of restored native habitat including wetlands and the remeandering Nippersink Creek. An Illinois Nature Preserve protects 400 acres of the central park. And then there is the hiking—over six miles of trails that take you up along a glacial kame, through a rolling woodland, and along a marsh and bog where the rare and threatened leatherleaf plant thrives. The landscape of Glacial Park was sculpted by the Wisconsin Glacier, which covered the land for thousands of years. Upon its retreat, it left behind rolling hills, kettle

© BARBARA I. BOND

Camelback Kame

holes, and eskers. The grasslands are home to compass plant, with it's tall yellow flower, and goldenrod in late summer.

Glacial Park has multiple trailheads, including one for early morning hikers who arrive before the main lots open. Begin at the main parking lot, which is south of the Wiedrich Education Center. From the lot walk south, past an information board, onto the mown grass trail. The first 0.5 mile winds through scattered, rolling oak and hickory. Just before the three-way trail junction around mile 0.6 you will emerge onto the prairie, pass a bench and interpretive sign, then reach the signed intersection for the Coyote Loop. Continue ahead to reach the signature glacial kame, Camelback. The Camelback runs north–south and divides the east savanna, marsh, and bog from Nippersink Creek.

Walk northwest another 0.25 mile to reach the "Y" with the kame trail. Curve

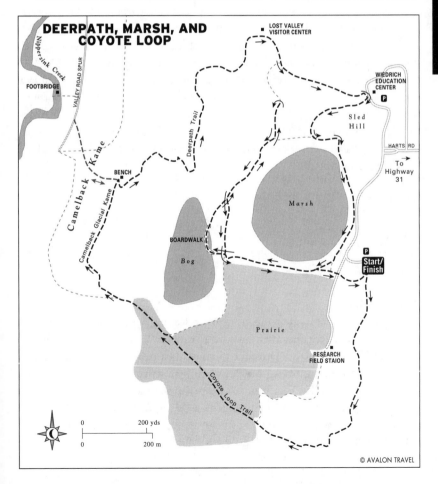

DEERPATH, MARSH, AND COYOTE LOOP

Nippersink Creek
FOOTBRIDGE
VALLEY ROAD SPUR
LOST VALLEY VISITOR CENTER
WIEDRICH EDUCATION CENTER
Sled Hill
HARTS RD
To Highway 31
Deerpath Trail
Camelback Kame
Camelback Glacial Kame
BENCH
Marsh
BOARDWALK
Bog
Start/Finish
Prairie
RESEARCH FIELD STAION
Coyote Loop Trail

0   200 yds
0   200 m

© AVALON TRAVEL

slightly right, then uphill, on the narrow path to the top of the kame and enjoy the view. There are wildflowers on the west side of the kame and the creek is clearly visible in the near distance. Walk downhill towards a bench and trail junction. When you reach the bench, at nearly 1 mile, you can turn left onto a trail that will take you down towards the creek and Valley Road Spur. It's only a detour of 0.14 mile one-way and it gives you a good view of the Camelback Kame (look for purple coneflower blooming along the west slope). If not, then turn right to a signed two-way junction, then left to get onto the Deerpath Trail. The trail wanders through the trees—it's a good habitat for birds and wildlife, including turtles. The path climbs up to the northern part of the trail, which is one of the highest sections. At 1.87 miles is three-way trail junction; keep left. In an additional 0.2 mile you reach the trailhead adjacent to the Weidrich Barn. Walk around the information sign, go right to get back on the trail. At 2.2 miles, turn left, then make a quick right on the Marsh Loop.

The Marsh Loop contours along the marsh edge. You reach a four-way junction at 2.7 miles, left is the Coyote Trail. Ahead is the bog boardwalk, it's short and worth checking out. Return to the trail and turn left to continue north to a viewpoint at about mile 3.3. The views are superb. From here, backtrack south on the Deerpath Trail. Then turn east at the trail junction to redo the first part of the Marsh Loop. It is 0.6 mile to the southeast corner of the marsh trail; turn left and walk east to your car. Your total mileage will vary depending upon how much exploring you do.

Options

For a longer hike, walk down from the Camelback Kame to Nippersink Creek. You can cross the bridge and walk around the west-side marsh on an equestrian trail; it's about a 2.4-mile loop. Return to the trail when you're finished for a total hiking distance of 6.4 miles.

Directions

From the I-90/State Route 53 intersection in Rolling Meadows, drive north on IL-53 for 8 miles. Exit onto Lake Cook Road west for 0.7 mile, then turn right on U.S. 12 W/N. Rand Road. Drive for 15 miles, then turn left at State Route 120 W/W. Belvidere Road. After 5.6 miles, turn right at State Route 31 N/N. Richmond Road. In 6 miles, turn left onto Harts Road at the Glacial Park sign. In 1 mile, turn left and drive south 0.2 mile to the parking lot. There is an information sign, trash receptacle, and vault toilet. A picnic area is adjacent to the lot.
GPS Coordinates: 16 T 391235mE 4696919mN

Information and Contact

There is no fee. Dogs on leash are allowed. Summer hours are 8 A.M.–6 P.M. daily. In winter, the park is open for cross-country skiing. Canoeing is available on Nippersink Creek; launch from Keystone or Pioneer Road Landing. For more information, contact Glacial Park Conservation Area, 6316 Harts Road, Ringwood, IL, 815/678-4532, www.mccdistrict.org.

The Lost Valley Visitor Center is open 8 A.M.–6 P.M. daily April–October; 8 A.M.–4:30 P.M. Monday–Friday and 9 A.M.–4 P.M. Saturday–Sunday November–March. For more information, contact Lost Valley Visitor Center, 18410 U.S. Highway 14, Ringwood, IL 60098, 815/338-6223.

❷ PIERCE LAKE TRAIL   BEST 🌙

Rock Cut State Park, Loves Park

Level: Easy/moderate   **Total Distance:** 4.5 miles round-trip

Hiking Time: 2-2.5 hours   **Elevation Change:** negligible

Summary: Enjoy bird-watching and a lakeside stroll along the Pierce Lake Trail.

Rock Cut State Park has grown quite a bit since the initial acquisition of 193 acres in 1930. Today the park covers 3,092 acres of diverse habitat for over 200 species of birds and a variety of small animals. Early park inhabitants were Native Americans until about 1830, when various European settlers began to arrive. Blasts through the solid rock for the Kenosha–Rockford railroad in 1859 gave the park its name. The rail lines were torn out in 1937. Most of the railroad grade is under Pierce Lake except for a small section in the Willow Creek area near the dam spillway.

Rock Cut State Park has an extensive trail system, with trailheads scattered throughout. Mountain biking, equestrian, and multi-use trails make up the bulk of the mileage; hikers may use any of the trails. The prairie restoration and hardwood forest north of Hart Road offer hikers the opportunity to view prairie wildflowers all summer long. Spring wildflowers carpet the forest floor, and you may

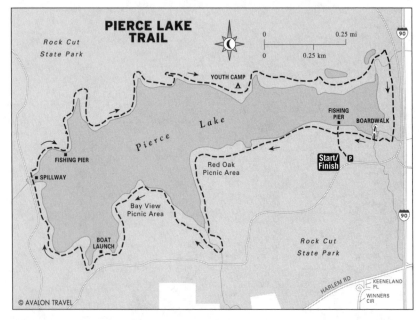

heron near the Red Oak Picnic Area

see a gray catbird or downy woodpecker in the trees. Watch for wild turkeys any time of year, if you are stealthy you may hear them before actually seeing them. They are quite a sight, especially when they are herding a flock of young.

Hiking the Pierce Lake Trail is a wonderful way to experience this state park. The trail winds through oak forest and openings, with nearly endless views of the blue lake waters. It is a good way to watch waterfowl and wading birds such as blue-winged teal and great blue heron. Begin walking west from the trail sign. In the first mile the trail works through dense woods before crossing the opening of Red Oak Picnic Area on the way to a narrow bridge. You will definitely feel small walking through these giant oaks. The trail is marked periodically with blue posts, usually near the start or end of a section or an intersection. While working your way around the inlet you will pass some huge maples. Ducks paddle quietly on the inlet and waders frequently fish along the shallow water near shore. Black cherry and occasional pines contribute to the dense woods. In some places, bright orange spotted touch-me-nots bloom.

There is a good view of the spillway from the point north of Bay View Picnic Area. Pass the boat launch area and concessions for 0.2 mile, then cross another overgrown wooden footbridge. At 1.7 miles you turn north into the trees through an overgrown section of narrow trail winding northward. After passing another picnic area, you cross the spillway bridge at just over 2 miles. This is a popular fishing spot, watch too for osprey.

After passing a fishing pier the trail zigzags to get around the camping area, turning westward at nearly 2.9 miles. It feels quiet along the next mile, where there is likely to be a lot of bird and animal activity. You may see goldfinch, tree swallows, sparrows, orioles, cottontails, or 13-lined ground squirrels. There are occasional bat boxes just off the trail; hopefully they are getting a lot to eat, so that there are fewer bugs to feast on you. Approaching 3.9 miles and the turn south, highway noise intrudes. The next 0.3 mile of trail was new in summer 2010. Cross the bridge, then turn west towards the wooden viewing platforms at 4.2 miles, where the path is paved. After taking in the views and listening to the birds, continue 0.3 more to reach the start.

Options

Hike through the northern woods on the multipurpose and equestrian trails to a short loop in the restored prairie, just west of the main entrance road. From the Puri Crest Picnic Area, walk north on trail marked with blue posts. Follow the trail north for 1 mile before turning left onto the equestrian trail. Hike west, cross the road at 1.3 miles. Continue hiking southwest, then south and east, to meet the Prairie Loop. Follow the 0.3-mile loop to the trailhead. From the trailhead, walk north about 0.1 mile, rejoining the trail heading east. Retrace your steps to the trailhead for a total hiking distance of about 3.3 miles.

Directions

From downtown Chicago and I-290, take the I-90 split and drive for 80.4 miles. Exit at E. Riverside Boulevard and drive east 0.7 mile. Turn north on Paulson Road and drive for 1.8 miles. Turn west on Harlem Road and continue 0.6 mile before turning north on Harlem Road for another 0.2 mile. Drive west into the park for 0.2 mile. Keep left on the park road for 0.1 mile to reach the Lions Club parking lot on the north side of the road. Restrooms, drinking water, and a map are available. Walk north towards the lake on the paved path. A map and information sign are posted at the trailhead.

Note: This is a fully wheelchair-accessible area.

GPS Coordinates: 16 T 337914mE 4690102mN

Information and Contact

There is no fee. Dogs on leash are allowed. The park is open daily 6 A.M.–10 P.M. April–October; 8 A.M.–5 P.M. November–February; and 8 A.M.–10 P.M. March. For more information, contact Rock Cut State Park, 7318 Harlem Road, Loves Park, IL, 815/885-3311, http://dnr.state.il.us.

3 BLACKHAWK SPRINGS–OAK RIDGE FOREST PRESERVE TRAILS

Winnebago County Forest Preserves, Cherry Valley

Level: Moderate

Total Distance: 9.6 miles round-trip

Hiking Time: 5 hours

Elevation Change: 260 feet

Summary: Wander along the Kishwaukee River on the quiet trails of Winnebago County Forest Preserves.

In quiet southeast Winnebago County is a 2000-acre parcel of forest preserve land. The five continuous preserves occupy slightly rolling to nearly flat terrain surrounding the main and south branches of the Kishwaukee River. The preserve trails wind along the river plain, wetlands, and through restored prairie and bur oak–hickory forest. The river and surroundings support a variety of wildlife including white-tailed deer, great blue heron, beaver, and wild turkey.

More than 20 miles of hiking trails wind through the three biggest preserves. This double-loop hike uses Perryville Road as a short connector between Blackhawk Springs and Oak Ridge Preserves. Although the preserves sit side by side, no trail connects the two systems. Deer Run trails are visible from Oak Ridge just north across the South Branch Kishwaukee River. Adventurous hikers can link this double-loop to Deer Run trails by fording the river at an equestrian crossing in the late summer.

Walk north across the river bridge on the paved bike trail. The paved path

Kishwaukee River

BLACKHAWK SPRINGS-OAK RIDGE FOREST PRESERVE TRAILS

continues north through the grassland; turn right to join the Grand Loop Trail. The trail heads northeast, then north, for 0.75 mile before turning westward through the oak savanna and woods. The forest floor is quite weedy and overgrown, and the trail is grassy for a while. Oak and hickory trees provide a thick upper canopy, and shade-loving maples fill in below. Now heading west, you notice a lot of wildflowers in the open field/grassland. Bergamot, clover, wild grape, and black-eyed Susan provide colorful habitat for the abundant butterflies. Monarch, small sulphur, and some fritillary flit around. Turn south at 1.27 miles, then turn sharply west at the four-way intersection. The woods are north, and to the south is open grassland. Watch for woodpeckers in the trees and hawks circling the grassland. Continue west, then south and across the bike path, which crosses a pretty bridge westward. The trail enters the woods and descends to the spring around 2.1 miles. Follow the trail towards the river, then along the north bank back to the bike trail and trailhead in just under 1 mile.

Walk to Perryville Road and turn south for 0.3 mile to Blackhawk Road. The preserve entrance is at a pull-out on the east side of the road. Walk around the gate and descend to a three-way intersection. This is the start of the Oak Ridge Loop. Turn southeast on the trail, which winds in and out of the woods for about the next 2 miles. Watch for wild turkeys and white-tailed deer along here. The turkeys can be startling, and a yearling deer nearly ran into me. At 4.1 miles, turn east for a 0.5 mile, then southeast again. Cross south between a prairie restoration and oak opening, and reach the main trailhead at about 5.7 miles. There is a restroom, water, and trail map here.

Head back north a short distance, then east/northeast towards a three-way junction and the Island Loop. Follow the arrow to the 1-mile loop around an old field and along the river. There are bluebird houses and some prairie wildflowers on this quiet loop. At the three-way intersection, turn north/northwest towards the river. Pass post 8 around 7.2 miles, jog west, then north through more oak savanna. After following power lines north, turn west at post 6, just south of a river bend. Now contour along the river channel northwest, then west. The river ford to the Deer Run Forest Preserve is at nearly 8.6 miles. Continue west along the river to the trail junction at 9.1 miles. Walk uphill 0.2 mile to exit the preserve and return along the road north 0.3 mile to your car at Blackhawk Springs.

Options

To add a couple of miles and some adventure to your day, ford the river at the equestrian crossing in Oak Ridge Forest Preserve. You will join a pretty 2.1-mile loop that winds through bur oak and hickory woods, and along a prairie restoration. Return to the river ford when you are done and resume the hike. Total distance for the combined hike is 11.7 miles.

Directions

From I-294/I-90 in Rosemont, drive west on I-90 for 60.2 mile. Take the I-39 S exit toward Rockford for 0.8 mile, then take Exit 122A for Harrison Avenue. Turn west and drive for 0.6 mile, then continue south on Perryville Road. Drive 2.8 miles and turn west to park at the Perryville Road parking lot.
GPS Coordinates: 16 T 336488mE 4673564mN

Information and Contact

There is no fee. Dogs on leash are allowed. The park is open from sunrise to 30 minutes after sunset daily. For more information, contact Blackhawk Springs Forest Preserve, 5800 Perryville Road, Cherry Valley, IL, 815/877-6100, www. wcfpd.org.

4 MARENGO RIDGE TRAILS

Marengo Ridge Conservation Area, McHenry County Conservation District, Marengo

🏠 🚴 ✈️ 🐕 🦌 👫 ♿

Level: Moderate

Total Distance: 5.2 miles round-trip

Hiking Time: 3 hours

Elevation Change: 290 feet

Summary: Enjoy the richness of oak woods and savanna along the rolling terrain of Marengo Ridge.

The rolling hills of McHenry County were shaped largely by the Wisconsin period of glaciation. For tens of thousands of years the advance and retreat of glacial ice left behind ridges of rocks and shallow depressions. About 24,000 years ago the Wisconsin Glacier formed the Marengo Moraine, which is the predominant feature of the 818-acre Marengo Ridge preserve. The Marengo Ridge Conservation Area protects the unique features of the moraine, including its oak savanna and woodlands. Due to the rugged terrain, much of the preserve contains parcels of native landscape. Settlers had to spare the land from becoming farmland due to the topography. Today hikers can walk along trails that ascend the moraine and enjoy views of the surroundings.

The trails of Marengo Ridge manage to cover most of the property in a series of interconnected loops. Hiking from Shelter #2 gives hikers good all-around views, and clearly illustrates the rolling nature of the land. Walking south on the trail, you will pass across grassland before looping through a small oak savanna with some very large trees and lots of wild black raspberry. The grassland fills with goldenrod, asters, clover, and sunflowers blooming much of summer; in the fall, various seed pods offer an interesting contrast to the grasses. These woods are home to several types of woodpeckers, nuthatches, chickadees, and northern flicker; also watch for goldfinch, red-winged blackbirds, and sparrows. You may even see a wild turkey or two along the west preserve trails.

Keep right just under 1 mile as you begin a gentle ascent along the moraine, heading to the central and north trails. After crossing the road, head through the walnut, black cherry, and oak woods. At 1.35 miles turn northeast onto the narrow path of the nature trail, leading to the pretty campground loop. There are dense woodland plants covering the forest floor, and a variety of trees including more black cherry and oaks. Turn right shortly at the loop, and walk the 0.5-mile path past vine-covered trees and across a couple of small boardwalks/bridges. Return to the main trail, and head north once more to the Kelly Hertel Nature Trail. Still in the trees, turn north at 2.7 miles then jog east to pass briefly through

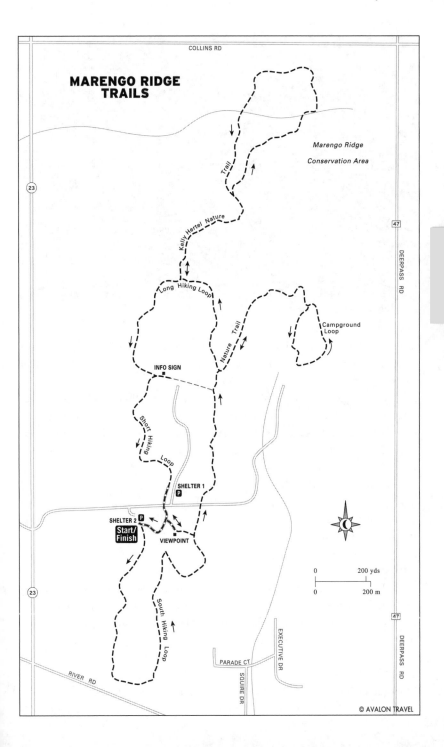

MARENGO RIDGE TRAILS

COLLINS RD

Marengo Ridge
Conservation Area

Kelly Herrel Nature Trail

Long Hiking Loop

Nature Trail

Campground Loop

INFO SIGN

Short Hiking Loop

SHELTER 1
P

SHELTER 2
P
Start/Finish

VIEWPOINT

South Hiking Loop

RIVER RD

PARADE CT

SQUIRE DR

EXECUTIVE DR

DEERPASS RD

23

47

0   200 yds
0   200 m

© AVALON TRAVEL

© BARBARA I. BOND

a footbridge along the nature loop

some grassland, then back into the trees to the nature loop. At 2.9 miles turn right on the loop, which is marked by a post. These woods have smaller trees and it's very shady and damp—there are moss-covered logs and lots of mushrooms. After crossing a couple of footbridges, which are very slippery when damp, re-trace your steps back to the main trail to head south. You will pass some glacial erratics, or boulders, along the trail, then cross a footbridge. There are some interpretive signs along this part of the trail. Continue south at 4.4 miles to reach the picnic grove and Shelter #1 at 4.8 miles. Here you'll find a water fountain, a restroom, and a map. The trail is paved now, and crosses the road southward to a Y intersection just prior to Shelter #1. Turn left on the paved trail to reach a viewpoint east that highlights the varied terrain. Return to the parking lot via the path, arriving at nearly 5.2 miles.

Options

For a shorter hike, begin on the south loop as written, then continue north along the long loop. Skip the campground and nature trails. The short loop is about 2.6 miles. For the nearly 0.3-mile (round-trip) accessible hike, follow the paved trail from Shelter #2 to the observation point.

Directions

From the junction of I-294 and I-90 in Rosemont, drive west on I-90 35.8 miles. Take the U.S. 20 exit towards Marengo and drive northwest on U.S. 20 for 8.9

miles. Turn north on IL-23 N/S. State Street and follow IL-23 north for 2.4 miles. Turn east on the first right after River Road, at the park entrance on the east side of the road. Turn south into the Shelter #2 lot, the first lot on the right. Walk on the path south towards the picnic shelter, then continue south. To reach the observation point, turn left just past the restroom and walk on the paved path a short distance.

GPS Coordinates: 16 T 367880mE 4682302mN

Information and Contact

There is no fee. Dogs are allowed on leash. For more information, contact Marengo Ridge Conservation Area, 2411 S. State Route 23, Marengo, IL, 815/338-6223, www.mccdistrict.org.

5 LEATHERLEAF BOG LOOP

Moraine Hills State Park, McHenry

Level: Easy

Hiking Time: 1.5 hours

Total Distance: 3.2 miles round-trip

Elevation Change: negligible

Summary: Hiking along the Leatherleaf Bog Trail offers a glimpse of the unique plant life and topography of Moraine Hills State Park.

McHenry County is known for its rolling hills and natural beauty. Nestled along the Fox River is the 2,200 acres of woodland, wetland, and lakes of Moraine Hills State Park. Moraine Hills is home to the Leatherleaf Bog and Pike Marsh Dedicated Nature Preserves and a far-reaching trail system that explores nearly every corner of the park. Hikers and bikers are presented with several choices of trails; each color-coded loop is well marked with signs and posts, and has restrooms and water along the route. St. John's wort and marsh marigold color the trails; look for marsh wrens amid the cattails and hawks lazily riding the summer thermals.

To reach the Leatherleaf Bog Trail, also called the Blue Loop, walk a short distance west from the parking lot to reach the main trail. Turn right and walk north on the limestone trail along the edge of the trees, and turn left at the sign for Opposum Run Junction. The trail rolls gently as you pass between marsh and bog and wind in and out of the trees. The forest contains bur oak and shagbark

west across Leatherleaf Bog

© BARBARA I. BOND

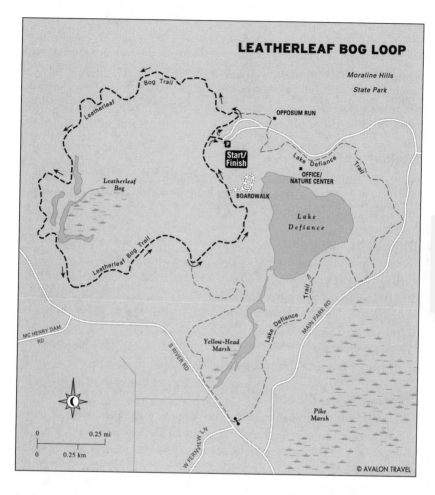

hickory, and is quite a contrast to the cattails and grasses of the wetlands. At 0.75 mile you'll pass a post, one of the many that periodically mark the trail.

Over the next 0.75 mile the trail passes through some grassland and more woods, providing a constantly shifting views of the bog. Walk uphill at 1.77 miles, and now you are above the bog in the dense woods once more. On the right, just before the 2-mile point, there is a short spur for the Fox Hollow Nature Path, a 0.5-mile pathway. Continuing east along the south end of the bog, look south as the woods give way to a nice view of the marsh lined with cattails. There is a bench and shelter on the left at 2.4 miles and you'll also pass the other end of the nature path. There are some aspens in the woods here; listen to the leaves rustle with just a hint of a breeze.

The trail ducks back into the woods, now turning northward towards the trailhead. Defiance Lake will soon come into view on the right through the trees at around 2.8 miles. The trail zigzags out of the woods and around 3 miles passes a boardwalk, which heads east through the wetlands. The boardwalk goes eastward through the wetland and along the north tip of Lake Defiance. Continuing on the Blue Loop a short distance, you will pass a signed trail junction at 3.1 miles before reaching the parking lot.

Options

Easily extend the Leatherleaf Bog hike by using the Lake Defiance Trail. Upon returning to Northern Woods continue ahead east on the trail, adding 4.2 miles to your hike (total mileage 7.4 miles).

Directions

From I-90/IL-53, take the IL-53 N exit. Drive 5.9 miles north and exit at U.S. 12/Rand Road. Drive northwest on U.S. 12/Rand Road for 12.6 miles. Turn left at IL-176 and drive west 3.6 miles to River Road. Keep right on River Road and turn right into the signed park entrance in 2.2 miles. The Northern Woods lot is at the end of the park road.

GPS Coordinates: Northern Woods lot: 16 T 398509mE 4686208mN
McHenry Dam lot: 16 T 397053mE 4684461mN

Information and Contact

There are no fees. Dogs on leash are allowed. The park opens at 8 A.M. daily; call for closing hours as they vary by season. In the winter cross-country skiing, sledding, and ice fishing are permitted. For more information, contact Moraine Hills State Park, 1510 South River Road, McHenry, IL, 60050, 815/385-1624, www.dnr.state.il.us.

6 LAKE DEFIANCE LOOP
Moraine Hills State Park, McHenry

Level: Easy · · · · · · · · · · · · · · · · · · · **Total Distance:** 4.2 miles round-trip

Hiking Time: 2.5 hours · · · · · · · · · · · · **Elevation Change:** negligible

Summary: Witness the impact of the Ice Age by wandering the peat shoreline of Lake Defiance, a kettle-hole lake at Moraine Hills State Park.

When the Wisconsin Glacier retreated, it left behind kettle holes, moraines, glacial till, and a forever changed landscape. Moraine Hills State Park preserves the geologic signature of the glacier in an area that spans 2,200 acres that is also home to wildlife and migratory waterfowl. Several Native American tribes passed through the Moraine Hills region over a century ago. Today outdoors enthusiasts can explore the lands that were donated to create the park. Well-signed hiking trails, two boardwalks, interpretive trails, two nature preserves, and a fishing lake all make Moraine Hills a prime destination.

From the Northern Woods parking lot, walk west on a short spur to the main limestone trail. Turn right onto the wide, well-maintained trail and hike to the Opossum Run trail junction, turning right. Cut through the picnic area and walk across the park road to pick up the Lake Defiance (red) Trail. Turn left onto the trail and walk eastward. You'll see the lakeshore to the south, along with the

Yellow-Head Marsh

LAKE DEFIANCE LOOP

Nature Center and interpretive trail. You will reach the oak-hickory woods at 0.78 mile. As you walk along the slightly rolling trail, take a look at the variety of trees. This is a great example of a thriving upland forest. Watch for distinctive shagbark hickory and beautiful red oak. The understory is crowded with shade-loving plants and in spring there are woodland wildflowers. Continue past a couple of spur trails to picnic areas as the trail winds southward.

The opening at 1.4 miles give you the chance to look at a marshy lake outlet filled with moss and cattails. The peat shore and dense growth is slowly encroaching on the open water. Lake Defiance is largely undeveloped so it's proceeding much as it would in a true wild state. After the open area you will turn north along the trees, then arc south. In 0.3 mile you'll come upon a narrow footpath to the lakeshore on the right. It's a good lunch spot.

The trail works southward through the woods and intermittent marshy openings as it approaches South River Road. Just before the road at 2.5 miles you will make a sharp right, keeping to the limestone trail. You will parallel a paved bike path as you walk north along Yellow-Head Marsh. The marsh is teeming with life—you may see any number of birds and hear the low hum of frogs.

The trail curves from the road, goes past a gate, and heads uphill into the trees. I saw great blue heron and a bald eagle here. Around 3.3 miles the trail continues winding through savanna as it works its way north. Prairie wildflowers bloom throughout summer and include purple coneflower, sunflowers, and butterfly milkweed. You reach the west entrance to the interpretive trail at 3.85 miles. Take a brief detour east onto the boardwalks. They go out onto this moss-covered part of the lake. Walk ahead and follow the boardwalk for three left turns, then a right to return to the main trail. Once on the main trail, follow it north 0.2 mile back to the Northern Woods Lot.

Options

Extend this hike by combining it with the 3.2-mile Leatherleaf Bog Loop or the Fox River Trail, an additional 3.5 miles from Pike Marsh (see listings in this chapter). Or, take it easy on the 2-mile Fox River Trail, a pleasant option if you start at the McHenry Dam lot. Walk east from the lot to reach the loop.

Directions

From I-90/IL-53, take the IL-53 N exit. Drive 5.9 miles north and exit at U.S. 12/Rand Road. Drive northwest on U.S. 12/Rand Road for 12.6 miles. Turn left at IL-176 and drive west 3.6 miles to River Road. Keep right on River Road and turn right into the signed park entrance in 2.2 miles. The Northern Woods lot is at the end of the park road.

To reach McHenry Dam, drive past the main entrance and turn left on McHenry Dam Road. The parking lot is at the end of the road; it is the west trailhead for the Fox River Trail Loop.

GPS Coordinates: Northern Woods lot: 16 T 398509mE 4686208mN
McHenry Dam lot: 16 T 397053mE 4684461mN

Information and Contact

There are no fees. Dogs on leash are allowed. The park opens at 8 A.M. daily; call for closing hours as they vary by season. In the winter there is cross-country skiing, sledding, and ice fishing. For more information, contact Moraine Hills State Park, 1510 South River Road, McHenry, IL, 815/385-1624, www.dnr.state.il.us.

7 SENTINEL AND SUNSET TRAILS   BEST ◖

Mississippi Palisades State Park, South System, Savanna

🏞️ 🦌 ✈️ 🌿 🐎 👫

Level: Strenuous

Hiking Time: 2-2.5 hours

Total Distance: 3.7 miles round-trip

Elevation Change: 870 feet

Summary: Experience a thrilling hike along the rugged cliffs of Mississippi Palisades State Park.

The highest point in Illinois, 1,257 feet, is in the far northwest corner of the state. That is no surprise to geologists—they know the area is in the Wisconsin Driftless Division. This land of canyons and cliffs, vertical rock faces, huge pillars, and deep river valleys was not scoured by glacial ice. Mississippi Palisades State Park has 2,500 acres of wooded ravines and canyons that radiate east from the Mississippi River. The namesake feature—palisades—are a line of vertical cliffs that rise up from the shore of Buffalo Lake, part of the Mississippi River backwaters. Hiking to the top of the palisades provides a tremendous sense of accomplishment, along with the great views of the mighty river and surroundings.

Walk south across the picnic area and across the bridge to the map and three-way intersection. To view the palisades briefly from the base, you can turn right and walk to just west of the cliffs. (I recommend turning left and heading to the overlook.) A sign describes Sentinel Preserve; hike east past the sign and climb the steps to a three-way junction. The oak forest is filling in with maple. Shade-loving plants crowd the forest floor and include a variety of ferns including maidenhair ferns, Virginia waterleaf, anemone, and poison ivy. Woodpeckers, including the yellow-bellied sapsucker, warblers, and thrushes fill the woods with life. Winter hikers may spy bald eagles over the river.

At the landing turn right and hike west towards the overlook. The trail is very slippery as it traverses west, in places wooden guardrails protect against accidental descents. There are more ferns, wild ginger, and false Solomon's seal along the way to the overlook, which you reach by turning right at a T intersection, descending some steps and reaching the platform at 0.58 mile. The views are wonderful.

Retrace your steps a very short distance, then keep right at the three-way junction to hike southeast on a wide trail. Black cherry and walnut fill in the forest now. The trail curves south. There is a bench at the three-way junction at 0.86 mile, keep right. There is also a sign for the Main Shelter pointing north. You will return this way.

Follow the trail across the gravel road to the sign for the Pine Trail and turn right. The trail winds downhill to a bridge across a ravine. At 1.4 miles I was

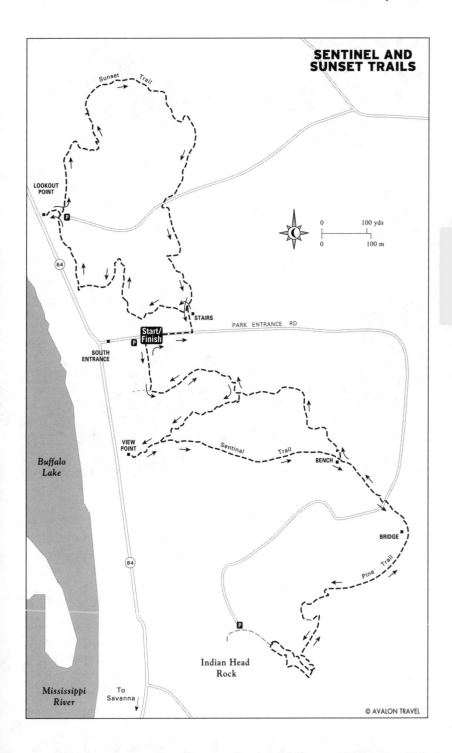

SENTINEL AND SUNSET TRAILS

Sunset Trail

LOOKOUT POINT

84

STAIRS

PARK ENTRANCE RD

Start/ Finish

SOUTH ENTRANCE

0   100 yds

0   100 m

VIEW POINT

Sentinal   Trail

BENCH

Buffalo Lake

BRIDGE

84

Pine Trail

Indian Head Rock

Mississippi River

To Savanna

© AVALON TRAVEL

view toward the Mississippi River

turned back by a washout. Otherwise, if favorable conditions allow, continue to Indian Head Rock. Retrace your steps to the bench and three-way junction. Turn north towards the main shelter, descend some steps to the landing, then retrace your steps to the Sentinel trailhead.

It is 0.2 mile to the trailhead for the Sunset Trail. Walk to the road and walk east to the trailhead on the north side of the road. Ascend the long staircase, new in summer 2010, then contour along the ridge through the pretty maple forest. Wind around, then ascend stone steps beside a huge rock outcrop on the way to a viewpoint at 0.3 mile. There are great views downriver, and you may catch a glimpse of deer, as well. Continue 0.1 mile to reach the viewing platform adjacent to the upper parking lot. After enjoying more tremendous views up and downriver, return to the trail, which continues north from the lot. Descend through the forest

0.2 mile, then ascend 0.2 mile as the trail makes an arc to turn south. At 0.9 mile you will cross the road before the final descent back to the trailhead.

Options

The north trail system has miles of trails that expose the natural beauty of the park without the steep cliff edges of the south trails. For a 3.5-mile loop, start at the High Point trailhead and hike north to join the Goldenrod Trail. Aspens are mixed within the oak and maple forest and lots of black raspberry (and poison ivy) clutter the wide, overgrown trail. Follow the Aspen Trail to its end at the campground road, then continue along the road back for about 1 mile to the trailhead. I saw deer along the quiet road, and the wildflowers attracted scores of butterflies.

Directions

From downtown Chicago, drive west on I-290 for 13.4 miles, then merge onto I-88 W and continue another 61.8 miles. Exit onto I-39 and drive north on I-39/U.S. 51 for 7 miles. Take Exit 104 and drive west on State Route 64 for 32.5 miles towards Savanna. In Savanna, turn north on Main Street/State Route 84 and drive 2.5 miles. Turn east at the south entrance and park on the south side of the road. The signed trailhead is just south of the picnic area.

GPS Coordinates: 15 T 735030mE 4667610mN

Information and Contact

There is no fee. Dogs on leash are allowed. The park is open sunrise–sunset daily. For more information, contact Mississippi Palisades State Park, 16327A IL Route 84, Savanna, IL, 815/273-2731, http://dnr.state.il.us.

8 CASTLE ROCK NORTH TRAILS

Castle Rock State Park, Oregon

Level: Easy/moderate

Total Distance: 3.6 miles round-trip

Hiking Time: 2 hours

Elevation Change: 380 feet

Summary: Castle Rock's north trails offer a wonderful cross section of the rolling hills of Rock River Hill Country and a chance to follow in the footsteps of Native Americans.

Castle Rock State Park occupies a sandstone butte on the west bank of the Rock River. Over 300 years ago at least three tribes of Native Americans lived here until the Blackhawk Indian War in 1812. The park is part of Rock River Hill Country, a distinct region of Illinois, and has unique geology, flora, and fauna. Dozens of different ferns have been identified in the park, as have native remnants of prairie and forest. Castle Rock is largely managed for preservation, the two trail systems are divided by the George B. Fell Nature Preserve. There is no access to the preserve,

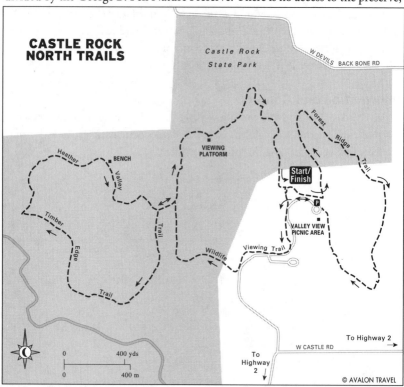

© BARBARA I. BOND

Rock River from Castle Rock

although the trails do skirt the northeast edge. Wildlife abounds—look for wild turkeys, white-tailed deer, beaver, and Blanding's turtle. In fact, I saw quite a few wild turkeys here on my last visit, including some with poults!

The three loops of this hike cover some of the most beautiful sites in Castle Rock State Park. Begin at the trail sign and walk right into the thick oak and hickory forest. It may seem confusing to sort out the trails because a self-guided nature trail covers the Wildlife Viewing–Heather Valley Loop. You can pick up a guide near the Aspen Ridge Picnic Area, along the trail. I hiked clockwise, which is the opposite of the trail guide. Hike west/southwest along the trail for 0.6 mile, turning left to continue south/southwest on the Heather Valley Trail. The trail goes in and out of the forest and along the edge of a meadow; look for purple or yellow coneflowers. A stand of aspens breaks up the oak/hickory woods, I love hearing the soft rustle of the leaves in even a slight breeze. Turn northwest at just under 1 mile on the Timber Edge Trail, marked by a sign with the park's unique map. It's pretty with the wildflowers and butterflies creating colorful contrasts to the green of the trees, lots of birds and rabbits too.

At 1.3 miles rejoin the Heather Valley Trail, which leads into the woods and another stand of aspens. Follow it back to the Wildlife Viewing Trail at 1.8 miles. The trail begins climbing, at 2.1 miles is a viewpoint with an idyllic view south across treetops and a meadow. You soon top out and begin the descent south back to the start. Walk out of the trees at the picnic area, continue east to catch the Forest Ridge Trail. The trail begins at the sign on the north side of the picnic area and heads north and uphill for 0.2 mile. You'll begin in an open field, pass a row of trees including some cedars, then as the trail makes a sharp turn back south you will descend to a footbridge. The trail passes some aspens as you go back into the woods, descending now to 0.7 mile before climbing once more. Several different kinds of fern grow here, watch too for wood anemone, may apple, and Virginia waterleaf. There are also squirrel boxes on some trees. After a short climb, you will reach the south trailhead and the end of the trail. Walk past the trailhead sign, a bench, and a pretty patch of prairie wildflowers as you return to the picnic area a few feet north.

Options

Explore another 4 miles of hiking trails by driving to the south trails in Castle Rock State Park. Begin from the parking lot, about 0.5 mile south of the scenic overlook. The trailhead is on the west side of IL-2. The Oak Ridge, Pond, and Fox Trails will total about 4 miles if you hike them all. Begin at the southwest corner of the parking lot to hike the Fox Trail first, then head west to the Pond Trail. Backtrack slightly to turn north onto the Oak Ridge Trail for a total distance of 7.6 miles.

Directions

From I-88 W/I-39 N, drive north on I-39/U.S. 51 for 7 miles. Take Exit 104 and drive west towards Oregon for 16.4 miles. After crossing the Rock River, turn south on S. 4th Street and drive for 0.6 mile, continuing on IL-2 S for 4.2 miles to reach the scenic overlook and great river views. To reach the north trails, backtrack north on IL-2 N for 0.6 mile and turn west onto the park road. Drive 1 mile to the Valley View Picnic area. Facing the restrooms, go left then up the steps and across the grass to reach the trailhead for the Wildlife Viewing Trail, marked by a sign with a map.
GPS Coordinates: 16 T 304411mE 4650407mN

Information and Contact

There is no fee. Dogs on leash are allowed. Trails are open daily from sunrise–sunset, except for brief firearm deer hunting closures. Check with Castle Rock State Park for exact closing dates. Download a map from the website, under the hunting section (dnr.state.il.us/lands/landmgt/parks/r1/lowdenmi.htm). For more information, contact Castle Rock State Park, 1365 W. Castle Road, Oregon, IL 61061, 815/732-7329.

🟦 LOWDEN-MILLER RIVER LOOP
Lowden-Miller State Forest, Oregon

🏞 🐾 👫

Level: Easy

Total Distance: 4.5 miles round-trip

Hiking Time: 2-2.5 hours

Elevation Change: negligible

Summary: Hike through the pine plantations and hardwoods of this former private forest.

Frank O. Lowden was ahead of his time. During several decades of the early to mid-20th century, hundreds of thousands of trees were planted on his family property in a grand experiment: Could specific tree plantings both grow well and control erosion? His dedication and vision paid off. The property became a premier hardwood and pine forest, now managed by the Illinois Department of Natural Resources. Sinnissippi Forest, as Lowden and his wife called it, features white pines more than 100 years old and a Christmas tree farm that's been in business since 1948. The forest has become a living laboratory for forest science

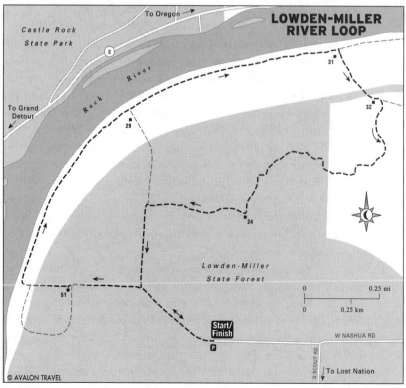

© BARBARA I. BOND

Trail junctions are marked with a numbered post and map.

and outdoor classrooms, and is a popular recreation destination. The Lowden family insured their legacy by selling more than 2,000 acres of forest to Illinois, resulting in the state forest we enjoy today.

Lowden-Miller has 22 miles of trails that crisscross the property. Intersections are marked with a numbered post, and many also have a map—this is the Lowden-Miller trail convention (the post numbers correspond to the state forest brochure and map). It allows for easy navigation of a relatively complicated web of trails. The wide trail first passes beautiful mixed stands of trees as it descends to the river in 0.75 mile. This section of trail starts in the forest of white pine, red and white oak, and some sumac. As you emerge from the trees you see a pretty stand of aspens at a Y intersection; keep left and walk along the edge of the open field towards a thick row of tall pines. At almost 0.6 mile is post 51. Continue straight ahead to the river trail and turn north. There were no other hikers out when I was there—just lots of butterflies and birds to keep me company. Occasionally a boat on the river broke the silence.

The trail now meanders along the river, we're going to follow it for the next 1.2 miles or so. The trees are thick around the trail, cottonwoods near the water tower above the river. Huge white, black, and bur oaks create a dense canopy, and you will see black cherry, and sugar maples too. Check out the peeling shagbark hickories, you can see how they got their name. Around 1 mile you start getting some views of the river and of the St. Peter's sandstone bluffs across the way.

Continue on the grassy, wide trail as it begins a gentle arc east around 1.5 miles.

Post 31 appears at 2.2 miles; turn right, then continue making rights at the next four posts. The trail does some gentle climbing through thick trees and more white pines until 2.9 miles. There are many birds around—lots of woodpeckers and warblers—and I saw a white-tailed deer along here. Reach post 24 at 3.3 miles, turn west and continue west another 0.4 mile. Turn south for a short walk through an open field—there are some pretty wildflowers taking hold here. At 3.95 miles, turn southeast and retrace your steps to the parking lot.

Options
Explore the Logger's Trail, an interpretive trail located at Parking Area 1 (see listing in this chapter). The 1.5-mile trail can be hiked solo for a short outing, or combine the two hikes for a total distance of 5.75 miles. The trails are easy to follow with a Lowden-Miller map.

Directions
From I-88 W/I-39N, drive north on I-39/U.S. 51 for 7 miles. Take Exit 104 and drive west towards Oregon. After 15.6 miles, turn south on S. Dayville Road. In 1.6 miles, keep right on S. Lowden Road. Turn west on W. Nashua Road in 0.7 mile. Drive to the end of the road and park at Parking Area 4. The trailhead is north of the parking lot and has a locked gate. (Note: There is another trailhead at the south end of the lot.) Walk around the gate to the left; the trail heads west.
GPS Coordinates: 16 T 303985mE 4647849mN

Information and Contact
There is no fee. Dogs on leash are allowed. The park is open sunrise–sunset daily. Check with Castle Rock State Park for short hunting closures (look on the website, under the hunting section, at dnr.state.il.us/lands/landmgt/parks/r1/lowdenmi. htm). For more information, contact Lowden-Miller State Forest, W. Nashua Road, Oregon, IL, 815/732-7329, www.dnr.state.il.us.

10 LOGGER'S TRAIL

BEST C

Lowden-Miller State Forest, Oregon

🦌 🛶 🌸 ⚙️ 🐐 👫

Level: Easy

Total Distance: 1.5 miles round-trip

Hiking Time: 1 hour

Elevation Change: negligible

Summary: Walk through history on this unique nature trail.

The 1.5-mile nature trail in Lowden-Miller State Forest offers a snapshot of both the human and natural history of the forest. In just a short distance, you will hike past more than 30 trail markers with information ranging from a poison ivy primer to details on how to distinguish various types of deciduous or coniferous trees. It's particularly fun with children or anyone who wants to familiarize themselves with the riches of the forest.

Walk northeast from the trailhead and into the shady forest. The packed-dirt trail is covered in places with a thick duff of pine needles and the forest floor is thick with woodland plants—sadly, some of them are invasive, like garlic mustard. Still, you may see some wood nettle, may apples, and false Solomon's seal. Shade-loving plants are definitely taking over. At post 1, keep right to begin hiking the interpretive trail. At this point, you'll regularly see lettered posts. This is the Lowden-Miller trail convention—most trail junctions correspond to a number on the state forest brochure map. (When I first saw the map, I was worried, thinking

the Logger's Trail

© BARBARA I. BOND

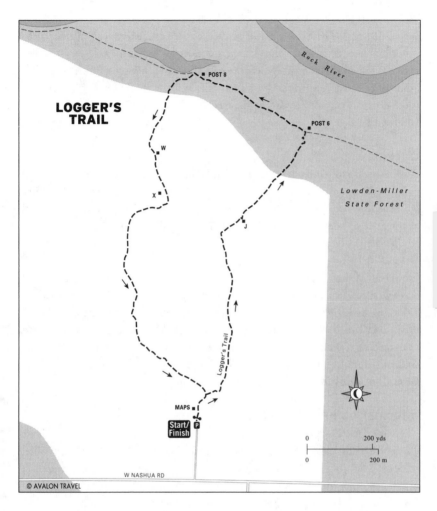

that the combination of numbers and letters would be confusing. In actuality, it works well in the field.) White oak, black cherry, shagbark hickory, and red and white pine line the trail. (Post F can help with your tree identification skills.) Just before mile 0.4, reach a three-way intersection marked by map post 12.

The corduroy trail at post J is fun to walk on; it's an example of how loggers used to get over boggy areas without getting stuck. You can see ferns growing happily in the dampest areas of the thick forest. Turn left at post 6 (at 0.6 mile) to continue on the Logger's Trail. (Check the forest trail map for this three-way intersection to gauge your overall location. Basically, this is the northeast corner of the property.)

From here, hike west past some very tall white pines to reach post 8, where you turn southward. There is a wetland on the west side of the trail; you may see some waterfowl here early in the day or perhaps a turtle (watch for frogs, too). You'll reach 1 mile between posts W and X; pass the trail junction with the shortcut. Some of the trees have vines—if it's not poison ivy, it might be Virginia creeper (post Z explains the difference). The next 0.5-mile rolls slightly down to where you began.

Options
With 22 miles of trails, it's possible to hike longer at Lowden-Miller. You can easily strike out on your own, with a state forest map in hand, or hike the pretty 4.5-mile Lowden-Miller River Loop, following the Rock River (see listing in this chapter). If you do both hikes, the total distance will be about 5.75 miles.

Directions
From I-88 W/I-39 N, drive north on I-39/U.S. 51 for 7 miles. Take Exit 104 and drive west towards Oregon. After 15.6 miles, turn south on S. Dayville Road. In 1.6 miles, keep right on S. Lowden Road. Turn west on W. Nashua Road in 0.7 mile. Turn north on an unmarked road in about 0.2 mile and drive to the end to park. The trailhead is at the north end of the lot. Walk around the gate to the start of the trail. Trail guides are in a box to the left.
GPS Coordinates: 16 T 305710mE 4648006mN

Information and Contact
There is no fee. Dogs on leash are allowed. The park is open sunrise–sunset daily. Check with Castle Rock State Park for short hunting closures (look on the website, under the hunting section, at dnr.state.il.us/lands/landmgt/parks/r1/lowdenmi.htm). For more information, contact Lowden-Miller State Forest, W. Nashua Road, Oregon, IL, 815/732-7329, www.dnr.state.il.us.

11 SHABBONA LAKE LOOP
Shabbona Lake State Recreation Area, Shabbona

🚻 🦌 ✈ 🛶 🐕 🚹 ♿

Level: Moderate   **Total Distance:** 6.2 miles round-trip

Hiking Time: 3 hours   **Elevation Change:** 260 feet

Summary: The quiet trails around Shabbona Lake include an artificial lake surrounded by restored prairie.

Shabonna Lake is named after Chief Shabbona, an Ottawa Indian influential in this part of DeKalb County who became a Pottawatomi chief after marrying into that tribe. In the 1830s, European pioneers were drawn to the rich soil in this area and settlers soon established farms here. In 1965, a plan was implemented to turn a tract of land into a lake and recreation site. By the late 1970s, the lake was finished, fishing piers built, and the recreation area we enjoy today completed. It now comprises 1,550 acres of lake, woodlands, and prairie restoration, and offers a variety of recreation opportunities to visitors. Hiking trails wind through the trees and around the lake in distances ranging from 1.2 to 7 miles.

Shabbona Lake is known as a prime fishing location. What most folks do not

© BARBARA I. BOND

Two sentinel oaks frame a bench along the Arrowhead Trail.

know is that the lake and its surroundings also offer a respite for hikers seeking quiet trails. The park is surrounded by farmland and is really an isolated collection of habitats. A variety of wildlife and bird species make the park home—you may see wild turkey, white-tailed deer, and migratory waterfowl.

Start walking north on the mown-grass Red Trail for 0.25 mile. At the three-way junction, continue ahead, towards the dam. (Note the "map" on the left.) Crossing the dam gives you a feel for the terrain; the lake views are beautiful. If you are quiet, you may see great blue heron just north, below the rim of the dam.

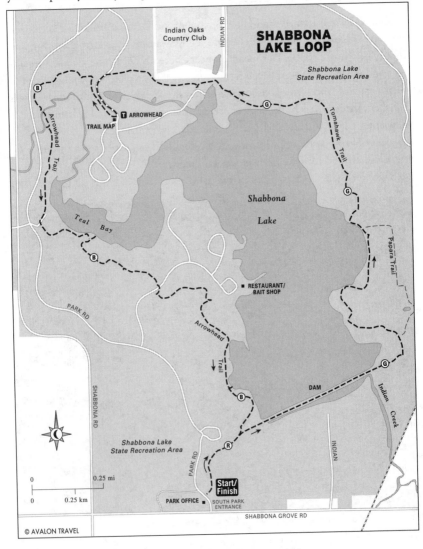

© AVALON TRAVEL

Judging by the number of boats, this is a productive fishing area. After crossing the bridge at the east end, you will descend to a trail junction. (If you turn right you can choose either to take the short Papara Trail through the woods, or the Snowmobile (red) Trail which tends to skirt the trees and stay more in the open.) Continue north on the Tomahawk Trail along the lakeshore for 0.75 mile, winding in and out of maple woods filled with chickadees and woodpeckers. Watch for osprey and great blue heron along here. After reaching an open field, cross a dike between a small pond just before turning west around 2.2 miles. The lake views from the northeast corner are lovely.

Now join the Red Trail along the north side of the lake; you'll reach the main road at 3.1 miles. Turn south along the road for 0.2 mile and at the signed trailhead for the Arrowhead (blue) Trail, turn northwest. The trail leads through open field and then returns to the woods, comprised of very large oak and scattered black cherry. You can hardly miss the sentinel oaks on either side of a bench around 3.5 miles. The trail is often noisy with birdsong. After a couple of creek crossings, you wind around Teal Bay. This is good spotting ground for Canada geese, ducks, and migrant species in fall. Turn south at 4.5 miles, away from the bay, and work your way southeast across grasslands filled with colorful sunflowers and prairie wildflowers. Follow the blue arrows to stay on the trail. At 5.4 miles, continue south at a three-way junction and enjoy the views of the lake across the grasses. At 5.9 miles, return to the junction near the lake map. Turn right to retrace your steps 0.2 mile to the trailhead through the pines.

Options

For a longer hike, it is necessary to retrace your steps a bit. Instead of turning back to the trailhead at the lake map, recross the dam heading east to the Papara Trail, and make a 1-mile loop through the trees. Both ends of the trail are marked with a post. Turn south at the end of the Papara Trail to walk along the lakeshore on the remainder of the Tomahawk Trail. Turn west to cross the dam and retrace your steps to the start. With the addition of this loop, your total hiking distance will be 9.75 miles.

Directions

From I-290 in Chicago, drive west for 13.4 miles to I-88 W. Continue west on I-88 another 26.9 miles. Take the IL-56 W/U.S. 30 exit toward Sugar Grove. Drive 4.2 miles southwest, then continue on U.S. 30 west for 22.5 miles. Turn south at S. Shabbona Road, then east on Shabbona Grove Road. The park entrance is 0.4 mile on the north side of the road. The park office is on the west side of the

parking area. The trailhead is on the east side of the parking area, adjacent to the large Snowmobile Trail information sign.
GPS Coordinates: 16 T 386224mE 4632041mN

Information and Contact

There is no fee. Dogs are allowed on leash. The park is open daily 8 A.M.–5 P.M. November–January; 8 A.M.–6 P.M. February–March; 8 A.M.–8 P.M. April; and 6 A.M.–10 P.M. May–October. The Touch the Earth Trail was specially developed for disabled visitors. For more information, contact Shabbona Lake State Recreation Area, 4201 Shabbona Grove Road, Shabbona, IL, 815/824-2106, http://dnr.state.il.us.

12 BLAZING STAR-
BLUESTEM-INDIGO TRAILS
James "Pate" Phillips State Park, Bartlett

BEST ᑕ

Level: Easy

Hiking Time: 2-2.5 hours

Total Distance: 4.5 miles round-trip

Elevation Change: negligible

Summary: Visit James "Pate" Phillips State Park and stand in three counties at once while bird-watching and identifying native plants and flowers.

James "Pate" Phillips State Park is the northern portion of a nearly 4,000-acre tract of conserved land. This chunk of land provides wildlife with a corridor of ecologically diverse land to use for migration, breeding, and feeding. The state park sits at the far northwest corner of DuPage County and overlaps into both Cook and Kane Counties. Preserving this land is a great example of cooperation among managing agencies—the City of Bartlett runs the nature center while DuPage County maintains the land. This young park is a work in progress. Drain tiles in the wetlands are being broken, a landfill is being shuttered, and Brewster Creek is being restored. The area is designated an Important Bird Area for several species of bird including sandhill crane, Henslow's sparrow, and the yellow-headed blackbird. You are likely to experience the resilience of nature on the trails of Phillips State Park.

© BARBARA I. BOND

rattlesnake master

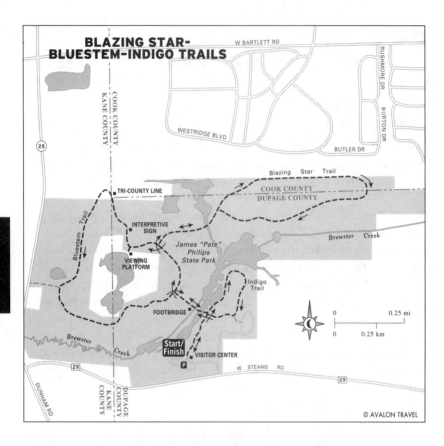

The trails of the park make three interconnected loops around the property. By walking the 4.5 miles of trails you'll cross Brewster Creek, and walk in and around prairie, wetlands, and a fen. Carry binoculars—I had a lot of fun bird-watching on one of my visits. Before hitting the trail take a moment to look at the gardens in front of the visitors center. These blooms attract lots of birds and butterflies and are beautiful all summer. The trail begins to the left of the visitors center and gardens. Walk north on the limestone path and at the four-way trail junction turn west towards the Brewster Creek Bridge. The bridge is a good spot to watch for beaver, ducks, or geese. The shore is a tangle of cattails and sedge; and as you continue west you'll pass some prairie willow too.

Turn north at the three-way intersection, then east onto the Blazing Star Trail. You'll be walking around the open grassland of the north park on this 1.5-mile loop. The next intersection, at 0.8 mile, will take you the 1.2-mile loop. There are a few trees to break up the grasses, some wildflowers include brown-eyed Susan, rattlesnake master, compass plant, and blazing star. At the start of the loop, retrace your steps southwest the short distance to the Bluestem Trail at 2.3 miles. Turn west (right) at the three-way intersection and in a short distance you'll reach a little spur (on the left) south to a viewing platform. This is where you can spend a bit of time—there are benches and an interpretive sign. Best of all is a wonderful view across the wetland. Egrets, great blue heron, and terns are just a few species of bird seen here; there always seem to be red-winged blackbirds and woodpeckers in the trees nearby.

Once back on the trail you will trace an irregular 1.2-mile loop encircling the wetlands. Yellow coneflower, culver's root, and blazing star are just a few of the flowers. There are plenty of scattered trees amongst the flowers, all of which attract birds like American goldfinch and dickcissel. A periodic interpretive sign explains some of the natural features.

At 3.65 miles turn southeast at the trail junction to cross Brewster Creek and join the Indigo Trail. This short loop features a pond just north of the trail, some large cottonwoods, and in the grassland yellow flax, pale beardtongue, and brown-eyed Susan.

Options
For more hiking, visit Pratt's Wayne Woods 2 miles southeast. Drive east on Stearns Road 0.8 mile, then turn south on Powis Road. The entrance is on the west side of the road; turn right and follow the road to the north end lot. The Lake Trail is 1.6 miles and is a pleasant loop. The combined hiking distance is 6.1 miles.

Directions
From I-290 W, take Exit 13B onto State Route 64 W/E. North Avenue. Drive 14.9 miles west and turn north on State Route 59 N/N. Neltor Boulevard. In 4.2 miles, turn left at W. Stearns Road and drive west 2.5 miles to the park entrance on the north side of Stearns Road.
GPS Coordinates: 16 T 395845mE 4647897mN

Information and Contact
There is no fee. Dogs on leash are allowed. Snowshoeing is allowed in winter. The park is open sunrise–sunset daily. Visitors center hours are 9 A.M.–4 P.M. Monday–Friday and 9 A.M.–1 P.M. Saturday. For more information, contact James "Pate" Phillips State Park, 2054 W. Stearns Road, Bartlett, IL, 847/608-3100, http://dnr.state.il.us.

Pratt's Wayne Woods is open from one hour before sunrise to one hour after sunset daily. More information is available online at www.dupageforest.com.

13 LAKE AND WEST TRAILS
Pratts Wayne Woods Forest Preserve, Wayne

Level: Moderate   **Total Distance:** 3.5 miles round-trip

Hiking Time: 2 hours   **Elevation Change:** negligible

Summary: Visit the wetlands, open meadows, and oak savanna of Pratt's Wayne Woods.

DuPage County's largest preserve is teeming with wildlife and natural beauty. Since 1965 the county has been acquiring land for Pratt's Wayne Woods and today 3,462 acres are home to white-tailed deer, beaver, and numerous species of bird including the sandhill crane. The preserve's numerous lakes, ponds, and marshes are hallmarks of the glacial ice that left this land scoured over 10,000 years ago. All this water contributes to a healthy waterfowl and amphibian population. Location is everything, and Pratt's abuts James "Pate" Phillips State Park, creating a nearly 4,000-acre parcel of land that is an important wildlife corridor. In particular, the restoration work at Brewster Creek is increasing the natural ap-

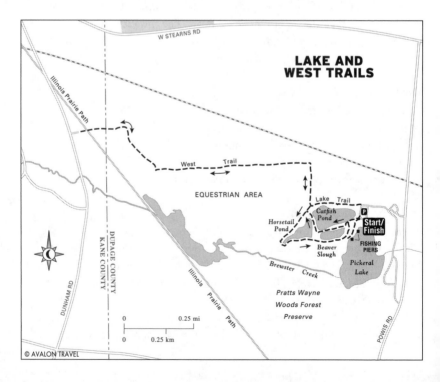

view across Catifish Pond from the Lake Trail

peal of this popular preserve. Hiking the trails amongst the meadows, ponds, or through the oak savanna is a wonderful way to spend a day.

Pratt's Wayne Woods has several miles of trails to explore. Walk west between Catfish Pond and Beaver Slough on the limestone path. Cattails edge the water and cottonwood and oaks dot the shore across the pond. The sound of chattering songbirds will keep you company, and keep an eye on the water for great blue heron, Canada geese, and wood ducks. Quickly turn right to walk north between Horsetail and Catfish Ponds, then make a quick right then left to continue north on a 0.16-mile connector trail leading to the West Trail. At about 0.5 mile turn west for a walk on the mown path through the equestrian area. The Wayne area has a long equestrian history and today is still the West Suburban center for horse lovers. In nearly 0.6 mile turn northwest and continue for another 0.2 mile, then west until you reach the trail's end at about 1.5 miles. The Illinois Prairie Path access is just south the trail, just prior to Dunham Road. Retrace your steps to Catfish Pond, and at nearly 2.6 miles turn west for the remainder of the Lake Trail.

Follow the trail southwest to the corner of Horsetail Pond. Tall black and bur oaks create a pleasing canopy. During spring you may see the delicate flowers of Solomon's seal and anemone along the trail. After crossing the footbridge, note the sign notifying hikers of nesting sandhill cranes. Now you are walking east, for 0.3 mile, until you reach the main trail. You quickly reach a junction; keep right to walk along the south shore of Beaver Slough. The trail curves north to reach a three-way junction; turn right to reach the trailhead at 3.1 miles.

Options

The East Loop lies across Powis Road and winds through an open meadow similar to the West Trail. For an additional 4.5 miles of hiking, drive north to James "Pate" Phillips State Park for an experience in a different landscape (see listing for Blazing Star-Bluestem-Indigo Trails in this chapter).

Directions

From the interchange of I-94/I-90 and I-290 in Chicago, drive west on I-290 for 16.3 miles. Take Exit 13B onto State Route 64 W/E. North Avenue. Drive 14.9 miles west and turn north on State Route 59 N/N. Neltnor Boulevard. In 2.2 miles, turn left at Army Trail Road and drive west 1.8 miles. Turn north on Powis Road, then turn west in 0.8 mile (at the signed preserve road). Drive 0.4 mile to the last parking lot. The trailhead is at the southwest corner of the lot.
GPS Coordinates: 16 T 396952mE 4646660mN

Information and Contact

There is no fee. Dogs are allowed on leash. The park is open from one hour before sunrise to one hour after sunset daily. For more information, contact Pratt's Wayne Woods Forest Preserve, Powis Road (north of Army Trail Road), Wayne, IL, 630/933-7248, www.dupageforest.com.

14 HORLOCK HILL PRAIRIE-PRESERVE LOOP TRAIL

Leroy Oakes Forest Preserve, Kane County Forest Preserve District, St. Charles

🪁 🌿 🏊 🎡 🐕 👫

Level: Easy

Hiking Time: 1.5 hours

Total Distance: 3.3 miles round-trip

Elevation Change: negligible

Summary: Leroy Oakes contains a native prairie, a historic schoolhouse, and a babbling creek – all for the enjoyment of hikers of all ages.

Leroy Oakes Forest Preserve has a little bit of everything. The two-acre Murray Prairie, a dry prairie remnant, is protected as an Illinois Nature Preserve. Just east of Murray is the Horlock Hill Prairie, a prairie restoration named for a local science teacher. Horlock is now a benchmark dry prairie due to its success. The Durant-Peterson House has been restored authentically as a mid-19th-century farmstead and is open for summer tours. There is also a mid-19th-century one-room schoolhouse. A collection of trails await exploration. The perimeter trails are the quietest, and a web of interconnecting paths offer lots of options. A short footpath explores Ferson Creek. The Great Western Trail (GWT) also winds through the preserve.

© BARBARA I. BOND

Horlock Hill Prairie

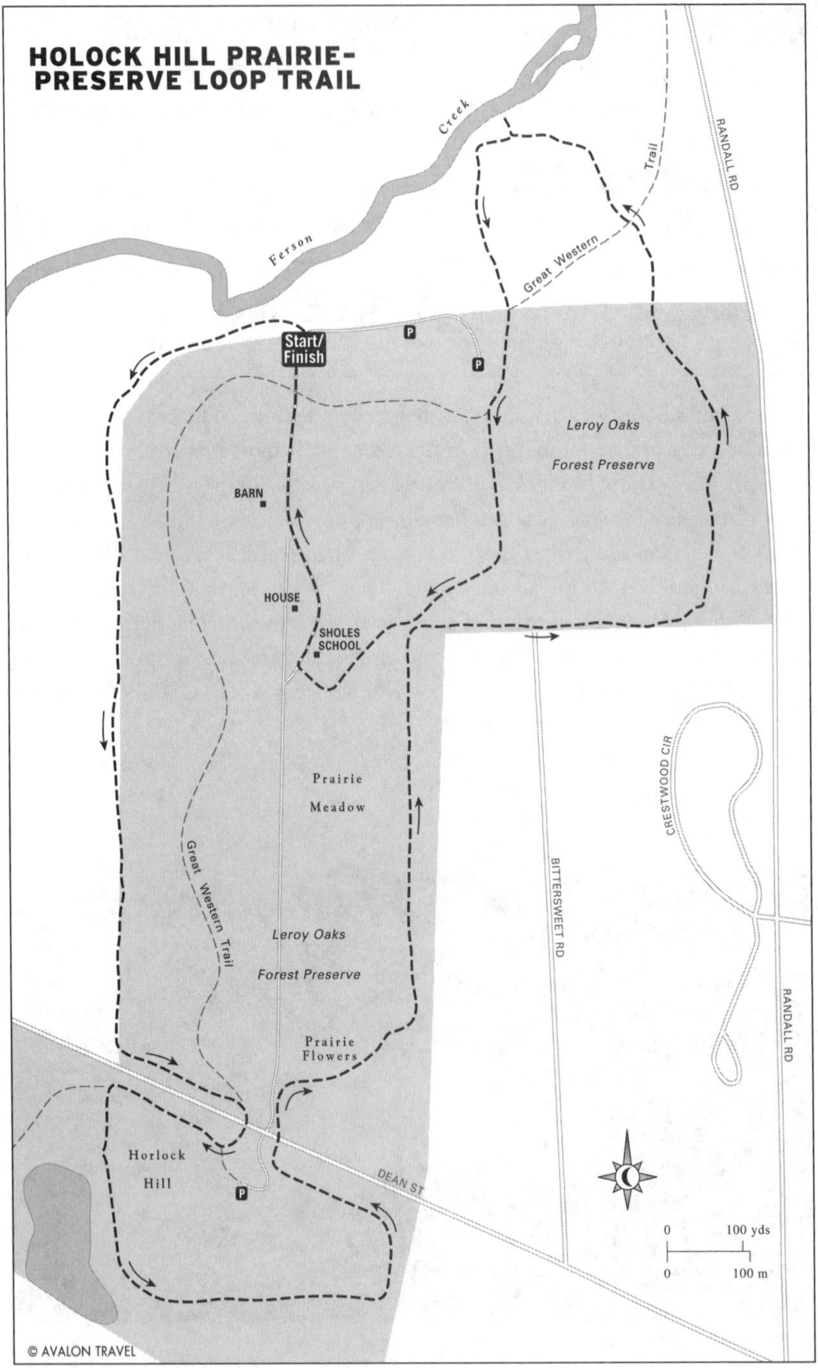

HOLOCK HILL PRAIRIE-PRESERVE LOOP TRAIL

Ferson Creek

RANDALL RD

Great Western Trail

P

P

Start/Finish

Leroy Oaks

Forest Preserve

BARN

HOUSE

SHOLES SCHOOL

Great Western Trail

Prairie Meadow

BITTERSWEET RD

CRESTWOOD CIR

RANDALL RD

Leroy Oaks

Forest Preserve

Prairie Flowers

Horlock Hill

P

DEAN ST

0   100 yds

0   100 m

© AVALON TRAVEL

Walk west across the grass onto the mown path. The trail begins a slow curve southward as it enters the forest of mostly spindly maples. The trail heads south about 0.6 mile before curving east to parallel Dean Street. The GWT joins the footpath; follow it as it curves south, crosses Dean Street, and then makes a hairpin turn to head west. At 0.8 mile is an interpretive sign and map on the left, as well as a memorial to Bob Horlock. Horlock was the innovative teacher who spearheaded the prairie restoration. Continue on the GWT less than 0.1 mile and turn south onto a mown path, which leads to a viewing platform. From the platform you can see both the Murray Prairie to the west and the Horlock Hill Prairie east. Continue south and resume walking on the mown path. The prairie blooms all summer with coneflowers, black-eyed Susan, compass plant, and more. As quickly as you began, the short trail curves back around to emerge at the south lot adjacent to five pines at 1.35 miles. Turn right to walk across Dean Street to resume hiking the main path. Walk north a scant 0.1 mile and turn right on the mown path.

The path crosses an old field with prairie flowers that include butterfly milkweed and rattlesnake master. The path heads towards some trees, then turns left to skirt the border briefly, then at 1.5 miles ducks into the trees. You'll hardly notice the preserve's high point. At 1.7 miles you reach a four-way trail junction; turn right. This will take you into what I think is the most remote-feeling section of the preserve—that is, after you pass some private property to the south. Turn north, following the trail through the dense trees. You'll cross the GWT at about 2 miles, on a slight descent towards Ferson Creek. The trail goes to a pretty spot on the south bank of the creek at 2.2 miles. Back on the trail you'll curve away from the creek southward across an open area with some huge old oak trees. (You're heading towards Picnic Shelter 1 and the GWT.) You reach a corner of the GWT around 2.5 miles, walk south then west, then take a left to go south on the mown path. Continue another few tenths, south then west, to reach the historic buildings at about 3 miles. Walk north for 0.3 mile to return to the parking lot.

Options

To shorten this hike, park south of Dean Street and walk the Great Western Trail to the mown path through the Horlock Hill Prairie. It's peaceful; there are lots of birds and butterflies and it's just about 0.7 mile total. The south lot has a covered picnic shelter, vault toilet, and garbage cans along with information signs. To keep going, take a walk on the 11.5-mile Great Western Trail.

Directions

From the junction of I-290 W and I-88 W, drive west on I-88 W for 0.5 mile. Take the IL-38 W exit, keep right and drive west on IL-38 W/E. Roosevelt Road for 22.8 miles. Turn right on Randall Road and drive north 1.2 miles. Turn left on Dean Street and continue 0.4 mile. There are signed park entrances on both the north and south side of Dean Street. Turn right and drive north on the entrance road about 0.3 mile. There are about a dozen parking spots on the left, just before the road curves east. The trailhead is west of the parking area.

GPS Coordinates: 16 T 388334mE 4642552mN

Information and Contact

There is no fee. Dogs on leash are allowed. The park is open sunrise–sunset daily. There are restrooms, picnic shelters, water, and information signs throughout the preserve. In winter snowshoeing and cross-country skiing are allowed. For more information, contact Leroy Oakes Forest Preserve, 37W370 Dean Street, St. Charles, IL, 630/232-5980, www.kaneforest.com.

15 FOX RIVER TRAIL: GENEVA TO BATAVIA LOOP

Fabyan Forest Preserve, Geneva

Level: Easy/moderate

Total Distance: 5.5-5.9 miles round-trip

Hiking Time: 2-3 hours

Elevation Gain: negligible

Summary: Sample the beauty along the Fox River while enjoying the history of the Fabyan Forest Preserve.

Geneva and its surroundings were home to Native Americans for thousands of years prior to the arrival of settlers in the early 19th century. Today a number of historic buildings dating from the early and mid-1800s still stand, including many residential homes. The Fabyan Forest Preserve consists of 350 acres on both sides of the Fox River, just south of downtown Geneva. The grounds are home to two buildings on the National Register of Historic Places, and also feature walking paths, flower gardens, and a Japanese-style garden that dates back to 1910. The Fabyan grounds also have a villa remodeled by Frank Lloyd Wright and an authentic windmill. The Fabyans moved the windmill to the grounds in 1914; according to some experts it is the best example of a Dutch windmill in the United States. The Fox River Trail passes through the preserve on both side of the river.

The Fox River Trail parallels its namesake river for nearly 36 miles, from

© BARBARA I. BOND

footbridge across the Fox River with Fabyan Windmill in the distance

Algonquin to Aurora. The trail offers residents of both McHenry and Kane counties a multitude of choices for recreation, including hiking and biking the trail. Hiking this loop of the Fox River Trail will expose hikers to interesting architecture and history along with beautiful natural features.

Walk east on South Street three blocks to River Lane. On the right is a signed path that leads over a train bridge across the Fox River. After crossing, head south along the Fox River Trail, passing the Geneva Water Treatment Plant. There is a water fountain (one for humans and one for pets) and bench on the left. The trail then crosses an open field, often filled with Canada geese in fall and spring. Continue south as the trail enters the woods, crosses a wooden bridge around 0.6 mile, and winds toward Fabyan. This shady section is pleasant in summer. Many birds frequent the trees and you can sometimes see deer in early morning. You'll quickly reach a Y intersection; go left to stay on the main trail. There are some large snags west of the trail and in spring, you may spot a bald eagle atop them.

The Fabyan Windmill sits just east of the trail, atop a short rise at about 1.2 miles. (The windmill is open for tours on a limited schedule.) The hill is popular in winter with local snow sport aficionados and kayaks often put in on the river here. The main and river trails merge just north of the windmill. The trail continues south past a parking lot

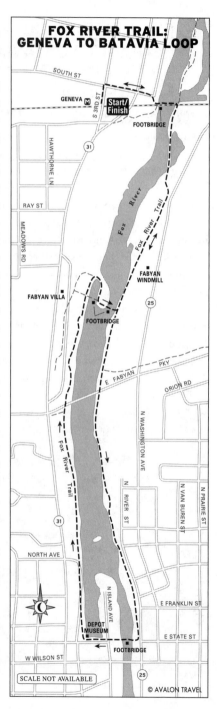

with two vault toilets and a picnic shelter. Ignore the trail that heads west across the river to the rest of the Fabyan Preserve grounds—you'll come back this way. The trail continues in the woods, crosses under the Fabyan Parkway, then opens up as it passes some houses and a park and boat ramp. The Batavia river crossing is at about 2.6 miles. Follow the trail signs to cross the bridge over the Fox River westward. At the west end of the bridge are a couple of drinking fountains and an interpretive kiosk with information and a map. Here, continue west (parallel to Houston Street) to the Depot Museum and turn north onto the Fox River Trail West.

You may pick up the Fox River Trail West after exiting the Riverwalk near the Batavia Depot Museum, set in a historic 150-year old train station. The first part of the trail passes residences to the west, with viewing platforms along the river on the east. Around 3.8 miles the trail continues along a dike, passing a spur trail heading west and another information kiosk. Cross the bridge and you'll reach the Fabyan grounds. As you approach, you can take in the complexity and beauty of the former home site, formal gardens, various outbuildings, a Japanese Garden, and atop the hill, the Fabyan Villa. The Japanese Garden was restored to its original beauty by volunteers and is open to the public. There are some oddities on the grounds, like a "Bear Cage" that was used to display a captive bear long ago. If you can, spend some time exploring the grounds. The flowers are beautiful in spring and summer. The Villa sits in splendor atop a hill and is the highlight of the property.

When done, continue north along the trail. Take a shortcut across the river on a pedestrian bridge at about mile 4.4, or continue on the main path, which makes a U-turn in a short distance. Enjoy the views south of the backwater and main river channel, then turn east to cross the river to the Fox River Trail. You will end up adjacent to the windmill and parking area. Turn left (north) to return to your starting point.

Options

The Batavia Riverwalk, maintained by the City of Batavia, is a beautiful trail with interpretive signs, viewing platforms, public art, and a collection of windmills. The Riverwalk, an inviting and relaxing 0.75 mile, begins on the west side of the footbridge; turn north and follow the path to begin. There is parking along Houston Street and North Island Avenue, adjacent to the Riverwalk.

Directions

From downtown Chicago, drive west on I-290 for 13.4 miles, merging onto I-88 W and taking this highway for 21.3 miles. Take the Farnsworth exit and turn right to go north on Kirk Road for 4 miles. Turn left on Fabyan Parkway, then right on IL-31. Drive north for 1.2 miles and turn left at the light onto 3rd Street. South Street is two blocks north. There is free parking along 3rd Street and the surrounding city streets. The hike begins at the corner of South 3rd and South Street, at the southeast corner.

Public transportation: From the Ogilvie Transportation Center in Chicago, ride Metra's Union Pacific/West Line to the Geneva Station. For schedules visit metrarail.com. From Geneva's Metra Train Station on South 3rd Street, walk north on 3rd Street one block to South Street.

GPS Coordinates: 16 T 391388mE 4637377mN

Information and Contact

There is no fee. Dogs on leash are allowed. The park is open sunrise–sunset daily. Maps are available for download www.kaneforest.com. A Batavia Riverwalk map is available at www.bataviaparks.org. For more information, contact Fabyan Forest Preserve, 1925 Batavia Ave., Geneva, IL 61350, 630/232-5980.

The Fabyan Villa Museum is open 1–4 P.M. Wednesday and 1–4:30 P.M. Saturday and Sunday May 15–October 13 and is closed in winter; admission is a $2 donation. The Fabyan Japanese Garden is open 1–4 P.M. Wednesday and 1–4:30 P.M. Sunday May 1–October with limited winter openings; the admission is $1.

16 NELSON LAKE LOOP   BEST **(**
Dick Young Forest Preserve, Kane Country Forest Preserve District, Batavia

🦌 ✈️ 🌿 🐕 👫 ♿

Level: Easy   **Total Distance:** 4.2 miles round-trip

Hiking Time: 2 hours   **Elevation Change:** negligible

Summary: A walk around Nelson Lake Marsh reveals several rare and threatened species.

Dick Young Forest Preserve (Nelson Lake Marsh) is one of Kane County's finest natural areas. Here, nearly 1,000 acres of marsh, prairie, savanna, and woodland are home to dozens of species of birds and plants. Butterfly lovers will appreciate sightings of meadow fritillary and Baltimore checkerspot amongst the significant butterfly populations. A huge depression was left by the Wisconsin Glacier's retreat more than 10,000 years ago. Now a 172-acre lake and marsh occupy that spot, including a layer of Houghton muck. Muskrat and beaver favor the lake and its shore, which has a rich collection of aquatic plant life. The preserve is an important birding site and home to the American bittern, various warblers, and dickcissel. A walk of any length is a pleasant outing at this beautiful preserve.

Walk towards the lake along the wide, accessible path. There is an elevated observation platform, with a ramp, at the end of the 0.2-mile path. It's a good place to get your bearings and listen to all the bird chatter. Turn north on the Nelson Lake Trail, which winds north then west for about a mile to reach the junction with the Big Creek Trail. Check out the huge oaks as you make your way through the savanna. It's an ambitious restoration project. The trail will wind through some

interpretive overlook on the Nelson Lake Loop

more oaks and hickories. There is a small pond south of the trail as it turns west, with cottonwoods and some aspens. The frogs can be loud in this area.

At post 4, turn north. As you leave the trees, watch for birds in the grass, you may flush a pheasant or two. The trail turns west, and there is an interpretive display a short distance past the main preserve entrance. From here, look south at the kettle pond ringed with cattails. Turn south at 1.95 miles, at post 13, onto the Mid-County Trail. The landscape is markedly different, all open sky and grassland as you pass through the prairie restoration. Turn east at 2.25 miles for a short walk on the mown Cutback Trail to reach a footpath through the grass. Turn south at the mown path and walk another 0.2 mile to reach a small observation platform in the trees at the west edge of the lake. After enjoying the quiet, turn around and walk west on the 0.2-mile West Overlook Trail to reach the Mid-County Trail at 2.6 miles. Turn south once more through the prairie. Watch for bobolink and goldfinches along here. Mid-summer you will see tall compass plant amongst the grasses. At 3.15 miles you get back on the Nelson Lake Trail, marked by post 10. The Audubon Bridge crosses the Lake Run stream and the trail continues south another few tenths of a mile before turning east around the south end of Nelson Lake. Trees are few until about 3.65 miles when the trail skirts the north edge of the woods and gradually turns northward. You may see a hawk in the trees or woodpeckers looking for insects. At nearly 4 miles you'll reach the junction with the Savanna Trail at post 8. This short trail goes around an open field and reaches the trailhead in the same distance as the Nelson Lake Trail. Continue north a short distance along the edge of some trees, then turn right on the limestone path to the trailhead.

Options

Combine the Nelson Lake, Coyote, and Meadowlark Trails to make a large 5.8-mile loop hike around the perimeter of the preserve. Follow the hike as described until post 13, continuing west on the Coyote Trail to post 14. Turn west onto the 1.9-mile Meadowlark Trail and make rights at the two trail junctions to return to the Audubon Bridge, where you'll resume the main hike as outlined.

Note: I recommend hiking the loop in the cooler spring or fall months, since it follows open prairie much its length. It's a good way to enjoy fall's prairie wildflowers such as tall goldenrod, blazing star, asters, and various sunflowers.

Directions

From downtown Chicago, drive west on I-290 for 13.4 miles and merge onto I-88 W. Drive west 23.9 miles, exiting at State Route 31 and drive north 3.9 miles. Turn left on Main Street and drive west for 3 miles to Nelson Lake Road. Turn south onto Nelson Lake Road; the east parking lot is 0.8 mile south on the west side of the road. Walk north past the old silo, then west on the wide limestone path to reach the trailhead.

GPS Coordinates: 16 T 386224mE 4632041mN

Information and Contact

There is no fee. Dogs on leash are allowed. The park is open sunrise–sunset daily. There are information signs and restrooms at the trailhead. Preserve maps may be available; trail intersections are numbered on that map. For more information, contact Dick Young Forest Preserve, Nelson Lake Road (south of Main Street), Batavia, IL, 630/232-5980, www.kaneforest.com.

17 REGIONAL-BOBOLINK TRAIL LOOP

Blackwell Forest Preserve, Warrenville

Level: Easy/moderate

Hiking Time: 3.5-4 hours

Total Distance: 7.0 miles round-trip

Elevation Change: negligible

Summary: The trails of Blackwell Forest Preserve offers hikers lots of scenic options and fun natural history.

Blackwell Forest Preserve occupies more than 1,300 acres of land shaped by the Wisconsin Glacier. The glacial retreat 12,000–15,000 years ago left a scoured, rolling landscape. The preserve serves as a nature island in the heavily populated Western Suburbs. Blackwell is home to several lakes and ponds, which provide opportunities for angling, boating, and bird-watching. The open prairie gives way to marshes and one trail loops through the thick woodlands along the West Branch DuPage River. Scattered oak savanna offers hikers some protection from the sun in summer, and provides habitat to songbirds, squirrels, and raccoons. Also notable is the site adjacent to McKee Marsh where workers discovered the skeleton of a woolly mammoth in the 1970s.

Hike southwest, then north, around White Pine Pond. The limestone trail is wide and well-maintained. Mount Hoy rises gently above the surrounding trees across the pond. As you walk, listen to the rich cacophony of birdsong. The trail drops into the hardwoods, then passes a stand of conifers. If it's a sunny day you'll get relief as the trail passes through a woodland with thick understory plants and wildflowers. Cross the footbridge and pass a split log bench as you enter the prairie near 1 mile. You may spy a meadowlark or a red-winged blackbird. Continue past the mown path on the right, which leads to the Youth Campground. The pretty avenue of trees signals that the Mack Road Crossing is close. Cross the road at about 1.7 miles.

At 2 miles you will reach the three-way intersection with the Bobolink Trail, which goes right. Turn right; the trail rolls slightly through some trees and then passes through grasslands. As the trail curves northward you'll find an interpretive sign, and a bench sits conveniently nearby. The trail turns west at 2.6 miles, then briefly enters the trees once more. At about 3.2 miles you will reach the Catbird Trail junction. Note that the Bobolink Trail ends here and the Regional Trail resumes. Turn right on the Catbird Trail and head north towards the Sanctuary Pond, which you'll see before reaching the curve west to the river. I love this short trail, the dense oak and hickory woods make it feel remote and there are lots of birds. You return to the main loop at 4 miles.

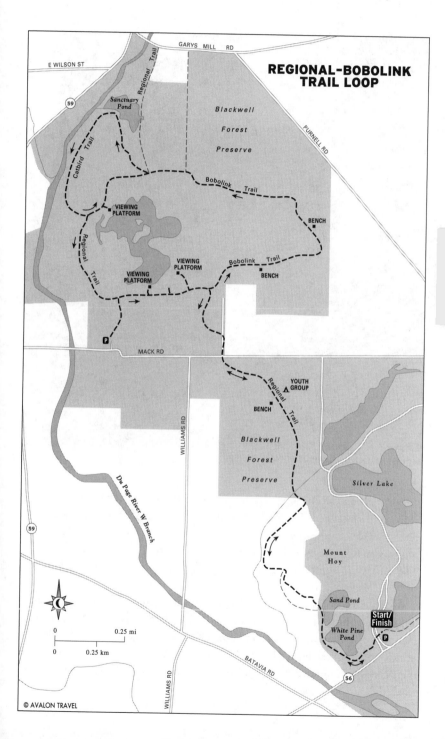

REGIONAL-BOBOLINK TRAIL LOOP

GARYS MILL RD

E WILSON ST

59

Regional Trail

Sanctuary Pond

Blackwell Forest Preserve

PURNELL RD

Catbird Trail

Bobolink Trail

VIEWING PLATFORM

BENCH

Regional Trail

VIEWING PLATFORM

VIEWING PLATFORM

Bobolink Trail

BENCH

P

MACK RD

Regional Trail

YOUTH GROUP

BENCH

WILLIAMS RD

Blackwell Forest Preserve

Silver Lake

Du Page River W Branch

59

Mount Hoy

Sand Pond

Start/Finish

P

0   0.25 mi

0   0.25 km

White Pine Pond

WILLIAMS RD

BATAVIA RD

56

© AVALON TRAVEL

limestone path and avenue of trees

Turn left on the Regional Trail, walk 0.1 mile, and turn right to reach the viewing platform and interpretive sign for the woolly mammoth discovery. The platform faces southeast across the pretty marsh, which is edged with encroaching grasses. Return to the Regional Trail and turn left to continue along the loop. The trail winds south through the trees, in springtime there is a vernal pool to the east. Listen for frogs near the pond.

At about 4.5 miles, a spur on the right leads to restrooms and a small parking lot. Just past the spur are two viewing platforms—both look north to the marsh. Here you can listen to the frogs and keep an eye out for goldfinches, a variety of ducks, woodpeckers, butterflies, and dragonflies. At about 4.8 miles you'll reach the three-way trail junction of the Regional and Bobolink Trails. Turn right to reach the start.

Options

Enjoy some shorter hikes by parking at the north end of Silver Lake to access the 0.9-mile Egret Trail. This short trail winds through the woods north of the campground. If you want to enjoy some views, park on the west side of Silver Lake and walk across the road to take the gravel trail to the top of the landfill mountain, Mount Hoy.

Directions

From the I-290/I-294 interchange, drive southwest on I-88 W for 14.5 miles. Exit at Winfield Road and turn right. Drive 1.5 miles north and turn left on IL-56/Butterfield Road. Drive nearly 0.5 mile to the south entrance to the Blackwell Forest Preserve. Turn right at the signed entrance (Main Drive) and park at the first lot on the right. The trail begins on the west side of Main Drive.
GPS Coordinates: 16 T 402288mE 4631159mN

Information and Contact

There is no fee for hiking. Dogs on leash are allowed; there is an off-leash dog area for those with a permit. There are no services at the trailhead; water and restrooms are available along the trail. Maps are available at most parking areas. For more information, contact Blackwell Forest Preserve, Butterfield Road and Main Drive, Warrenville, IL, 630/933-7248, www.dupageforest.com.

18 HERRICK LAKE LOOP
Herrick Lake Forest Preserve, Wheaton

🛶 🎋 🚣 🦌 👫 ♿

Level: Easy/moderate   **Total Distance:** 5.7 miles round-trip

Hiking Time: 3 hours   **Elevation Change:** negligible

Summary: Spring wildflowers and grassland birds make Herrick Lake trails a great outing.

Herrick Lake Forest Preserve is a mainstay of the DuPage County preserve system. As with much of northern Illinois, this area was at one time covered in thick sheets of glacial ice. When the Ice Age ended, it left behind rocky moraines and depressions, which later became ponds or wetlands. Today the 885 acres provides habitat for over 200 animal species, and supports at least 470 different plant types. The preserve contains mature woods with white, red, and bur oak. Fields of native prairie and European grasses support birds like dickcissel, bobolink, and eastern meadowlark. Wetlands, pothole ponds, and a marsh attract frogs and muskrats, too.

Walk north from the picnic area on the rolling Lake Trail. You will enjoy clear lake views, which allow plenty of time to look for birds, usually Canada geese or ducks. At the south end of the lake turn east, then, at the three-way junction, turn onto the Meadowlark Trail. You will wind southward through the woods skirting the golf course for the next mile; watch for woodpeckers in the trees here. The trail reaches open grassland just before 1.6 miles, where there is a four-way intersection with the Regional Trail, marked by post 7.

Walk southwest now onto the 1.9-mile Green Heron Trail. You will climb slightly for about a half mile then slowly descend past scattered pines, oak, black cherry, and cedar trees. At the southern tip of the trail is post 9, at 2.6 miles. Now walk north through more woods until your reach the open grassland and marsh around 3 miles. Continue in and out of the trees until you get past the four-way trail junction and onto the Bluebird Trail at 3.45 miles. This is one of my favorite trails—the views north are usually across bright yellow compass plant and yellow coneflowers. It is usually filled with grassland birds and you may see a bobolink along with various sparrows.

At 3.8 miles is a three-way with the Regional Trail at post 11. Turn right to walk southward, continuing through mostly open space for the next 0.8 mile. You will pass the four-way intersection with Bluebird Trail as you continue west. At nearly 4.5 miles there is a nice view south across the marsh; you may spot an egret or two on the water early in the day and frogs usually can be heard along here too. Hike

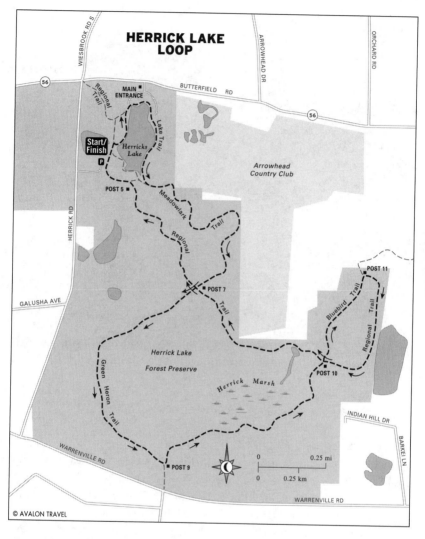

through the woods for a short distance as the trail curves northward and past another four-way intersection. Back in the woods at 5.1 miles, watch for poison ivy along here, sometimes as a vine climbing up maple trunks. Keep left at post 5 (a three-way junction) to walk the short distance northwest back to the start.

Options

For a more robust hike, add more mileage by hiking the Regional Trail to its terminus in Danada Forest Preserve. Start; at 3.8 miles (post 11), continue straight instead of turning south. Follow the Regional Trail for 2.8 miles until it ends

preserve pond north of Herrick Lake marsh

next to Rice Lake and Leask Lane. Retrace your steps to post 11 and resume the hike as written. The total hiking distance is about 11.4 miles.

Directions

From downtown Chicago, drive west on I-290 for 13.4 miles and then merge onto I-88 W. Drive west on I-88 for 13.2 miles. Take the Naperville Road exit and merge onto Freedom Drive for 0.1 mile. Turn west on Warrenville Road and drive for 1.5 miles. Turn north on Herrick Road and drive 1 mile north. The entrance for the South Picnic Area is on the east side of Herrick Road. Walk east from the lot to the information board to reach the trailhead.

GPS Coordinates: 16 T 404838mE 4630969mN

Information and Contact

There is no fee. Dogs on leash are allowed. Accessible trails, a boat dock, and restrooms are available at the East Shelter area. The park is open from one hour after sunrise to one hour after sunset daily. For more information, contact Herrick Lake Forest Preserve, Herrick Road (between Warrenville and Butterfield Roads), Wheaton, IL 60189, 630/933-7200, www.dupageforest.com.

19 DANADA REGIONAL AND NATURE TRAILS
Danada Forest Preserve, Wheaton

Level: Easy

Hiking Time: 2 hours

Total Distance: 3.4 miles round-trip

Elevation Change: negligible

Summary: Some of the oldest bur oaks in the area keep hikers company along the Danada Forest Preserve's nature trail.

Danada Forest Preserve is part of a string of DuPage County preserves for wildlife and bird habitat that also create a recreation corridor for residents. When the last glacial era ended over 10,000 years ago, it left in its wake the gently rolling terrain of Danada Forest Preserve. Danada is a unique preserve with 789 acres of oak savanna, prairie, and wetlands surrounding the palatial estate, equestrian center, and farm of the late Daniel and Ada Rice. Within the preserve, restoration and preservation efforts have resulted in wetland, prairie, and woodland habitats that

oak savanna along the Nature Trail

provide for a wide variety of animal and plant life. A 35-acre prairie restoration site west of Naperville Road provides nesting for grassland sparrows and bololink, and the blooms of prairie blazing star, coneflower, and goldenrod are a delight to onlookers. Visitors today can visit and enjoy 3 miles of hiking trails along the wide, limestone regional trail or along the double-loop nature trail. Whichever you choose, a hike at Danada Forest Preserve is a refreshing way to bird-watch or enjoy native wildflowers.

The trailhead is marked by numbered post 14. (The numbered posts coincide with map locations to help hikers stay oriented.) Walk north on the limestone path from the trailhead, towards Danada House. Follow the path for the nearly 0.2 mile as it crosses the property to reach the edge of the trees at post 15. You will quickly reach post 16 at the Nature Trail trailhead, which is sometimes called Parson's Grove. Walk south through the mature mixed oak and hickory woods. There are huge bur oaks amongst the trees and the grove is known for early wildflowers like spring beauty, shooting stars, and anemone. (The grove area is actually a restored oak savanna, which thrives today due to hours of volunteer effort.) After turning north, pass a three-way intersection to rejoin the regional trail at 0.75 mile.

Note post 17 on the right as you walk north through the thinning trees. The trees largely end at the edge of a rolling grassland. At 1 mile, the trail descends along the east side of Rice Lake. There are scores of goldfinch and sparrows enjoying the endless flowers, and heron and egrets fish the shallow waters along the lake's edge. The trail gently rolls around the lake for the next 0.4 mile to the trail's end at Leask Lane at 1.8 miles. Retrace your steps up the hill, pass post 17, then keep right at about 2.7 miles to start hiking the Regional Trail. Follow the Regional Trail south along the edge of the trees before turning sharply north on a gravel path at 2.85 miles. This wide path follows the edge of the trees and shortly turns south to rejoin the Regional Trail just north of the equestrian center at 3.2 miles. Turn west to walk the short distance to the start of the hike.

Options

The west end of Danada Forest Preserve provides a longer hiking experience. From the trailhead at post 14, follow the path through the tunnel under Naperville Road. Just before the trail makes a hairpin curve, look north over the restored prairie; it's full of birds and wildflowers all summer long. At 1.45 miles, reach the junction with the trails of Herrick Lake Forest Preserve. Retrace your steps to the trailhead for nearly 3 additional miles, or 6.4 miles combined hiking distance. If you still want more, continue about 1.9 miles on the Regional Trail to the Herrick Lake Loop (see listing in this chapter).

Directions

From downtown Chicago, drive west on I-290 for 13.4 miles, then merge onto I-88 W. Drive west on I-88 for 13.2 miles. Exit at Naperville Road, following the signs, then turn north on Naperville Road. Danada is 0.8 mile north on the east side of the road. Pull into the large parking lot. Along the west edge is a path with a preserve map and bench. Numbered post 14 serves as the trailhead.
GPS Coordinates: 16 T 407920mE 4630053mN

Information and Contact

There is no fee. Dogs on leash are allowed, except on the nature trail. The park is open from one hour after sunrise to one hour after sunset daily. For more information, contact Danada Forest Preserve, 3S501 Naperville Road, Wheaton, IL 60189, www.dupageforest.com.

20 WEST AND SCHULENBERG PRAIRIE LOOP

BEST C

Morton Arboretum West, Lisle

🛩 🌲 🔆 👫 ♿

Level: Moderate

Total Distance: 4.6 miles round-trip

Hiking Time: 2-3 hours

Elevation Change: 190 feet

Summary: Walk through oak savanna and a model planted prairie in this exploration of Morton Arboretum's west side.

It's likely that these days, Joy Morton would hardly recognize the 735-acre arboretum he founded in 1922. Today's 1,700-acre Morton Arboretum is not all formal gardens, oak woodlands, and conifer plantations. Schulenberg Prairie, in the far west corner, is Morton Arboretum's model planted prairie. It's both home to important native plant and animal communities and a direct link to Illinois's prairie past. In the 1960s, arboretum curator Ray Schulenberg began planting a native prairie. Schulenberg and his staff collected seeds, cleared invasive species, and planted seedlings. What a difference five decades can make. Today a walk through the original prairie plot and the adjacent expansion are a wonderful introduction to the world of native plants. Blooms burst forth in the springtime—prairie false indigo, compass plant, purple and yellow coneflower, and others decorate the green grassland with color. The peripheral savanna of oak and hickory forms a woodland habitat with widely spaced trees and large open areas—an important component of the prairie ecosystem. By combining the west-side trails with the prairie trails, hikers can really enjoy the diverse landscape of the arboretum.

The trails at Morton without specific names are referred to as "Main Trail Loop #" (ML#). Walk west on ML 2 through the sometimes-dense oak and hickory woods along the rolling wood-chip trail. Passing Pine Hill to the south, follow the signs to the Prairie Visitor Station (PVS) in 0.8 mile. At the PVS, take a look at the interpretive panels, then walk the 0.25-mile wheelchair-accessible loop north of the shelter. After that, walk west, then south on the Prairie Trail.

Walk across a footbridge, then take a short detour west onto a mown-grass Acre Trail that follows the north bank of Willoway Brook. The grassland is beautiful and full of birds like goldfinch and sparrows. Walk southward across a second footbridge, keeping an eye out for wading birds like great blue heron. When you reach a gravel road, turn back east for 0.2 mile to return to the Prairie Trail at about 1.6 miles. Turn southeast, in and out of the trees, for the next 0.2 mile. The prairie stretches south, interrupted only by a couple of stately oaks in the middle. Turn southwest, still in the trees, then westward at the sign for the prairie loop.

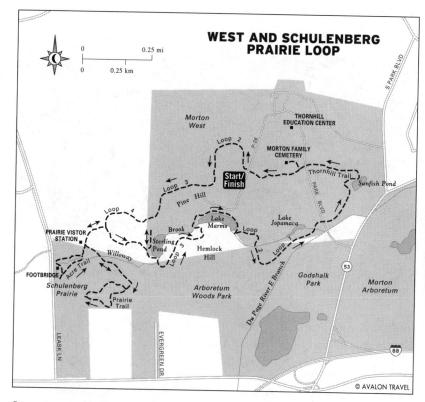

Lingering on this short loop might lengthen your hike significantly—there are so many flowers and grasses to look at and it is very peaceful and quiet.

Return to the PVS on the Prairie Trail around 2.6 miles. Turn southeast onto ML 4 for a short while, towards Sterling Pond, then join ML 3. Take the quick turn north and uphill along the pond's wooded west side for nice views across the water. Return to ML 3 and work your way eastward through huge maples to Lake Marmo. At 3.2 miles turn north, just before Hemlock Hill, and take a shortcut trail to join ML 2. This will take you along the north lakeshore, passing a huge Freeman maple before you turn south. Before joining ML 1, you'll pass an enormous stand of arborvitae. Wind along the creek, past Godshalk Meadow, reaching Sunfish Pond at 4.1 miles. After going north around the pond, continue through the meadow to the trail junction; turn west to reach the start in 0.5 mile along the Thornhill Trail and ML 2.

Options

To spend a day exploring arboretum history and some formal gardens, begin at the Thornhill Education Center. You may walk south along the paved Joy Path

© BARBARA I. BOND

Schulenberg Prairie

and link to the Thornhill Path west for a combined 1-mile loop. You will pass the spur to the Morton Family Cemetery, which is worth the short walk.

Directions

From downtown Chicago, drive west on I-290 13.4 miles, merging onto I-88 W. Continue 10.6 mile to the exit for State Route 53. Drive north 0.5 mile to entrance on the east side of the road. Follow the road from the entrance station to the stop sign. Turn right, drive through the underpass, and continue north on the Main Route West Side. After you pass the Thornhill Education Center, turn left on an alternate road and park at pull-out P26 on the west side of the road. The roads are well signed. The trail is a few feet north of the parking area and is signed.
GPS Coordinates: 16 T 410234mE 4629976mN

Information and Contact

Entrance to the Arboretum is $11 for adults (age 18–64), $10 for seniors (age 65 and over), and $8 for youth (age 2–17). Dogs are not allowed. The park is open daily 7 A.M.–sunset. There is a visitors center (daily 9 A.M.–6 P.M. May–Oct., 9 A.M.–5 P.M. Mar.–Apr. and Nov.–Dec., 9 A.M.–4 P.M. Jan.–Feb.), library, bookstore, café and restaurant. Snowshoe rentals are available in winter. For more information, please contact Morton Arboretum, 4100 SR-53, Lisle, IL, 630/968-0074, www.mortonarb.org.

21 BIG ROCK TRAIL SAMPLER
Morton Arboretum, East Side, Lisle

Level: Easy/moderate

Hiking Time: 2.5 hours

Total Distance: 4.3 miles round-trip

Elevation Change: negligible

Summary: Hike the east-side trails of the Morton Arboretum to visit the restored native woodlands.

Morton Arboretum's east side covers nearly two-thirds of the grounds acreage. One way to sample the diverse environments present amongst the six trails is through this sample loop. The Big Rock Visitor Station provides easy access to much of the rich east-side forest. There you can check out a wonderful collection of interpretive panels, visit a geological relic, and hike through the oak woodlands that are part of an experimental restoration project. Before the area was affected by human development in the 19th century, the oak savanna and forests here contained trees

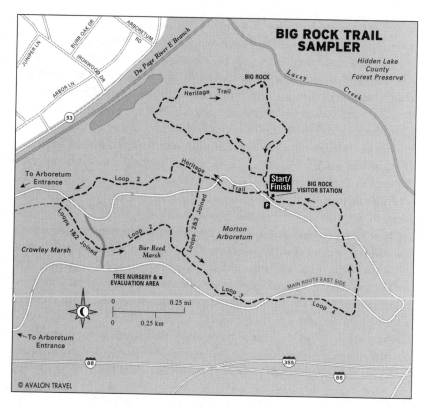

footbridge and woodchip trail along Morton Arboretum's east side

of different ages, which formed a beautiful open canopy that let light filter to the forest floor where a variety of flowers, shrubs, and wildlife thrived. Generations of fire suppression and overuse changed these native forests, creating thick canopies where shade-loving opportunistic species moved in. Hiking the trails through the restoration areas gives outdoors lovers the chance to imagine what these forests once were like—and perhaps become inspired to get involved in the conservation efforts. The Arboretum trails have a utilitarian naming system, but they are well-signed for hiking enjoyment; once you understand their conventions it's easy to stay on track. In the woods, watch for woodpeckers, warblers, or chickadees, then turn your eyes skyward for hawks along the west side of the trail.

Walk west from the Big Rock lot onto the East Side Main Loop 3 (ML3). ML3 winds through the sometimes dense forest along a wood-chip trail, if you are hiking after a rain, watch out because tiny frogs are often hopping about. Solomon's seal, trillium, and other wildflowers thrive here in spring and summer. The trail passes the southward trail junction with the Joined Loops 2 and 3, continuing west as ML2 and curving south at 0.86 mile or so onto Joined Loops 1 and 2. This short connector trail heads towards Crowley Marsh. Turn left onto ML2 once more and walk a few tenths further to the boardwalk that passes through Bur Reed Marsh. Cattails, rushes and sedges, reeds—it's definitely a whole different ecosystem and it's a startling change. Take a moment to enjoy the view from the platform, and even close your eyes and listen for frogs. Continue east and at nearly 1.35 miles the trail dips south sharply, heading past the Joined Loop 2 and 3 trail (which goes north) towards the southern part of the arboretum. You will walk past the tree nursery and evaluation area, a great place for snowshoe exploration in winter.

Over the next 0.75 mile the trail gently climbs. As you reach ML4 you will begin to walk through a patch of forest that feels remote. At 2.2 miles the trail turns northward, crosses the main road, and continues winding through the trees. You cross the main road one more time, and rejoin ML3 before ending at the Big Rock Visitor Station at just under 3 miles.

At Big Rock you have the choice to hike either the Heritage or Woodland Trail separately, or combine them into a pleasing loop. The Heritage Trail shows how this area may have appeared prior to settlement. Walk north from the shelter onto the trail, keeping left at the two trail junctions. Big Rock, at the bend in the trail, is one of the highlights. This huge rock is a glacial erratic, although the story is that it got moved to its present location. Pass Big Rock and turn west at 3.25 miles to wind through a more open landscape of scattered trees and lots of wildflowers. It's very quiet in this part of the arboretum. In 0.25 mile you enter the trees again, turning east/southeast at 3.7 miles. Continue in the woods to complete the loop at 4.3 miles.

Options

For a different experience, visit the west-side trails of Morton Arboretum. The possibilities are endless: from the Prairie Visitor Station, hike the Acre and Prairie Trails or follow the West and Schulenberg Prairie Loop (see listing in this chapter). The Prairie Visitor Station also has a short accessible trail with interpretive panels.

Directions

From downtown Chicago, drive west on I-290 for 13.4 miles, merging onto I-88 W. Continue for 10.6 miles to the exit for State Route 53. Drive north 0.5 mile to park entrance on east. Follow the road from the entrance station to the stop sign. Turn left at the stop sign and follow the East Side Main Road until reaching the Big Rock Visitor Station (the road is signed).
GPS Coordinates: 16 T 413068mE 4629945mN

Information and Contact

Admission to the Arboretum is $11 for adults (age 18–64), $10 for seniors (age 65 and over), and $8 for youth (age 2–17). Dogs are not allowed. The park is open 7 A.M.–5 P.M. in winter; 7 A.M.–7 P.M. summer. There is a visitors center, library, and restaurant. Snowshoe rentals are available in winter. For more information, contact Morton Arboretum, 4100 SR-53, Lisle, 630/968-0074, www.mortonarb.org.

22 FULLERSBURG-GRAUE MILL LOOP

Fullersburg Woods Forest Preserve, Oak Brook

Level: Easy

Total Distance: 3.0-4.0 miles round-trip

Hiking Time: 1.5-2 hours

Elevation Change: negligible

Summary: Fullersburg Woods Forest Preserve offers hikers a wealth of options, including a wildflower trail and a historic grist mill.

Fullersburg Woods is bounded on three sides by the meandering waters of Salt Creek. This has created a preserve full of wildlife and natural beauty. Once the oak woodland thrived and the waters of Salt Creek were pristine, but popularity of the preserve has degraded the land and water due to overuse. However, recovery efforts have been in process and the land is being restored. Fullersburg Woods Nature Education Center has taught generations about the importance of natural resources and the center is a cornerstone of DuPage County's outdoor education and recreation programs. The Interpretive Trail provides an introduction to the preserve, and the Multipurpose Trail allows further exploration of the Paul Butler Nature Area in the northwest corner of the preserve. Don't miss a trip south along

a historic bridge built by the Civilian Conservation Corps in the 1930's

© BARBARA I. BOND

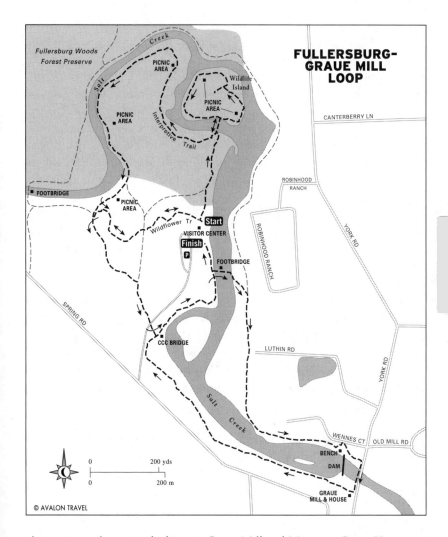

the scenic creek to visit the historic Graue Mill and Museum, Graue House, or Fuller House. The gristmill is the only water-powered mill still operating in the state and the mill property was a station of the Underground Railroad; it is on the National Register of Historic Places.

Begin by heading north on the Interpretive Trail towards the small "wild-life island." As you walk you'll note the nearness of the creek to the east, it almost looks like a small pond. You quickly reach the bridge leading to the island. The short island loop is quiet and has good opportunities for watching wildlife. Beavers, white-tailed deer, and a variety of songbirds and waterfowl are commonly seen. Even if you don't see beaver, look for the telltale chew marks on downed trees along the water's edge. After the loop, cross back over the bridge and turn right onto the trail to follow the creek as it winds north, then turns back on itself southward at 0.56 mile. Continue south, you will approach a three-way intersection just ahead of a picnic shelter. This is a shortcut back to the nature center. Continue straight and pass the shelter, and you will quickly reach the intersection with the Multipurpose Trail. Turning right here takes you over the bridge to the Paul Butler Nature Area. If you go left, you'll return to the nature center. Along the way you can take a short detour along the Wildflower Trail; pick up a guide at the nature center for help identifying the most commonly seen flowers.

From the main trail near the nature center, extend your hike by backtracking west to the Multipurpose Trail, then turn left to head south. You'll exit the trail briefly at 1.9 miles, cross the entrance road then pick up a dirt connector trail that passes a pretty bridge which was built by the Civilian Conservation Corps in the 1930s. (Don't cross the bridge unless you want to explore a trailless area along the creek.) Turn left and you quickly reach the main bridge across Salt Creek; cross over and turn right to go south along the east side of the creek. You'll hear the rush of water over a spillway before the Graue Mill comes into view to the west. Cross the York Road overpass then visit the historic buildings in the area. When you're done, head northward on the west side of the creek on the well-graded trail. You'll be back at the nature center and parking lot in about a mile.

Options
For a short option that still gives you a feel for the preserve, first hike the Wildflower Trail, then walk the island loop to experience the quiet of the preserve and to view wildlife. Watch for white-tailed deer in the morning; along the main trail, you may catch a flash of blue from the indigo bunting.

Directions
From downtown Chicago, drive west on I-290 for 13.4 miles, then merge onto I-88 W for 0.5 mile. Take the State Route 38 W exit towards Roosevelt Road/I-294 S and drive south on I-294 2.9 miles. Exit onto US-34 W/Ogden Avenue and drive west 0.8 mile, turn north on York Road and continue for 0.2 mile. At Spring Road, turn west and drive 0.5 mile to the preserve road on the north side of the street. Turn right and drive 0.2 mile to the main lot. Walk north to the nature center and trailhead.
GPS Coordinates: 16 T 422548mE 4630689mN

Information and Contact

There is no fee. Dogs on leash are allowed. Preserve and trail hours are from one hour after sunrise to one hour after sunset daily. Visitors center hours are 9 A.M.–5 P.M. daily. For more information, contact Fullersburg Woods Forest Preserve, 3609 Spring Road, Oak Brook, IL 60523, 630/850-8110, www.dupageforest.com.

The Graue Mill and Museum are open 10 A.M.–4:30 P.M. Tuesday–Sunday mid-April–mid-November. Admission to the mill and museum is $3.50 for adults, $3 for seniors, and $1.50 for children (age 4–12). For more information, contact Graue Mill and Museum, 3800 York Road, Oak Brook, IL 60523, 630/655-2090, www.grauemill.org.

23 MAIN-GREENE VALLEY LOOP

Greene Valley Forest Preserve, Naperville

Level: Easy/moderate

Total Distance: 6.4 miles round-trip

Hiking Time: 3-3.5 hours

Elevation Change: 175 feet

Summary: Enjoy seemingly endless views from atop Greene Valley Hill before hiking the varied terrain of Greene Valley Forest Preserve.

Greene Valley Forest Preserve is a 1,400-acre greenspace in heavily populated suburban Naperville. The preserve sits on a triangle of land between the east and west branches of the DuPage River. The preserve has the typical landforms associated with the glacial period that ended over 10,000 years ago. One unique constructed feature of the preserve is the area high point, Greene Valley Hill, which is 980 feet tall. Sadly there are no trails to the top; however, the scenic viewpoint is open on weekends and the pretty hill adds to the preserve's beauty. The preserve has over 10 miles of trails, allowing hikers of all types to take advantage of this area resource.

Greene Valley has a trail system that can take intrepid hikers to practically every corner of this large preserve. With several trailheads, water fountains, and restrooms, it is easy to see why this is a popular spot with area residents. Walk northeast from the trailhead on the wide, limestone Main Trail. Walking towards a stand of trees past sunflowers, yarrow, and gray-headed coneflowers, it's hard to believe you are surrounded by residential neighborhoods. There are lots of birds here, including goldfinches and red-winged blackbirds, and monarch, red-spotted purple, and sulphur butterflies flit about the grassland. You will pass rows of sumac trees, some aspens, and scattered pine and juniper trees. The Main Trail crosses 79th Street, then curves south to a trail junction at 1.3 miles. Turn east on the connector trail, then head north on the Greene Trail.

The next 1.5 miles mostly cover the savanna of the east preserve. Keep right at 1.8 miles on the Valley Trail, which will make a wide turn south. Greene Valley Hill comes into view across the open grassland, providing some pleasant visual relief. At 2.8 miles continue south, then west on the Oak Spur Trail. The southern preserve contains mature oak woodland with some magnificent trees. You head towards, then enter, the woods at 3.4 miles. After completing the 0.5-mile loop, retrace the trail back to the junction with the Greene Trail. At 4.5 miles turn north, then west, and follow the Green Trail north past black-eyed Susans and bergamot to the connector trail. Turn west, cross Green Road, then at 5.1 miles hike south on the continuation of the Main Trail. The trail enters the oak and

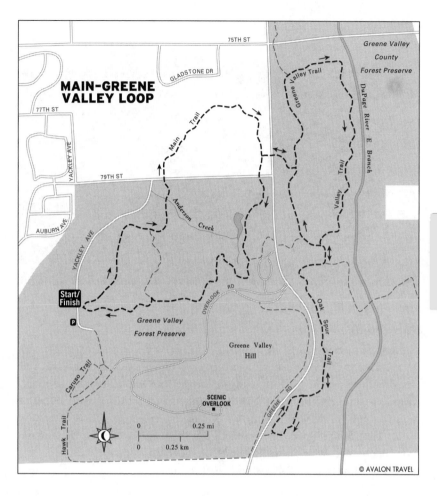

hickory woods, which are undergoing restoration south of 79th Street. There are some pretty shagbark hickories here; the bigger trees have very shaggy trunks. At 6 miles, you emerge from the woods. Continue on a slight uphill through the grassland, with its wildflowers and sparrows, for the last 0.4 mile to reach the start.

Options

To learn more about preserve trees, hike the 0.8-mile Caruso Trail (dedicated to a young man who died in 2004 while serving in the Marines) also called the Tricky-Tree-Trek Trail. Trail materials are available at the ranger residence on the property, or by contacting the Fullersburg Woods Nature Center. If you hike either of these trails, be sure to wear long pants; portions of the trails are overgrown and poison ivy abounds.

© BARBARA I. BOND

Greene Valley Hill

Directions

From the junction of I-88 W and I-355 in Lisle, drive south on I-355 for 4.5 miles. Take the 63rd Street exit and turn right on 63rd St./Hobson Road and drive southwest 1.4 miles. Turn south on Greene Road and follow it for 1.1 miles, then go west on 79th Street for 0.5 mile. Turn south on Yackley Avenue and drive south 0.6 mile to the west parking lot. (On the preserve map, Yackley Avenue is called Thunderbird Road.) The trailhead is at the east side of the lot. Walk to the information sign, which is slightly north on the trail.
GPS Coordinates: 16 T 409500mE 4620760mN

Information and Contact

There is no fee. Dogs on leash are allowed; an off-leash area is available for permit holders. The park is open from one hour after sunrise to one hour after sunset daily. For more information, contact Greene Valley Forest Preserve, Thunderbird Road, Naperville, IL, 630/933-7200, www.dupageforest.com.

24 LAKE RENWICK-BUDDE LAKE LOOP

BEST ◖

Lake Renwick Preserve and Heron Rookery Nature Preserve, Plainfield

🏞️ 🌿 🛶 👪 ♿

Level: Easy   **Total Distance:** 3.0 miles round-trip

Hiking Time: 1.5 hours   **Elevation Change:** negligible

Summary: Bring binoculars and a field guide for this hike along Renwick and Budde Lakes and past a huge heron rookery.

Lake Renwick Preserve and the Heron Rookery Nature Preserve are an important birding site in Illinois. The preserve was created to protect the nesting habitat of five species of then-threatened or endangered birds. As of 2010, four of the five species were no longer at risk, thanks to the success of the preserve. Breeding and nesting birds are protected by the preserve's closure in March and April. Bird-watching is restricted May through fledge (usually Aug. 1) in order to keep disturbances to a minimum; limited outings with preserve staff are available (check website for schedule). Two artificial islands have been outfitted with weird-looking structures to provide nesting opportunities for the double-crested cormorant, great blue heron, and great egrets that nest here annually.

Like much of the surrounding area, Lake Renwick used to be prairie. The

© BARBARA I. BOND

Lake Renwick heron rookeries

land was settled in the early 19th century; the gravel mining industry took root thereafter. When springs were opened by mining, freshwater filled the quarries to create lakes. The lakes were popular in summer, and were used for ice harvesting in winter. In the 1940s the area was closed due to increasing pollution. Birds came anyway, and nesting activity was documented throughout the years. Active preservation efforts began after mining ended in 1983.

Hiking the limestone path of the Heron Rookery Nature Preserve is all about bird-watching. There are butterflies in the wildflowers; wild grape, quaking aspen, and tall goldenrod also grow along the path. However, the reason people come here is to see the birds. Even in summer the two lake rookeries have some birds hanging around. I was here in late August and there were a lot of double-crested cormorants on the platforms.

Walk towards the visitors center on the path, passing restrooms and a trail information sign. Ignore the four-way intersection and continue north for 0.2 mile where the trail is joined by a parallel trail. As you proceed northward, the views west across the lake open up and the two rookeries come into view. If it is the first time you have seen an artificial nesting area, it definitely takes a moment to adjust. If you have binoculars or a spotting scope, there is a nice open spot around 0.4 mile where the views are unobstructed. Birds also frequently fly overhead on their way to or from the adjacent pond or larger Turtle Lake.

Walk north to the end of the preserve, where the trail turns east and goes through a tunnel. The limestone path ends around 0.8 mile and a paved path begins. This is the 1.25-mile loop that goes around Budde Lake. Turn north and follow the path as it follows the lakeshore. At 1.5 miles you will turn south past a nice outside amphitheater. At the trail junction, turn east towards the fishing platform just ahead. This is the Turtle Lake area of the preserve and is a good spot for a lunch break and more bird-watching. Great blue heron and egrets are often found near the lake shore.

When you are through, retrace your steps to the trail junction and walk west along the path, which now runs between Budde and Turtle Lakes. This is the "Woods Walk." You will reach the underpass in just under 0.5 mile and enter the Heron Rookery Nature Preserve once more.

Walk south 0.5 mile, and keep right at the Y intersection to reach the a gazebo with viewing scopes. As the path continues south in the woods you will begin seeing some interpretive boards—they explain the history of the area. Listen for woodpeckers, too. At 2.8 miles is another Y intersection, keep left to reach the visitors center directly. Or, keep right to complete another 0.4-mile loop. End at the information sign and map adjacent to the visitors center, totaling around 3 miles.

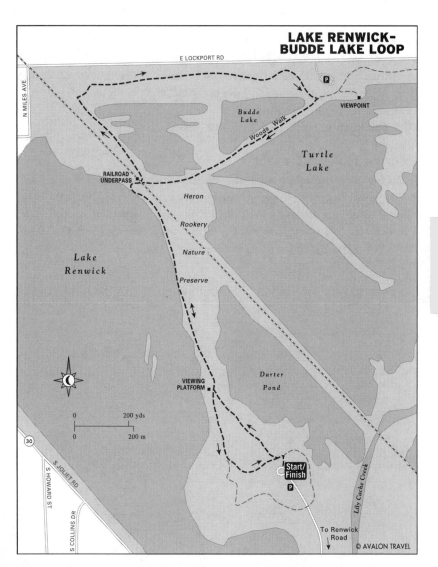

Options

If you want to focus on nature and bird-watching, shorten this hike by walking the 0.5-mile loop from the visitors center. Walk north along the path for 0.2 mile, then make a sharp turn left onto the west side of the loop. This will take you to the viewing platform. To return to the parking lot, just continue south, keeping left at the first three-way trail junction in 0.2 mile.

Directions

From downtown Chicago, take I-55 S for 36.5 miles. Take Exit 257 for U.S. 30 and drive northwest 1.1 miles. Turn east on E. Renwick Road and drive 0.4 mile. Turn north into the preserve and drive to the lot. Walk north towards the trail-head sign and visitors center to begin hiking.

GPS Coordinates: 16 T 401462mE 4605504mN

Information and Contact

There is no fee. Dogs are not allowed in the nature preserve. The preserve is open 8 A.M.–sunset August 15 through February, but it's closed March–August 15. The visitors center is open May 1–August 15. For more information, contact Lake Renwick Heron Rookery Nature Preserve, 23144 W. Renwick Road, Plainfield, IL, 60544, 815/727-8700, www.fpdwc.org.

CHICAGOLAND SOUTH

© BARBARA I. BOND

BEST HIKES

❰ Bird-Watching
Prairie View Loop, **page 251.**

❰ Children
Dells Trails, **page 239.**
Twin Oaks-Bunker Field Trails, **page 264.**

❰ Geologic Wonders
Lemont Quarry Loop, **page 230.**
West Overlooks and Canyons, **page 242.**
East Canyons, **page 245.**

❰ History Buffs
I&M Canal Trail: Iron Mile, **page 233.**
Twin Oaks-Bunker Field Trails, **page 264.**

❰ Lakefront or Riverside Hikes
Lemont Quarry Loop, **page 230.**

❰ Wildflowers
Prairie Creek Woods and Grass Frog Trails, **page 261.**

South of Chicago lies a great expanse of land

once covered with far-reaching grasslands and scattered trees. This is the land of Illinois's Grand Prairie, a natural division that was home to thousands of acres of tallgrass prairie, wetlands, and marshes. Although agriculture has converted much of the area, we can still enjoy hikes through large tracts of land undergoing restoration. One exciting aspect of the restoration trend is the establishment of the Prairie Parklands Macrosite. This is a collection of public and private lands, over 40,000 acres worth, in several counties. The goal is to eventually link these sites into continuous corridors to support plant and animal life. Several hikes outlined here travel through sections of this ambitious project.

Canyons, waterfalls, industrial sites, and transportation canals contribute to an eclectic landscape with miles of trails for hikers to explore. The Illinois & Michigan Canal only enjoyed a short span of time as a transportation canal after it was completed in the mid-1800s. Today the miles of towpath that parallel the canal provide hikers with an unsurpassed opportunity for historic hiking. The Heritage Quarries in Lemont are a great example of how one township converted an eyesore into beautiful lakes. Coyotes, wading birds, and amphibians now populate the area. Nearby are two other canal hikes, each with their own version of natural and human history and array of flora and fauna.

One of my favorite hiking destinations in this region is the Midewin National Tallgrass Prairie, in south-central Will County. The huge property is the site of the former Joliet Army Ammunition Plant. Today more than 15,000 acres have been dedicated as a preserve for restoration, conservation, and recreation. Miles of trails have been built at Midewin, and even more will be established in years to come. The huge ammunition plant structures are in the process of being dismantled, but you can still hike amongst historic World War II-era TNT storage bunkers at this unusual site – not to mention enjoy the grasslands that are being brought back to life.

Further west is another restoration site with a unique history. The prairies at Goose Lake Prairie State Natural Area feature highly adapted plant and animal communities. Prairie dropseed, Indian grass, prairie dock, and rattlesnake master are just some of the grasses and wildflowers that make this landscape so beautiful in the summertime. Birders may see a host of grassland species, including the reclusive Henslow's sparrow. The threatened Blanding's turtle also calls the prairie marshes home; you might spot this slow-moving amphibian rustling along a marshy trail. If you enjoy quiet trails with expansive views, then Goose Lake might be the place for you.

Farther west along the Illinois River are a string of state parks that have dramatic geologic features and provide miles of trails. The sandstone bluffs of Buffalo Rock State Park provide hikers with stunning views south across the Illinois River. (Buffalo Rock is also home to one of the largest outdoor art works in the country, the Effigy Tumuli.)

It would be hard to live in northern Illinois and not already know about the canyons, waterfalls, and overlooks of Starved Rock State Park. This natural area contains miles of trails amid a series of canyons carved into the St. Peter sandstone by Ice Age floodwaters. The trail systems wind through forests of mixed oak, hickory, and maple, traveling in and out of narrow canyons. The river bluffs have wonderful views of the Illinois River, and bald eagles are often visible, either nesting in trees or soaring overhead. The park is open year-round; visits to the icy waterfalls are popular in winter. Nearby Matthiessen State Park has canyons and bluffs also formed by violent geologic processes, resulting in yet another beautiful and dramatic landscape. The canyons of Matthiessen are also home to unusual and rare species of fern, moss, and liverwort.

South Chicagoland contains a wide array of unusual hiking opportunities. Hikers of all ages and experience levels will find something intriguing along the trails here, whether exploring the historic trails of Joliet and Lemont, visiting the wide-open prairie of Midewin, or meandering through the canyons of Starved Rock.

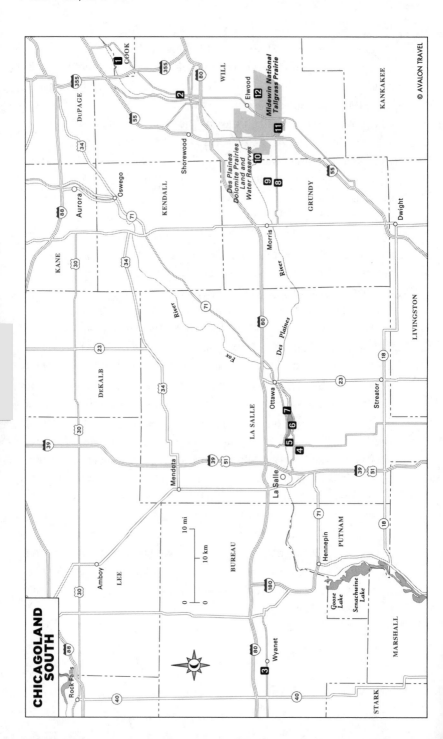

TRAIL NAME	LEVEL	DISTANCE	TIME	ELEVATION	FEATURES	PAGE
1 Lemont Quarry Loop	Easy	3.0 mi rt	1.5 hr	negligible		230
2 I&M Canal Trail: Iron Mile	Easy/moderate	4.1 mi rt	2.5 hr	negligible		233
3 Hennepin Canal Trail	Easy/moderate	10.5 mi rt	5-6 hr	negligible		236
4 Dells Trails	Moderate	3.2 mi rt	2-2.5 hr	390 ft		239
5 West Overlooks and Canyons	Moderate	6.6 mi rt	3.5 hr	900 ft		242
6 East Canyons	Moderate	6.5 mi rt	3.5 hr	850 ft		245
7 River Bluff-Effigy Tumuli Trails	Easy/moderate	3.0 mi rt	1.5 hr	150 ft		248
8 Prairie View Loop	Easy	3.4 mi rt	1.5-2 hr	negligible		251
9 Tall Grass Nature Trail	Easy	2.7 mi rt	1.5 hr	negligible		254
10 I&M Canal Trail: East Side	Moderate	11.25 mi one-way	5-6 hr	negligible		257
11 Prairie Creek Woods and Grass Frog Trails	Easy	5.5 mi rt	2.5-3 hr	negligible		261
12 Twin Oaks-Bunker Field Trails	Easy/moderate	3.3-4.3 mi	2-2.5 hr	negligible		264

1 LEMONT QUARRY LOOP   BEST C
Heritage Quarries Recreation Area

🛩 🏵 🏊 🎡 🐴 👫 🚌

Level: Easy   **Total Distance:** 3.0 miles round-trip

Hiking Time: 1.5 hours   **Elevation Change:** negligible

Summary: Historic Lemont is home to a unique collection of retired quarries that can be explored on foot or by boat.

In 1848, the 96 miles of the Illinois & Michigan Canal were completed, contributing to a water route that reached from the Gulf of Mexico to the east coast. The village of Lemont, near the east end of the canal, was one of many cities that benefited from the construction. Dolomite limestone of high quality was discovered here and mined extensively during the latter part of the 19th century. Many significant buildings in Chicagoland were built from Lemont stone, including the distinctive Chicago Water Tower. Once the quarries were closed, they filled with spring water, creating the peaceful and scenic lakes we enjoy today. Lemont set aside land as part of its overall vision to create a beautiful park featuring the canal towpath trail and a trail that winds around the attractive quarry lakes.

Walk west 0.1 mile towards the steel plant, then make two right turns on the canal towpath. You are now heading west on the north side of the I&M Canal, along the southern shore of Consumers Quarry. The blue of the lake water is quite a contrast to the whitish gray of the limestone along the rugged, rocky shore. Turn left in 0.5 mile to walk north between the lakes. The limestone trail is wide and flat, and leads through a surprisingly dense and overgrown tangle of brush and smallish trees. Sumac trees form small stands in places and you'll see some ash, walnut, and honey-locust. This is an area in transition; hopefully restoration efforts will continue.

After a short distance, the trail again heads eastward along the north side of several smallish lakes called the Great Lakes Quarries. Great blue heron are often seen on these lakes. The next 0.4 mile is really dense, watch for riverbank grape and poison ivy, it's almost a relief to reach a three-way junction at 1.0 mile. This is a short spur that leads to the edge of the water. Continue east through the trees to the picnic area around mile 1.4. If you planned ahead, this is a great place to lounge around, enjoy the view of the clear water, and do a little floating if you brought your inflatable raft or kayak.

Resume your hike on the path, which makes a wide arc south, then west, along the southern shore of the lake. Wind in and out of the trees for the next few tenths of a mile, and turn onto the Joe Forzley Bridge at about 1.8 miles to cross back

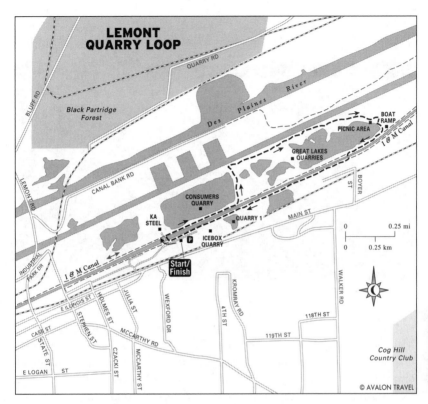

to the south towpath trail heading west. The next 0.3 mile is quiet; watch for great blue heron on the canal. Quarry 1 and the Icebox Quarry are the last lakes south of the path and they are very scenic. Wildflowers bloom along the shore of Icebox Quarry, including yarrow, clover, and blazing star. From Icebox Quarry it is 0.4 mile back to the parking lot.

Options

Add about 1.5 miles to this hike by hiking (out and back) to downtown Lemont along the I&M Canal Trail. From the parking lot, hike west on the I&M Canal Trail and continue past the steel plant. Stop to read the historic facts posted on the canal mileposts; at about 0.3 mile there is a covered bench. Once you reach Stephen Street, continue west to explore the town or return the way you came.

Directions

From downtown Chicago, take I-55 S for 22.9 miles. Take Exit 271A for S. Lemont Road. Drive south on Lemont Road for 2.9 miles, then continue onto State Street for 0.2 mile. Turn left (east) on E. Illinois Street and drive for 0.3 mile. Turn left

Consumers Quarry

and drive north on Holmes a short distance; take the first right and drive east on Main Street. In 0.2 mile, turn left onto Talcott Avenue and follow the road east 0.2 mile, past the steel plant entrance to a signed parking area and the trailhead for the Heritage Quarries. The trailhead is at the north edge of the parking lot; a trailhead information sign is at the east end of the parking lot.

Public Transportation: From Chicago's Union Station, take the Heritage Corridor line to Lemont Station. From there, walk east on New Avenue to Main Street, continue two blocks to Stephen Street. Turn north and walk two blocks, crossing the canal. Turn right on the north side of the canal and pick up the I&M Canal Trail eastward. Walk 0.7 mile to the lot and trailhead.

GPS Coordinates: 16 T 417866mE 4614447mN

Information and Contact

There is no fee. Dogs on leash are allowed. The park is open dawn–dusk daily. There is no swimming, however kayaking is permitted. For more information, contact the Heritage Quarries, Talcott Road, Lemont, IL 60439, 630/257-1550, www.lemont.il.us.

2 I&M CANAL TRAIL: IRON MILE   BEST **C**
Joliet Iron Works Historic Site, Joliet

🛶 🎣 🌿 ⊛ 🐾 🚻 ♿

Level: Easy/moderate   **Total Distance:** 4.1 miles round-trip

Hiking Time: 2.5 hours   **Elevation Change:** negligible

Summary: Walking along the interpretive trail through the old Iron Works provides a fascinating look at a bygone era.

A visit to the Joliet Iron Works Historic Site offers a great opportunity to take in the region's industrial and transportation history. Before the arrival of the Iron Works in the 1870s, Joliet was home to a limestone quarry, a railroad, the I&M Canal, and the state penitentiary. By the 1900s, the Iron Works were a mainstay of the local economy.

Walking the winding paths through the Joliet Iron Works is a fascinating experience. Interpretive signs illuminate both the culture and backbreaking labor of the old steel-making operation. Start hiking north from the trailhead along the limestone I&M Canal Trail (also called the bicycle trail on the map). Before hiking onto the interpretive trail, look across the railroad tracks and note the gigantic warehouses, plants, and buildings. The broken windows and rusty corrugated metal are a stark contrast to the quiet of the trail. In 0.2 mile, turn left at the sign for the start of the Iron Mile, which winds through the historic site on a

looking south at the Skull House

primarily concrete pathway. Frequent signs explain the significance of the ruins—one of my favorites is the Skull House, which you can see up close on the return hike.

Return to the I&M Canal Trail (bicycle trail) at 0.9 mile, and turn north to explore some of the old towpath trail. The tree-lined path leads to locks 3 and 4 after about 0.5 mile. Sumac trees, odd mushrooms, and a tangle of bushes pepper the trail. Pass an old elevated railroad bridge over the canal at milepost 31; then, at 1.4 miles, jog left to cross the canal. Look for wildlife along the trail here; great blue heron like to sit on the water between the locks and I saw a big snapping turtle laboriously making its way across the path to a rather stagnant-looking pond of water. The trail continues north, shortly crossing back over the canal. Milepost 30 is a good turnaround point. Retrace your steps to the Iron Mile, then continue south on the bicycle path. You will pass by the Skull House around 3.7 miles, just before the trail ends at 4.1 miles. The Skull House remains include more than a dozen arches in the crumbling wall. This imposing sight is one of the larger structures on view.

Options

Extend this hike 3 miles by exploring the trails at nearby Pilcher Park. Pilcher Park offers a pleasant contrast to the Iron Works, with a dense oak and maple forest, a host of woodland wildflowers, an accessible trail, and a

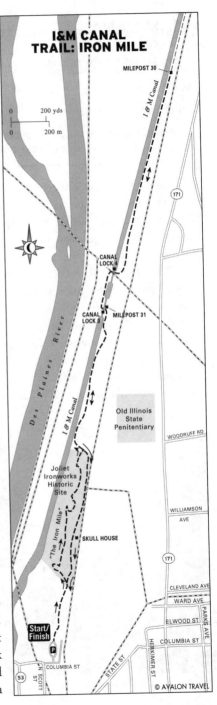

greenhouse. Pick up the purple trail from the North trailhead just west of the Nature Center. The Outer Loop Trail follows a shallow ridge through shady woods, switching to the light blue Artesian Trail past the pavilion and to the greenhouse. Tour the greenhouse, then enjoy a pleasant walk west through the oak and hickory woods along the pink Hummingbird Lane Trail back to the Nature Center.

Directions

Joliet Iron Works: From downtown Chicago, take I-55 S for 22.3 miles. Take Exit 269 for I-355 S and drive 5.2 miles south. Exit at IL-171/Archer Avenue and drive south for 7.9 miles. Turn west at Ohio Street for 0.4 mile, then north at N. Scott Street. Drive 0.2 mile to Columbia Street, turn right, then left into the parking lot. Walk north to the signed trailhead, at the end of the lot.

GPS Coordinates: 16 T 409920mE 4598730mN

Pilcher Park: From Joliet Iron Works, exit the parking lot, turn west on Columbia Street, and make a left and drive south on N. Chicago Street for 0.3 mile. Turn east on E. Jackson Street for 0.5 mile, then south on Collins Street for 0.3 mile. Turn east on Cass Avenue and drive 2.4 miles, continuing on Longwood Drive/Highland Park Drive for another 0.6 mile. Turn left on Pilcher Park Drive to reach the nature center and lot. The trail begins west of the nature center, at the North Trails sign.

GPS Coordinates: 16 T 414731mE 4598197mN

Information and Contact

Joliet Iron Works is open 8 A.M.–sunset daily. There is no fee. Dogs are allowed on leash. Water, restrooms, and a picnic shelter are available at the trailhead. For information, contact Will County Forest Preserve District, 17540 Laraway Road, Joliet, IL, 815/727-8700, www.reconnectwithnature.org.

Pilcher Park is open daily 9 A.M.–4:30 P.M. June–August; 9 A.M.–3 P.M. September–May. There are no fees. Dogs are allowed on leash. For more information, contact Pilcher Park, 2501 Highland Park Drive, Joliet, IL, 815/741-7277, www.jolietpark.org.

3 HENNEPIN CANAL TRAIL
Hennepin Canal State Park, Sheffield

🛶 ⛷ 📷 🐕 ♿

Level: Easy/moderate

Total Distance: 10.5 miles round-trip

Hiking Time: 5-6 hours

Elevation Change: negligible

Summary: Experience a part of history by walking the Hennepin Canal towpath.

The vision for a canal connecting the Mississippi and Illinois Rivers was a grand one, particularly in 1834. Construction took so long that by the time the canal was completed in 1907, it was already obsolete. Still, the engineering innovations were valuable and boats were able to use the canal until 1951. Today, the remaining 32 locks and 6 aqueducts provide visitors with a glimpse of history and worthy hiking destinations. The towpath is part of the National Recreational Trail system and has undergone several improvements over the last decade. This hike—from the visitors center complex eastward to Lock 21—is a great introduction to the Hennepin Canal Trail.

At the visitors center, start walking past the fishing lagoon and turn east onto the towpath. The wide, packed-dirt trail runs south of the canal. The first thing you will notice is how quiet it is; there seem to be no sounds except the twittering of birds and the rustle of leaves. Watch for great blue heron; they love the quiet

Hennepin Canal towpath and Lock 21

© BARBARA I. BOND

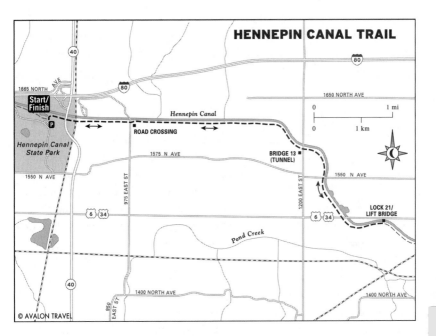

waterway. (I saw them in trees and on the water.) Dense woods filled with huge cottonwoods and old oaks accent the trail's wild and remote feel. The north bank is particularly overgrown, with a lot of foliage growing right into the water.

A road crossing at mile 1.2 allows a brief view of the canal from above. Continue along the path east, then south, at 3.2 miles, noting the slight rise over the next couple of miles. At 3.5 miles, enter a short metal tunnel marked BR 13 MI 19—you'll then pass through another one about 0.5 mile later. After the second tunnel, the landscape clears to views west across farmland. Hawks lazily circle, and you might see some red-winged blackbirds. On the east side of the canal lie a few pools of water with birdhouses and thick trees. There is a metal tunnel on the canal, similar to the pedestrian tunnels, just big enough for a couple of kayakers to pass through.

At 4.8 miles, look for another pool and tunnel, with a campground across the canal. You will reach Lock 21 around 5.25 miles. The trail spurs, allowing a walk across the old lift bridge to explore. There is a historic marker on the north side of the canal, and a couple of benches and restrooms; when done, return the way you came.

Options

Turn this hike into a bike-and-hike! Bring your bicycle along and ride the canal path, taking some time to explore the westbound path. A ride 5.5 miles west will take you across a historic bridge and down nearly 50 feet. End your ride at the junction with the north–south feeder canal. The total distance for the westward ride is 11 miles.

Directions

From downtown Chicago, take I-55 S for 43.1 miles. Take Exit 250B for I-80 W and drive 81.4 miles. Take Exit 45 for State Route 40 S and drive south 1.5 miles. Make the first right at 1550 N Ave/County Road 1550 N and drive west 0.3 mile. Turn right and drive north on the park entrance road for 0.7 mile. Turn into the parking lot on the northeast side. (There are some information signs and park brochures here.) To reach the trailhead for the canal towpath, walk towards the visitors center at the north corner of the parking area. Follow the path towards the fishing lagoon's east end and north to the trail.
GPS Coordinates: 16 T 274967mE 4584438mN

Information and Contact

There is no fee. Dogs on leash are allowed. Trails are open daily, except for closures around the main visitor complex during hunting season (check the website for closure dates). Visitors center hours vary. For more information, contact Hennepin Canal State Park, State Route 40 and County Road 1550 N., Sheffield, IL, 815/454-2328, www.dnr.state.il.us.

4 DELLS TRAILS

BEST ☾

Matthiessen State Park, Oglesby

Level: Moderate

Hiking Time: 2-2.5 hours

Total Distance: 3.2 miles round-trip

Elevation Change: 390 feet

Summary: The sandstone canyons of Matthiessen State Park will leave you with an unforgettable experience.

Matthiessen State Park, in the upper Illinois River Valley, has a rich geologic past. The canyons and bluffs of this small natural area are the results of massive geologic forces that folded the earth's crust. Periodic raging floodwaters later helped shape the canyons we enjoy today. Mosses, liverwort, and ferns cling to the damp canyon walls, while the canyon floor supports frogs and other amphibians. Park trails allow you to explore the hardwood forest along the bluffs and descend into the cool, shady canyon for views of dramatic waterfalls.

Once a private park owned and developed by Frederick W. Matthiessen, today the 1,900 acres of state land comprise a significant natural area. Hiking and picnicking are popular during the warmer months, and stunning fall colors attract

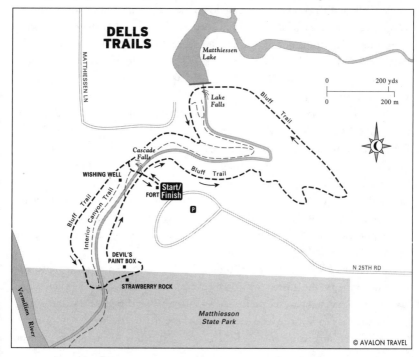

Dells canyon

additional visitors at the height of autumn. Begin your hike at the trailhead across from the restrooms. Note that trail intersections have directional signs with trail maps. Walk past the restored fort and down the steps. The mixed oak and maple woods provide plenty of shade, and in spring wildflowers like anemone, spring beauty, and columbine dot the forest floor. Turn right and walk eastward on the Bluff Trail. The deep layers of the canyon walls are intriguing as they rise above the small canyon stream. The stream drains Matthiessen Lake, flowing to the Vermillion River in a single mile.

The trail continues eastward nearly 0.6 mile, then turns northwest along the forested bluffs to the tip of Matthiessen Lake and Lake Falls at just under 1 mile. Benches all along the trail invite you to linger. Cross the bridge and turn south. Here you can stay on the Bluff Trail or descend the steps down into the canyon towards Cedar Point. The steps go down to a viewpoint; continue down to the canyon floor, turn right, and follow the trail curving west towards Cascade Falls. The walls are a vertical garden of ferns and moss. In some places, water seeps out of the porous rock. Walk across concrete stepping stones, then up the steps to reach the bridge and view of Cascade Falls.

Back on the Bluff Trail, walk through the oak and hickory forest southwest 0.5 mile to the bridge. Listen for woodpeckers and chickadees in the woods, and watch for nuthatches and the pretty scarlet tanager. You can just make out a staircase at the east end of the bridge; descend the stairs to the canyon once more. Check out the surprising colors of the Devil's Paint Box to the east before you head upstream. Minerals leaching out of the rock tint the water with orange-red hues. The canyon walls here are vibrant green with moss.

Cross the footbridge, then walk upstream about 0.4 mile to reach Cascade Falls, at the head of the canyon. The falls plunge nearly 50 feet to a pool of water surrounded by steep canyon walls and an overhang. This is a popular spot on a hot summer day. Retrace your steps to the top of the stairs and continue 0.4 mile or so east, then north back to the stairs; turn right and climb to the fort and parking lot.

Options

Spend the day in the cool shady canyon by skipping the Bluff Trail. Descend from the parking lot, turn left and walk to the stairway just before crossing the south bridge. Enjoy exploring the canyon, then retrace your steps to return for just 1.5 total miles of hiking.

Directions

From downtown Chicago, take I-55 S for 43.6 miles. Take Exit 250B for I-80 W and drive west for 45 miles. Take Exit 81 for State Route 178 and drive south towards Utica. In 2 miles, turn left at W. Canal Street, then right to follow State Route 178 S/S. Clark Street. Drive 3.2 miles south to N. 25th Road; turn west and continue 0.8 mile into the large parking lot. The trailhead is near the fort at the top of the stairs.

GPS Coordinates: 16 T 330393mE 4573424mN

Information and Contact

There is no fee. Dogs on leash are allowed. Off-trail hiking is not permitted. The park is open daily 7 A.M.–8 P.M., but closes seasonally during hunting seasons. For more information, contact Matthiessen State Park, N. 25th Road and State Route 178, Oglesby, IL, 815/667-4868, www.dnr.state.il.us.

5 WEST OVERLOOKS AND CANYONS BEST 🄲

Starved Rock State Park, Utica

Level: Moderate

Total Distance: 6.6 miles round-trip

Hiking Time: 3.5 hours

Elevation Change: 900 feet

Summary: Explore Starved Rock State Park on this overlook and eight-canyon sampler hike.

Over 14,000 years ago, catastrophic glacial floodwater scoured the Illinois River Valley, creating canyons and bluffs of St. Peter sandstone. Thousands of years later, various Native American tribes called this beautiful region home. Today the dramatic chasms and cliffs form a unique ecological niche, offering a plethora of outdoor wonders to modern residents of northern Illinois. The well-established Starved Rock trail system invites hikers to gaze from on high at Starved Rock or Eagle Cliff, or hike into the shady and cool depths of St. Louis Canyon to explore the etched sandstone walls covered with mosses, liverwort, and ferns.

Hiking from the visitors center trailhead is a great way to begin exploring the 13 miles of Starved Rock trails. Park trails are marked throughout with yellow (away) or white (return) circles indicating whether you are heading away from or toward the visitors center. Walk east from the visitors center and follow the signs

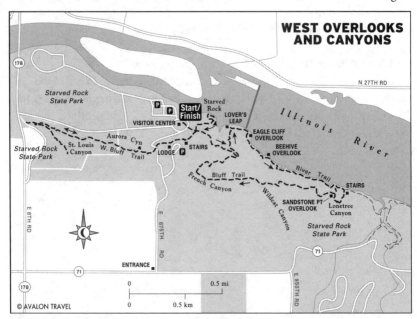

WEST OVERLOOKS AND CANYONS

St. Louis Canyon

for Starved Rock, the popular bluff-top viewpoint high above the Illinois River. Near the bluffs and river, the forest fills with tall black and white oak, cedars, and some white pine. As you head towards the stairway, keep your eye out for a lovely green vine along the trail—it's most likely poison ivy, which thrives here in its many forms. Atop Starved Rock views of the dam, Plum Island, and the Illinois River abound—it's a great place to spot eagles and waterfowl. An interpretive sign explains the Starved Rock legend.

Head east for the next 2 miles, climbing more steps to the overlooks and hiking along the river shore. As you descend the stairs, return to the main trail and turn left. In 0.3 mile, at a three-way intersection marked by a sign, turn left toward Lover's Leap Overlook. This is the River Trail; hike up and over three overlooks, then drop down to continue east along the river. At 2 miles you'll reach the Bluff Trail. Turn south and climb more than 150 steps to Sandstone Point Overlook at 2.2 miles. Watch for pileated woodpeckers and white-tailed deer in early morning. After enjoying the views, continue west through the woods for the next 1.5 miles. The Bluff Trail peters out halfway; keep left towards French Canyon, then follow the signs back to the visitors center.

At a four-way junction at nearly 3.8 miles, hike south and follow the sign to the West Bluff Trail and the four canyons, including St. Louis. (You'll spend about 0.3 mile getting past the lodge area.) Once on the trail, slow down and enjoy peering into the beautiful canyons—the next 2 miles are among the prettiest in the park and maples provide plenty of shade. At 4.5 miles, you're still amidst trees heading down some steps alongside the deeply etched, rust-colored sandstone formations. The trail junction to St. Louis Canyon is at 4.8 miles; make almost a hairpin turn to follow it along the creek southeast to the head of the canyon. The terraced walls have overhangs and shelves covered with glossy ferns, mosses, and liverwort. When finished, hike the 1.5 miles back to the visitors center the way you came.

Options

For a shorter outing, hike either the trail to St. Louis Canyon (3 miles) or the Sandstone Point Loop (3.8 miles). Both hikes begin and end at the Visitor Center trailhead.

Directions

From downtown Chicago, take I-55 S for 43 miles. Take Exit 250B onto I-80 W and continue for 45 miles. Take Exit 81 for IL-178 and drive south towards Utica. In 2 miles, turn left at W. Canal Street then turn right to follow IL-178 S/S. Clark Street. In 1.3 miles, turn left into the park (signed) and drive 0.8 mile to the visitors center parking lot on the left. (The route is well-signed.) The trailhead is on the east side of the visitors center; stop inside and pick up a map.

Note: If you continue on the road another 0.5 mile, you will reach the entrance to the lodge, which has ample parking and trail access.

GPS Coordinates: 16 T 333091mE 4576219mN

Information and Contact

There is no fee. Dogs on leash are allowed. The park is open 5 A.M.–9 P.M. daily; closed during hunting season. The visitors center is open 9 A.M.–4 P.M. daily. Stay on the trail to avoid poison ivy and bring insect repellent in summer, when mosquitoes are ubiquitous. For more information, contact Starved Rock State Park, State Route 178 and 71, Utica, IL 61373, 815/667-4906, www.starvedrockstatepark.org.

6 EAST CANYONS

Starved Rock State Park, Utica

BEST ☾

Level: Moderate

Hiking Time: 3.5 hours

Total Distance: 6.5 miles round-trip

Elevation Change: 850 feet

Summary: Visit the dramatic canyons of Starved Rock's east trails.

It is easy to see why Starved Rock State Park is so popular. The dramatic sandstone canyons and bluffs have made this a favorite destination for modern Illinoisans. When torrents of glacial meltwater rushed over the area 14,000 years ago, it scoured away the soft surface stone. The resulting canyons and bluffs of hard St. Peter sandstone remained and the eight canyons of the park's eastern region provide a variety of perspectives on the area's geology. The unique and dramatic half-dome of the Council Overhang is a major attraction.

The park's trail system is well established—grab a map and explore! Begin this eastside hike from the Parkman's Plain trailhead, about 2 miles east of the main park buildings. (Park trails are marked throughout with yellow/away or white/return circles, indicating whether heading away from or towards the Visitor Center.) The first 2 miles of this hike follows the river and visits two impressive and popular canyons. Walk north through a woodland of oaks, maple, and black

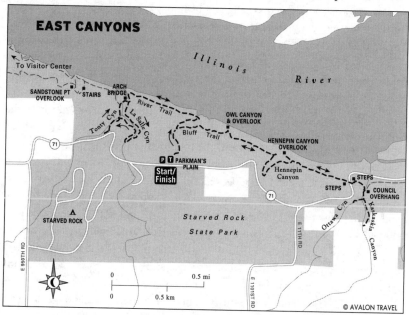

Tonty Canyon

cherry. Shade-loving plants crowd the forest floor—look for may apple, wood nettle, lopseed, and ferns, or trillium in early spring. The trail descends nearly 100 feet, then turns left to head west along the river. At 0.8 mile, the trail turns south; you'll pass an arched bridge and continue to LaSalle Canyon. Follow the trail as it travels under an overhang and behind a waterfall. This is a great relief on a hot summer day—there are usually lots of people here. Continue ahead, enjoying the ferns and moss as they climb the damp stone walls. Follow the signs to Tonty Canyon. The deep, dark canyon overhang highlights the waterfalls, with more green moss and ferns covering the walls—this is one of the most dramatic canyons in the park.

Return to the trail, cross the arch bridge, and retrace your steps nearly to the trailhead. Look for a trail sign and the continuation of the River Trail at 2.7 miles. Now hiking east in the forest, the trail follows a rolling section that persists until the final short climb to the trailhead. There is a lot of bird action in the trees—nuthatches and woodpeckers cling to tree trunks. The verdant forest is shaded by an oak and hickory canopy; ravines and rocky outcrops add texture and color. Cross two small creeks, then, around 3.4 miles, take a short walk to the river overlook. The Hennepin Canyon overlook (at 3.8 miles) provides more dramatic viewpoints east. In 0.25 mile, the trail follows some steps down and across the road. Return to the trail, following another set of steps down to Council Overhang. Appreciate the moment and look up as you walk by—it is huge! The cliffs here are chalky white, rusty orange, and several shades of green; it's a fun spot to take photos. The trail hugs the base of the cliffs, then heads into the open to a Y-junction and sign. Ottawa Canyon is to the right; Kaskaskia is to the left. Visit them both—they are very different. (I went to Ottawa first, then Kaskaskia. The head of Kaskaskia is at 4.7 miles.) Retrace your steps nearly 2 miles to return to the trailhead.

Options

For a little more exploring, continue to Illinois Canyon after leaving Kaskaskia. From the trail junction near Council Overhang, hike east 0.7 mile to Illinois Canyon. Return to the trailhead by retracing your steps. The total distance will now be 1.6 miles longer, a total of about 8.1 miles.

Directions

From downtown Chicago, drive west on I-55 S for 43 miles. Take Exit 250B onto I-80 W and drive for 45 miles. Take Exit 81 for IL-178 and drive south towards Utica. In 2 miles, turn left at W. Canal Street then turn right to follow IL-178 S/S. Clark Street. In 1.3 miles, turn left into the park (signed) and drive 0.8 mile to the visitors center parking lot on the left. Pick up a map, then return to the park road and continue east, then south to IL-71. Turn east on IL-71 and drive about 1 mile to the Parkman's Plain Trailhead on the north side of the road. There is ample parking, a trail sign, and a restroom. The trailhead is at the northeast corner of the lot, with a trail map and gate.

Alternately, you can take I-80 W to Exit 90. Drive south on State Route 23 S/Columbus Street for about 3 miles, cross the Illinois River, and turn west on Courtney Street. In 0.4 mile, continue west on State Route 71 W/Hitt Street and drive 7.3 miles to the trailhead on the north side of the road.
GPS Coordinates: 16 T 335427mE 4574821mN

Information and Contact

There is no fee. Dogs on leash are allowed. The park is open 5 A.M.–9 P.M. daily; closed during hunting season. The visitors center is open 9 A.M.–4 P.M. daily. Stay on the trail to avoid poison ivy and bring insect repellent in summer, when mosquitoes are abundant. For more information, contact Starved Rock State Park, State Routes 178 and 71, Utica, IL, 815/667-4906, www.starvedrockstatepark.org.

7 RIVER BLUFF–EFFIGY TUMULI TRAILS
Buffalo Rock State Park

🏕 ✈ 🧭 🏃

Level: Easy/moderate

Hiking Time: 1.5 hours

Total Distance: 3.0 miles round-trip

Elevation Change: 150 feet

Summary: Buffalo Rock State Park offers a unique hiking experience high above the Illinois River and around the massive earthen sculptures of the Effigy Tumuli.

Buffalo Rock State Park has a varied and colorful history. In the 17th century, Buffalo Rock was the site of a French trading and missionary fort and a meeting place for Native Americans. The unique geology of the area eventually made it valuable for coal extraction and the adjacent lands later became home to a strip-mining operation, resulting in environmental degradation. Fortunately, the area has undergone restoration and, in 1983, an artist created five earthen mounds—called the Effigy Tumuli, named to honor the Native American burial grounds here—as part of a restoration project. Although best seen from the air, hiking among these earthen sculptures is a unique experience, highlighted by tremendous views above the Illinois River.

Buffalo Rock sits like a sandstone island above the surrounding land and Illinois

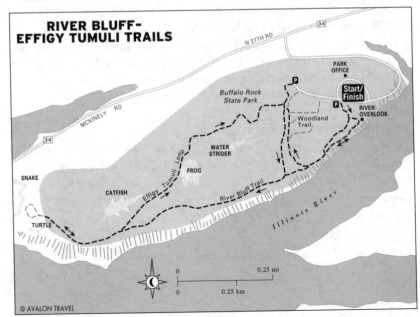

© AVALON TRAVEL

Effigy Tumuli

River. The park features oak and hickory woodlands and an expanse of restored grassland where the Effigy Tumuli rise. The River Bluff Trail is a great way to experience the Buffalo Rocks landscape. From the trailhead, hike south to the River Bluff Trail, turning east at a sign to for the overlook. After enjoying the expansive views, descend to the River Bluff Trail as it heads southwest along the edge of the bluffs. The wide trail works its way through oak and hickory forest. In no time, you'll reach a signed three-way junction with the Woodland Trail; turn right and enjoy the cool forest. Walk across a small footbridge and at 0.5 mile turn left to reach the Effigy Tumuli Loop.

Turn south and walk along the edge of the woods towards the river. As you gaze across the grassland, note the rise of these grass-covered effigy mounds. The trail curves west along the bluffs; look for an overgrown viewpoint right before the signed trail junction at 1.15 miles. Follow the Effigy Trail west to reach the first mound in a short distance. The effigy mounds were planted with native prairie seed in the shape of animals—catfish, turtle, snake, frog. Interpretive signs encourage hikers off the trail and on top of the mounds to better appreciate the scope of the project. Take a moment to explore their grassy forms. As raptors soar overhead, look for red-winged blackbirds, goldfinch, and sparrows; you may even catch sight of an osprey looking for its next meal.

The trail curves northwest, then reaches a loop in front of the immense "snake" mound. Some groves of oak, hickory, and black-cherry trees break up the open grass. Retrace your steps back to the trail junction and keep left to walk along the north side of the remaining mounds. The trail follows the edge mounds before reaching the water strider, then continues northeast. At about 2.5 miles, turn south and walk a very short distance to retrace your steps on the Woodland Trail. Follow the signs to return to the start.

Options

For a completely different hiking experience, visit nearby Matthiessen State Park and hike the Dells Trails (see listing in this chapter). A walk around the sandstone canyons will add about 3 miles to your hike.

Directions

From I-55 S/I-80 W, drive west on I-80 for 35.9 miles. Take Exit 90 and drive south on State Route 23 S/Columbus Street for 1.8 miles. Continue south on La Salle Street for 0.5 mile, turning west on W. Main Street. Drive 0.4 mile west then south onto Clay Street for 0.2 mile. Turn right and drive 1.9 miles west on Ottawa Avenue and continue 1.6 more miles on N. 27th Rd/McKinely. Turn south onto the park road and follow it as it winds 0.5 mile around the bluffs to the parking lot. (The parking lot is on the south side of the road.) The trailhead is at the southeast corner of the lot; walk around the restrooms to begin.

GPS Coordinates: 16 T 340133mE 4576567mN

Information and Contact

There is no fee. Dogs on leash are allowed. The park is open sunrise–sunset daily. Restrooms, drinking water, and picnic tables are available. For more information, contact Buffalo Rock State Park, P.O. Box 2034, Ottawa, IL 61350, 815/433-2224, www.dnr.illinois.gov.

Note: In early fall of 2010, the Effigy Tumuli Trail was temporarily closed. Call the park superintendent for current conditions.

8 PRAIRIE VIEW LOOP BEST C

Goose Lake Prairie State Natural Area, Morris

Level: Easy

Total Distance: 3.4 miles round-trip

Hiking Time: 1.5-2 hours

Elevation Change: negligible

Summary: Walk through tall prairie grasses en route to a hilltop viewpoint and enjoy a unique perspective of Goose Lake Prairie.

Goose Lake Prairie State Natural Area contains more than 2,500 acres of reclaimed and restored land. The area was once part of an immense stretch of grasslands that extended for hundreds of miles. Today, Goose Lake Prairie has the largest remnant of tallgrass prairie in Illinois, and over half of the acreage is a dedicated Illinois Nature Preserve. The terrain, which ranges from flat to rolling, offers hikers an opportunity to experience this natural beauty up close. A hike to the overlook offers views of the surrounding grassland, lakes, and marshes, and an opportunity for both bird- and wildlife-watching.

The signed trailhead is at the south end of the Visitor Center parking lot. Walk across the footbridge onto the mown-grass path. Take a look around, particularly east, and you'll see that you are surrounded by prairie. If visiting in late summer, some of the grasses will be several feet high. As you head towards the loop, you'll pass a spur trail on the right for the Prairie Grove Picnic Area. Lots of red-

© BARBARA I. BOND

Goose Lake Prairie, the largest remnant of tallgrass prairie in Illinois

winged blackbirds and barn swallows can be found here, as well as birdhouses; these were built for Eastern bluebirds, but are mostly inhabited by swallows. In the southern distance, you can begin to make out a couple of small hills—this is your destination.

Pass some old fencing and barbed wire—a farming remnant—to find yourself surrounded by golden Alexanders. At 0.9 mile is the northwest corner of the loop and a broadly mown area with a bench on the west side. At the loop, hike counterclockwise on the mown path. The Overview—the spoil mounds and viewpoint—is coming into view as the vegetation thickens. If hiking late in the day, listen for pheasant and keep a lookout for white-tailed deer. Turn right at 1.3 miles onto the

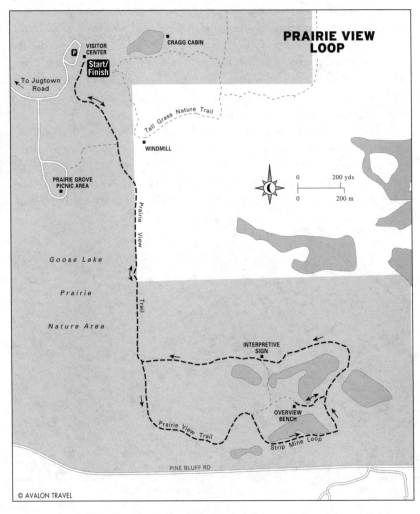

© AVALON TRAVEL

first path and follow it as it winds east uphill, then curves north. Turn left again near the top and walk to the viewpoint and a bench. The views are predictably good, with great expanses of the preserves' lakes, ponds, marshes, and wetlands. You may even spot the occasional tree, further evidence that this is a recovering landscape (since native prairie is, by definition, treeless). Enjoy.

Return to the trail to continue the path as it curves west around the northern-most pond. At about 2.1 miles, near a three-way trail junction, note a sign detailing the history of the strip-mining operation and subsequent reclamation. Continue west along the loop, for a short distance hiking through an extremely wet and marshy area. The prairie grasses along here are quite tall. Once you reach the start of the loop at 2.5 miles, turn right to walk north back to the trailhead.

Options

Shorten this hike to 2.8 miles by skipping the Overview. When you reach the loop, hike counterclockwise and keep left at the two trail junctions. This allows you to spend a little more time enjoying the ponds and watching for waterfowl. After enjoying the ponds, continue ahead to the start of the loop, then retrace your steps and return to the visitors center.

Directions

From downtown Chicago, drive 53 miles on I-55 S. Take Exit 240 for Lorenzo Road/Pine Bluff Road. Turn right and drive west approximately 7.5 miles to Jugtown Road. Turn north on Jugtown Road and travel 1 mile to the park entrance on the right.

GPS Coordinates: 16 T 389734mE 4579392mN

Information and Contact

There is no fee. Dogs on leash are allowed. The park is open sunrise–sunset daily. The visitors center is open 10 A.M.–4 P.M. daily. Drinking water is available behind the visitors center. In the winter, cross-country skiing is allowed. Trail maps are available for download (www.gooselakeprairie.org/glpsna_hikingtrails.htm). For more information, contact Goose Lake Prairie State Natural Area, 5010 N. Jugtown Road, Morris, IL 60450, 815/942-2899, www.dnr.state.il.us.

⑨ TALL GRASS NATURE TRAIL

Goose Lake Prairie State Natural Area, Morris

🐾 🛶 🐎 🐕 👫 ♿

Level: Easy	**Total Distance:** 2.7 miles round-trip
Hiking Time: 1.5 hours	**Elevation Change:** negligible

Summary: Envision being surrounded by grassland as you hike along the trails of Goose Lake Prairie, a glacier-sculpted preserve.

Once part of an immense grassland that stretched for hundreds of miles, today Goose Lake Prairie State Natural Area has the largest stand of remaining tallgrass prairie in Illinois. The preserve even has a kettle pond, which includes a few glacial erratics (large boulders deposited by the Wisconsin Glacier over 10,000 years ago). Goose Lake Prairie is also home to a rich collection of birds and wildlife. White-tailed deer, Blanding's turtle, red fox, and cottontail rabbits, as well as red-winged blackbirds and marsh hawks, are commonly sighted. If you are patient, you may even see the shy Henslow's sparrow around the marsh.

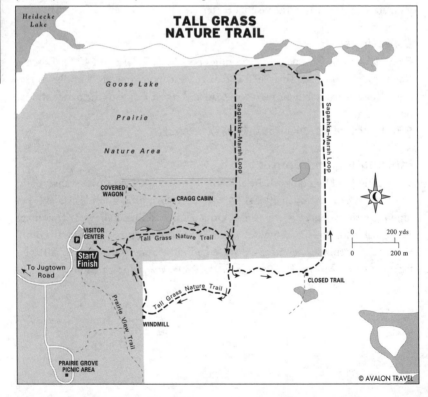

© BARBARA I. BOND

an old marsh boardwalk south of the Sagashka Trail

Pass the visitors center to begin hiking the signed Tall Grass Nature Trail. Walk east towards the Sagashka and Marsh Trails. The Nature Trail has numbered interpretive signs; be sure and pick up a key from the visitors center. As you head east, note the kettle pond to the north, glacial erratics, and a cabin. The cabin is a replica of pioneer John Cragg's 1835 home, known to have been a station on the Underground Railroad. In 0.2 mile, pass a left turn for the continuation of the Handicapped Trail. This wide, flat trail is wheelchair-accessible and includes a ramp to and from the east entrance of the visitor center. Continue east to a three-way junction with the Sagashka–Marsh Loop; turn right to hike south towards the Marsh Trail. Take a deep breath as you walk through the grasses and take in the many unique smells associated with the prairie; you may even catch a hint of popcorn scent from the northern prairie dropseed. Turn left at 0.5 mile and walk east once more on the Marsh Trail. Pass a closed boardwalk where the marsh is surrounded by cattails and reeds; this stretch is home to turtles, frogs, and snakes. It's one of the most scenic areas in the preserve.

The grasses here differ from those along the Nature Trail. Look for switch grass, prairie cordgrass, or bluejoint closer to the marsh edge; you may also see ducks on the marsh. The Marsh Loop turns north around 0.8 mile, heading towards a collection of ponds. The brilliant color of blueflag iris marks quite a contrast along the trail. After reaching the ponds at 1.3 miles, the trail curves west, then back south, at 1.55 miles. Continue south, ignoring any left turns for the next 0.45 mile; you are now back on the continuation of the Interpretive Trail. At about 2.1 miles, the trail curves westward, passing a windmill at around 2.4 miles. Listen for rustling in the grasses—I looked down and watched as a Blanding's turtle made his way through the grass. The trail winds back to the east side of the visitors center, where a handicapped ramp and a drinking fountain are situated at 2.6 miles. From there it's just 0.1 mile back to the parking lot.

Options

For a 1.2-mile hike with a lot of human history, take the Handicapped Trail. From the east side of the visitors center, head east. In 0.2 mile, turn left to circle the pond toward Cragg Cabin. Take a moment to observe the cabin, then continue past a bench and covered wagon to return to the visitors center.

Directions

From downtown Chicago, drive 53 miles on I-55 S. Take Exit 240 for Lorenzo Road/Pine Bluff Road. Turn right and drive west approximately 7.5 miles to Jugtown Road. Turn north on Jugtown Road and travel 1 mile to the park entrance on the right.

GPS Coordinates: 16 T 389734mE 4579392mN

Information and Contact

There is no fee. Dogs on leash are allowed. The park is open sunrise–sunset daily. The visitors center is open 10 A.M.–4 P.M. daily. There is drinking water fountain behind the visitors center. During winter, cross-country skiing is allowed. Trail maps are available for download (www.gooselakeprairie.org/glpsna_hikingtrails.htm). For more information, contact Goose Lake Prairie State Natural Area, 5010 N. Jugtown Road, Morris, IL 60450, 815/942-2899, www.dnr.state.il.us.

10 I&M CANAL TRAIL: EAST SIDE

McKinley Woods Forest Preserve and Stratton State Park, Channahon and Morris

Level: Moderate

Total Distance: 11.25 miles one-way

Hiking Time: 5-6 hours

Elevation Change: negligible

Summary: Hike along the historic I&M Canal and walk in the footsteps of French explorer Louis Joliet.

In 1673, French explorer Louis Joliet realized the potential for a waterway connecting Lake Michigan to the Illinois and Mississippi Rivers. Nearly 150 years later, the idea was resurrected and construction began on the 96-mile Illinois & Michigan Canal. In 1848, the canal opened and commerce flourished. The success was short-lived, however, as transportation options widened—85 years later, the canal closed to boat traffic. Today, hikers and bicyclists can enjoy this important waterway. The wide, flat trail of the old towpath is dotted with mile markers noting historic facts, locks, aqueducts, and tons of natural history.

McKinley Woods Forest Preserve is one of the many parks with access to the I&M Canal Trail. From the trailhead, hike south across a footbridge to the

© BARBARA I. BOND

I&M Canal Lock 8

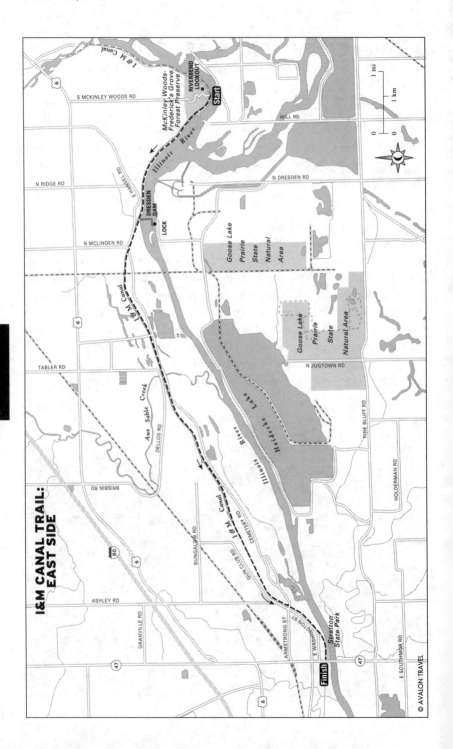

I&M CANAL TRAIL: EAST SIDE

© AVALON TRAVEL

towpath and turn west. The canal forms a pool west of McKinley Woods and is covered with flowering American lotus by midsummer. Watch for muskrat or turtles along here, and great blue heron all along the canal. At almost 1.0 mile is canal milepost 48. (You will see these mileposts regularly; each contains bits of canal trivia and the mileage to the next historic destination.) The trail runs along the north bank of the Illinois River until the Dresden Island Lock and Dam. At 2.65 miles, you can take a quick detour towards the river and check out the dam. After returning to the trail, turn slightly northwest away from the river en route to the Dresden Mill Barn at 3.6 miles.

Over the next couple of miles, the trail crosses the road, runs along some power lines, and then leads under the train bridge. Huge sycamores hug the north canal bank in places. At 5.6 miles, cross a footbridge and arrive at Aux Sable Village, now home only to the old locktender's house and lock #8. It is a peaceful and beautiful spot.

The trail continues west, passing a pool of water and a quarry at 6.5 miles. The next few miles are very quiet—the canal banks are overgrown with small trees and vines, including riverbank grape and smooth sumac. Watch for great blue heron here—I even saw one walking across the path! After passing milepost 55 at 8.4 miles, turn right, prior to a smaller quarry to the north. The path turns south towards the river once more, crossing Cemetery Road at 10.3 mile. Upon approaching William G. Stratton State Park, the trail reaches the river and turns west. At 11.25 miles, you will reach the east end of the large parking area at Stratton. Continue west to enjoy the picnic tables, boat launch, restrooms, and drinking water. If you are hiking this as a long out-and-back, it's a wonderful place to fuel up. Stratton State Park is popular with motor boaters, and provides another option for enjoying the park.

Options

For a short and beautiful hike, take the 1.4-mile Trail of Old Oaks at McKinley Woods Forest Preserve. The trailhead is at the north end of the Riverbend Lookout parking lot. The Trail of Old Oaks winds along ravines and bluffs, descends to parallel the canal, then climbs around 100 feet back to the trailhead.

Directions

From downtown Chicago, drive 45.9 miles on I-55 S. Take Exit 248 for U.S. 6 towards Joliet/Morris. Drive west on U.S. 6 W/W. Eames Street for 3.5 miles. Turn south on S. McKinley Woods Road for 2 miles. Enter the park and continue past the Riverbend Lookout parking lot to the Frederick's Grove parking lot. The trailhead is at the southwest corner of the parking circle.

To reach Stratton State Park, follow the McKinley Woods Forest Preserve directions to U.S. 6 W. Continue west past McKinley Woods Road and another 8.8 miles to Ashley Road/County Rd 1000 E. Turn south and drive 1.5 miles, continuing 1.1 miles on Washington Street. Turn south on Price/Grigg Street and drive 0.1 mile into the parking lot. (Restrooms are at the west end of the lot.) **GPS Coordinates:** 16 T 396291mE 4582021mN

Information and Contact

There is no fee. Dogs on leash are allowed. The preserve is open daily 8 A.M.–8 P.M. April–October; 8 A.M.–5 P.M. November–March. For more information, contact McKinley Woods Forest Preserve, McKinley Woods Road, Channahon, IL, 815/727-8700, www.dnr.state.il.us.

William G. Stratton State Park is open sunrise–sunset daily. For more information, contact William G. Stratton State Park, 401 Ottawa Street, Morris, IL, 60450, 815/942-0796.

11 PRAIRIE CREEK WOODS AND GRASS FROG TRAILS   **BEST 🌙**

Midewin National Tallgrass Prairie, Wilmington

Level: Easy   **Total Distance:** 5.5 miles round-trip

Hiking Time: 2.5-3 hours   **Elevation Change:** negligible

Summary: Explore a corner of the vast grasslands and then enjoy the unique Prairie Creek Woods, Midewin's only forest.

Midewin National Tallgrass Prairie is the largest contiguous holding of public land in the Chicagoland area. The work in progress is the most ambitious restoration of native prairie ever attempted. Although most of the land still consists of introduced plant species, gradually the native grasslands are taking hold. Roughly 9,000–10,000 acres of Midewin are now open to the public. Much of Midewin was formerly the Joliet Army Ammunition Plant. Prairie Creek Woods are unique to the property; this is the only forest in the area. Hikers will enjoy the oak, maple, and hickory woodlands. Bring your binoculars, too; Midewin is home to a large variety of birds.

Part of the fun at Midewin is hiking through the contrasting sites. This hike is hugely variable—the Grass Frog Trail visits recovering grassland and marshy

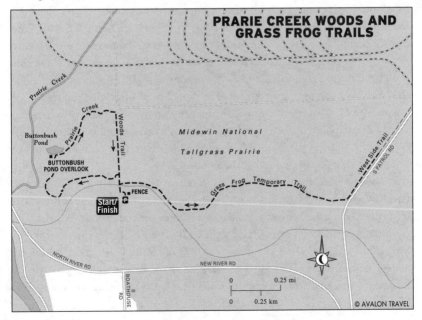

Buttonbush Pond overlook and interpretive sign

wetlands that support reeds, cattails, and the leopard frog. From the trailhead, walk north on the roadbed a few yards and turn right onto the mown path marked by an interpretive sign. The trail winds along the edge of some trees for about 0.5 mile then curves away from the creek through tall grasses. You'll see some little bluestem along here, along with other prairie grasses. As more native grasses are restored, the character of the trail will change. There is a lot to see along this trail; butterflies, dragonflies, and birds are constantly flitting about. Watch for the Henslow's sparrow, a shy bird that is abundant at Midewin. You might see a Northern Harrier, too. As you walk you might notice the plant life changing over to marsh plants as the ground gets boggy. The trail continues easterly, then turns north to meet the West Side Trail at its southernmost point. Hike to the West Side Trail to turn around at the 2-mile mark.

When you reach the roadbed upon your return, turn right to reach the Prairie Creek Woods Trail. You will quickly reach the trail entrance on the left, marked by a rustic wooden fence. At 4.3 miles you'll enter the cool woods. Bur oak and pignut hickory make up part of these woods. Look for may apples and other shade-loving forest plants. Wind along the trail towards Buttonbush Pond, which sits along the west side of the trail at about 4.7 miles. There is a nice viewing platform with benches, and interpretive signs where you can linger to watch great blue heron or egrets and listen to the frogs.

Once you get back on the trail you will cross a footbridge, then exit the woods crossing quickly through a bit of grassland before reaching the road at about 5.2 miles. Turn right on the road for 0.3 mile to the trailhead.

Options
For a short hike with historic significance, visit the Explosives Road trailhead to hike the Newton Trail, named for George Newton. Newton died in 1865 and although there is another site called Newton's Grave, he has a gravestone at the small fenced cemetery here. The 1.5-mile loop can be hiked in either direction. The mown-grass path passes through grasslands and the planted trees that remain from farming days. Bring a wildflower guide—there's a great variety on this short route. There are picnic tables, an interpretive kiosk with maps and brochures, a trail register, and an outhouse at the trailhead.

Directions
From downtown Chicago, take I-55 S for 53 miles. Take Exit 241 towards Wilmington, then turn east on County Road 44/N. River Road. Drive for 1.7 miles, then turn north on Kankakee River Drive (unpaved). There is no street sign, but on the south side of River Road is a sign for Boathouse Drive. Drive north 0.3 mile to the trailhead parking lot on the right.
GPS Coordinates: 16 T 402021mE 4577123mN

Information and Contact
There is no fee. Dogs are allowed on an eight-foot leash only and may not leave the trails. The visitors center is open 8 A.M.–4:30 P.M. Monday–Saturday and has wonderful displays on local human and natural history, guidebooks, drinking water, and restrooms. For more information, contact Midewin National Tallgrass Prairie, 30239 S. State Route 53, Wilmington, IL, 815/423-6370, www.fs.fed.us/mntp.

12 TWIN OAKS-BUNKER FIELD TRAILS

BEST ☾

Midewin National Tallgrass Prairie, Morris

🦌 ✈️ 🧭 🐎 👨‍👩‍👧

Level: Easy/moderate

Total Distance: 3.3-4.3 miles

Hiking Time: 2-2.5 hours

Elevation Change: negligible

Summary: This hike on the site of the former Joliet Army Ammunition Plant explores old buildings and 70-year-old bunkers.

Midewin National Tallgrass Prairie covers a large portion of the former Joliet Army Ammunition Plant. Established in 1996, this ambitious restoration project has served as the largest ongoing attempt to restore former farm or industrial land to its native state. Although the trail system is still a work in progress, recreation opportunities abound at Midewin. In 2010, several permanent trails were either completed or nearing completion. The east-side interim trails offer hikers a chance to experience both the human and natural history of the site.

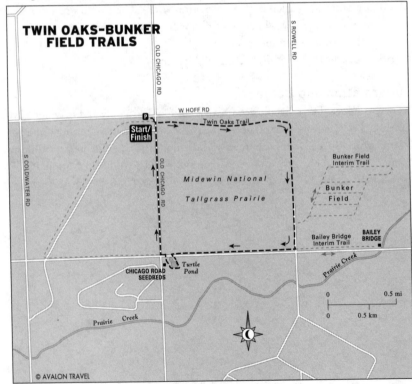

© BARBARA I. BOND

Bunker Field

The Twin Oaks Interim Trail takes intrepid hikers past the immense skeletons of World War II–era arsenal buildings, which are being dismantled for salvage. Where else do you have the chance to walk across a field of a 1940s TNT bunkers made of concrete and camouflaged with dirt and grass? If you want to, you can even go inside! On a hot summer day, the thick concrete walls keep the interior nice and cool.

To start your hike, sign the trail register and walk east past the demonstration garden to Old Chicago Road. Turn right and walk a few yards, then turn left at the sign onto the Twin Oaks Trail. As you walk along, huge frames come into view. Closer, it becomes obvious that these are rows of buildings. The trail goes east about 1 mile before turning right at a sign for Bunker Field. There are a lot of songbirds along here and hawks often circle the grasslands—a good indication that the land is indeed recovering. Soon you'll begin to see bunkers on the east side of the trail. (At first, the field looks like it has large grass hills; as you get closer, you realize what they are.)

Cross a footbridge and pass a bog; at about 1.75 miles, you'll reach the signed trail junction with the Bunker Field Trail. Turn left onto the mown-grass path and venture out to one of the bunkers. If you want to, you can hike the whole area; the distance, including the perimeter and walking around the bunkers, is just over 3 miles. Otherwise you'll only need to walk about 0.5 mile to reach an open bunker and check out the cool interior. When done, return to the trail sign and turn left to resume the Twin Oaks Trail. (Note: Trail mileage does not include a visit to this bunker.)

At 1.9 miles, a sign for the Wauponsee Glacier Trail and Bailey Bridge appears. Turn right; it's nearly 1 mile to the Turtle Pond and seedbeds from here. Turtle Pond has a pretty 0.3-mile loop that includes some picnic tables and a bike rack. You're likely to hear lots of frogs, and a sharp eye may catch a glimpse of a turtle. Walk along the west side of the pond, alongside the fenced seedbeds. Native seed production has been a major part of the Midewin restoration. At 2.2 miles is an interpretive sign where you can rejoin the trail.

Continue west a short distance, then turn right on Old Chicago Road as it heads north 1 mile to the trailhead. The Twin Oaks Trail continues ahead; however it is not as scenic—I recommend the shortcut.

Options

For a longer hike, turn left at the sign for Bailey Bridge and walk about 0.6 mile. There is an interpretive sign on the left just before the World War II portable bridge—it's a unique part of local history. Retrace your steps when done, then resume the main hike as described.

Directions

From downtown Chicago, take I-55 S for 53 miles. Take Exit 241 towards Wilmington and turn left on County Road 44/N. River Road. Travel 4 miles on New River Road to State Route 53. Turn north and drive 1.0 mile to the Midewin Supervisor's Office/Visitor Center. To reach the trailhead, drive north on State Route 53 to Hoff Road. Turn right onto Hoff Road and drive east 2 miles to the parking lot at the intersection of Hoff and Chicago Roads. The trailhead is at the southeast corner of the parking lot.

GPS Coordinates: 16 T 409887mE 4582790mN

Information and Contact

There is no fee. Dogs on leash are allowed. The park is open sunrise–sunset daily. The visitors center is open 8 A.M.–4:30 P.M. Monday–Saturday and has guidebooks, drinking water, restrooms, and wonderful displays about local human and natural history. In the winter, cross-country skiing is allowed. For more information, contact Midewin National Tallgrass Prairie, 30239 S. State Route 53, Wilmington, IL, 815/423-6370, www.fs.fed.us/mntp.

INDIANA AND MICHIGAN

© BARBARA I. BOND

BEST HIKES

◖ Bird-Watching
Dune Blowout-Woodland Loop, page 293.

◖ Children
West Beach Trails, page 281.

◖ Geologic Wonders
Mount Baldy, page 278.

◖ History Buffs
Bailly Homestead-Chellberg Farm Trails,
 page 287.

◖ Lakefront or Riverside Hikes
West Beach Trails, page 281.

For anyone in the Chicago area, hiking the trails

of nearby Indiana and Michigan is fun and eye-opening. The most well-known hikes in this region are along the numerous trails of the Lake Michigan shoreline. The northwest corner of Indiana is home to the spectacular scenery of the Lake Michigan dunes. Along a 15-mile stretch of lakeshore is a complex landscape of young beach dunes, older dune ridges and black oak forest, bogs, wetlands, and marshes. There are seemingly limitless opportunities for recreation on this land, which today is protected by the Indiana Dunes State Park and Indiana Dunes National Lakeshore. But this wasn't always so. Starting in the mid-1800s, increasing settlement and urbanization encroached upon the fragile landscape. However, conservation and preservation efforts began soon after 1900, fueled by the passion of some key individuals and communities.

Chicago botanist and professor Henry C. Cowles studied the Indiana dunes and was fascinated by the natural diversity of the changing landscape. He pioneered the concept of succession – the process whereby a set of natural features are gradually replaced – and walked the dunes and their surroundings again and again as he educated generations of students. Cowles generated enthusiasm for conservation and preservation. Years after his death, the Indiana Dunes National Lakeshore was established, protecting this wonderful resource for generations to come.

The Indiana dunes have miles of trails. Beginning at the west end, the trails of West Beach are a wonderful introduction to the succession that threatens the dune landscape. It's here that thousands of visitors get their first impression of the beauty of these dunes. A short walk along the Dune Succession Trail is a great way to learn about the ways this landscape adapts to change.

Farther east is Cowles Bog, where trails wind through a large wetland complex that contains black oak and maple woods in addition to the marsh and wetlands. Hiking here is a wonderful way to spend a day. Nearby is the Bailly Homestead, where history buffs can hike along trails that explore the settlement property of a former fur trader. If you are up for a little more exploration, the Little Calumet River Trail allows for a longer hike through a prairie restoration and marshy woods with lots of bird activity and summer flowers.

Surrounded by national park lands are the dunes and woodland of Indiana Dunes State Park. A challenging hike to the tops of the three highest dunes rewards with a seemingly endless view across Lake Michigan. If you like wildlife and birds, the woodland trails just east of the dune peaks may offer just your kind of hiking. The oak and hickory woods provide a rich habitat for woodland and migratory birds. Bring your binoculars! The blowout trail offers views of the dramatic shoreline nearly the entire way and an up-close look at the powerful forces shaping the young lakeside dunes. Mount Baldy is the moving dune (one that is slowly moving inland) of the far east corner of the national lakeshore – and is one of the most beloved places in this region. Hikers set out in the woods and walk up the steep, sandy trail to a starkly beautiful landscape. Standing atop the windswept dune really helps you appreciate the forces at work here. Wild grape, cottonwoods, and bunches of marram grass all fight the powerful wind that is slowly blowing back the big dune.

Michigan has its own lakeshore parks with sand dunes and dense woodlands. Warren Dunes State Park has a well-developed trail system and is a popular birding site with the local chapter of the Audubon Society. Visit Warren Dunes for challenging steep climbs and beautiful lakeshore views, along with the opportunity to walk for miles along the beach.

These trails in Indiana and Michigan cover a wide territory – they ascend heavily wooded ridges, cross ravines, wind through the spring wildflowers of the forest, and emerge in windswept dunes. If you make the trip east and get some sand in your shoes, you'll be glad you did.

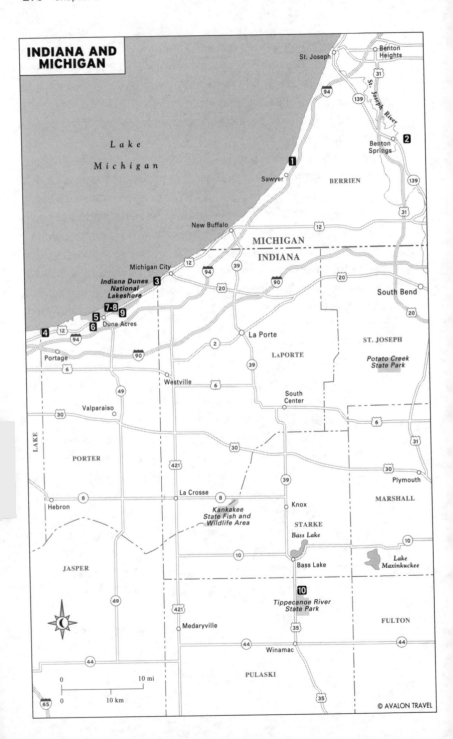

INDIANA AND MICHIGAN

TRAIL NAME	LEVEL	DISTANCE	TIME	ELEVATION	FEATURES	PAGE
1 Woodland–Beach Loop	Moderate	5.0 mi rt	2.5–3 hr	570 ft		272
2 Love Creek Trails	Easy	3.8 mi rt	2 hr	200 ft		275
3 Mount Baldy	Moderate	1.2 mi rt	30 min	100 ft		278
4 West Beach Trails	Easy/moderate	3.5 mi rt	2 hr	270 ft		281
5 Cowles Bog Trail	Easy/moderate	4.7 mi rt	2–2.5 hr	240 ft		284
6 Bailly Homestead–Chellberg Farm Trails	Easy/moderate	4.6 mi rt	2–2.5 hr	190 ft		287
7 Three Peaks	Moderate	1.7 mi rt	1 hr	320 ft		290
8 Dune Blowout–Woodland Loop	Moderate	4.0 mi rt	2 hr	125 ft		293
9 Ly-co-ki-we Trail	Moderate	7.0 mi rt	4 hr	140 ft		296
10 River Bluff–Oxbow Trails	Moderate	9.6 mi rt	4.5–5 hr	190 ft		299

1 WOODLAND-BEACH LOOP

Warren Dunes State Park, Michigan

Level: Moderate

Hiking Time: 2.5-3 hours

Total Distance: 5.0 miles round-trip

Elevation Change: 570 feet

Summary: A hike at Warren Dunes rewards with spectacular views atop tall Lake Michigan dunes.

Warren Dunes State Park is a nearly 2,000-acre sand dune and woodland natural area on Lake Michigan's eastern shore. The park's popular beach, year-round camping, and well-marked trail system have made the diverse landscape a well-known destination. Warren Dunes has several peaks ranging from 738 feet to 771 feet, and all about 240 feet above nearby Lake Michigan. The property once belonged

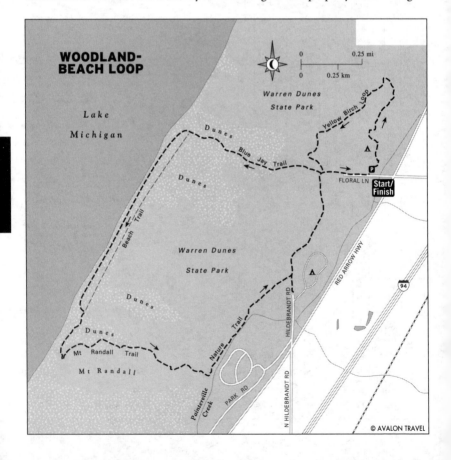

to wealthy conservationist Edward K. Warren. Warren valued the land for its natural beauty; his goal was to preserve his 1,500-acre purchase in its wild state. Today more than 1 million visitors annually enjoy Warren's vision.

The mature oak and hickory forest, dramatic dunes, and miles of beach waterfront all make the trails at Warren Dunes rewarding. The rolling terrain of woodlands and sand dunes create trails with some short and challenging ascents. This lopsided figure-eight hike includes plenty of up and down through enough varied terrain to keep any hiker happy. The payoffs are great views and nearly a mile of walking along the sandy shore of Lake Michigan.

trail to Lake Michigan

From the Yellow Birch Loop trailhead, turn north onto the path. The first mile loops through a shady maple forest on the north side of the campground. Walk over boardwalks through two low areas before making a sharp ascent of nearly 750 feet—all in less than 0.5 mile! Some large tulip trees dot these woods, along with American beech and black cherry. Ferns, may apples, snakeroot, and other shade-loving plants fill the forest floor. The trail winds south after a 0.5 mile, reaching a junction at post 8 in 1 mile.

Turn west onto the wide, packed-dirt path, which quickly heads uphill. The forest is an overgrown tangle—shagbark hickories hide amid the oaks and the mid-canopy fills with smaller beech and maple trees. The trail narrows and becomes sandy as you approach the dunes and emerge from the woods. Suddenly there are only a few aspens and marram grass on the sand as you begin a 0.5-mile descent to the lakeshore.

Approaching the beach, you'll pass a Blue Jay Trail sign partially buried in the sand. Turn south onto the beach and enjoy the next 0.9 mile by following the shore or walking south along the Beach Trail at the edge of the trees. Continue until you're close to the parking lot and to post 1, reaching the Mount Randall Trail, which climbs east for 1 mile up through the woods on a narrow trail and steps. The trail winds around deep ravines and climbs, peaking at around 3.5 miles. Wooden posts with "boots" now mark the trail as it descends somewhat steeply. At 3.6 miles and post 3, turn north onto the Nature Trail as it parallels Painterville Creek a short distance. Look for a quiet bench tucked away by the creek where you can listen to the frogs sing and groan. Beautiful, tall black oak, maple, and more tulip trees shade the trail. Continue north and follow the numbered trail markers to post 8 at 4.76 miles. Turn east onto Floral Lane, passing post 9, which is nearly obscured by foliage. Return to the parking lot at 5 miles.

Options

For more beach and less hiking, walk to the north end of the parking lot and onto Trail 1 to reach the Mount Randall Trail. After 0.5 mile or so of walking, reach the highest point in the park and enjoy the drama of the deep ravines and thick trees. Return the way you came for a 1-mile hike, then spend the rest of your time enjoying the beach.

Directions

From Chicago, take I-94 east to Exit 16 towards Bridgeman. Turn left and drive south on Red Arrow Highway for 0.7 mile. Turn west onto Floral Lane and drive 0.1 mile, then turn north into the Organization Camping lot. Walk north on the footpath through camp, following it west a short distance to the Yellow Birch Loop sign.

GPS Coordinates: 16 T 534928mE 4640950mN

Information and Contact

A Recreation Passport program (www.michigan.gov/recreationpassport) went into effect in late 2010. Passes are available at state park facilities; fees vary. Dogs are not allowed on the beach, however leashed dogs are allowed on the east side trails. The park is open sunrise–sunset daily. The website map does not have all the trails marked, however maps along the trails are accurate. Trails have posts with numbers and maps at trail junctions, making navigation easy. For more information, contact Warren Dunes State Park, 12032 Red Arrow Highway, Sawyer, MI 49125, 269/426-4013, www.dnr.state.mi.us.

2 LOVE CREEK TRAILS

Berrien Center, Michigan

Level: Easy

Hiking Time: 2 hours

Total Distance: 3.8 miles round-trip

Elevation Change: 200 feet

Summary: A visit to Love Creek rewards outdoors enthusiasts with opportunities for bird-watching, spotting white-tailed deer, or just enjoying the rich color of spring wildflowers.

Berrien County lies in the far southwest corner of Michigan, bordered by Lake Michigan to the west and bisected by the St. Joseph River, and the region features a rich history of agriculture and industry. Love Creek County Park sits nestled in the Love Creek Valley, just east of a bend in the St. Joseph River, surrounded by fruit orchards and farmland. The 150-acre park's namesake creek runs through mature forest, a prairie restoration, and a small marsh.

Begin hiking north from the nature center on the Blue Pond Loop. (Love Creek uses colored arrows on wooden posts as trail markers.) After crossing the creek, the trail works its way north through a forest of American beech and maple. The canopy is dense, as is the forest floor, covered with shade-loving plants such as may apple and wood nettle. Follow the trail gently uphill, then down, past shagbark

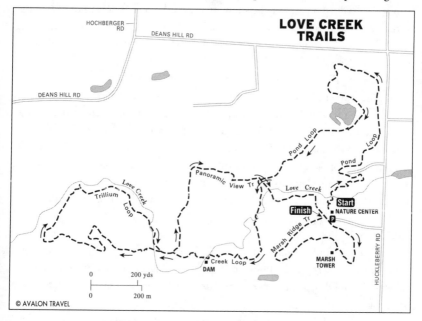

hickory and birch (watch for poison ivy throughout the woods). Woodpeckers thrive in these woods. Continue hiking south toward a trail junction at 1.2 miles. Keep left at the second Yellow Trail arrow and continue south. Follow the Yellow (then Green) trail to a creek crossing and then a bench at 1.55 miles.

Clamber down some steps, then turn left continuing west on the Green Trail. Cross another footbridge with the remains of an old dam just north. (If you approach the creek stealthily, you may catch a great blue heron standing sentinel in the shallow water.) After a short distance, keep left to continue west on the Red Trail, heading downhill and then back up. Just after 2 miles, you'll come across a well-placed bench and lots of huge tulip trees in the woods; there may

old wooden footbridge

even be wild leeks flowering in some places. This area is home to lots of trillium and spring wildflowers after the snow melts. As the trail follows along the ridge and above a deep ravine, keep left on the Red Trail at 2.5 miles. Cross the creek, then keep left once more to follow the Black Trail as it heads north and uphill through the trees.

Follow the Black Trail east as it zigzags past a bench; at the second Yellow Trail post, turn right and follow the signs to the nature center. To continue on the Marsh Ridge Trail to the viewing tower; walk south and pick up the Orange Trail across the parking lot (near the southwest corner). The Orange Trail finds its way south to the marsh platform, curving west to reach the platform in 0.2 mile. Frogs might hop across the path or the occasional garter snake might slither by. After enjoying the views from the platform, return to the path and complete the loop back to the nature center parking lot with a total distance of 3.8 miles.

Options

For a different kind of hike in the same region, visit Fernwood Botanical Gardens and Nature Preserve and enjoy 4 miles of trails adjacent to the St. Joseph River. The public buildings and garden trails are wheelchair-accessible; wheelchairs are available for visitor use.

Directions

From I-80/I-90 E in Indiana, take Exit 72 for U.S. 31 N. Drive 15.5 miles north, entering Michigan. Take Exit 13 toward Berrien Springs and turn left to drive northeast on Snow Road. After driving for 1.4 miles, continue onto W. Ferry Street for 0.5 mile. At Deans Hill Road, turn left and drive north, then east, for 1.9 miles. Turn south onto Huckleberry Road. The park entrance will be on the west side of the road in 0.5 mile.

To reach Fernwood Botanical Gardens and Nature Preserve, drive north on Huckleberry Road and turn west, then southwest, onto Deans Hill Road for 1.9 miles. Turn south onto old U.S. 31 and drive for 0.8 mile. Turn west onto Range Line Road and continue for 1.6 miles, then travel south on Range Line Road for 4.1 miles. Fernwood will be on the west side of the road.

GPS Coordinates: 16 T 558154mE 4644394mN

Information and Contact

The county park entrance fee is $3 per vehicle for Berrien County residents ($5 per vehicle for nonresidents). Dogs are not allowed. The park is open year-round; trails are open sunrise–sunset daily. The interpretive center is open 10 A.M.–5 P.M. Tuesday–Sunday. For more information, contact Love Creek County Park, 9228 Huckleberry Road, Berrien Center, MI 49102, 269/471-2617, www.berriencounty.org.

The Fernwood Botanical Garden and Nature Preserve is open 10 A.M.–5 P.M. Tuesday–Sunday (Nov.–Apr.); 10 A.M.–6 P.M. Tuesday–Saturday and noon–6 P.M. Sunday (May–Oct.). Entrance fees are $7 for adults, $5 for seniors, and $3–4 for children. Dogs are not allowed. For more information, contact Fernwood Botanical Garden and Nature Preserve, 13988 Range Line Road, Niles, MI, 269/695-6491, www.fernwoodbotanical.org.

3 MOUNT BALDY

BEST ◖

Indiana Dunes National Lakeshore, Indiana

Level: Moderate

Total Distance: 1.2 miles round-trip

Hiking Time: 30 minutes

Elevation Change: 100 feet

Summary: Hike to the top of Mount Baldy, the highest moving dune at Indiana Dunes National Lakeshore.

Mount Baldy towers 126 feet above Lake Michigan. The isolated dune offers intrepid hikers beautiful views across the lake and an opportunity to visit the quiet beach below the summit. Mount Baldy is covered with marram grass, which has adapted for life on sand dunes through a deep root system. Marram grass and cottonwoods help protect the windward side of the dune from erosion.

Mount Baldy is starving. At least, that is how the National Park Service describes the process eroding the tall lakeshore dune. It is also moving away from the lake at a rate of about four feet per year—the result of being too popular with

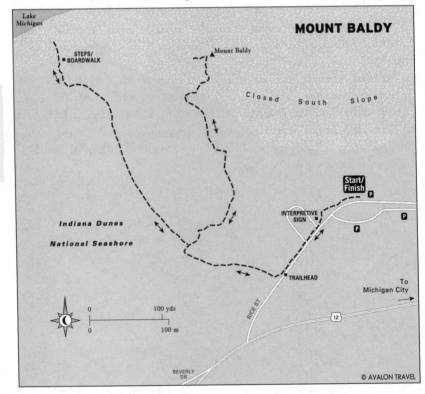

view from the top of Mount Baldy

visitors. Hikers walking up and down the south side summit trail have hastened the dune's slow migration southward. To learn more about the forces affecting Mount Baldy, check out the interpretive display at the trailhead.

The hike begins at a fence in front of Mount Baldy's south slope. Take a look at the few trees here, as they illustrate how tough life can be on a sand dune. Many trees have several feet of sand covering their trunks and the slope is nearly devoid of any other growth. Walk west around the dune's base to the trailhead and turn onto the sandy trail. (It seems weird to be in the woods, yet hiking on sand!) The trail climbs up and down again, before turning northeast towards the top. Now the work begins—for every step you take, you also slide backwards a bit. This slow progress upward allows you to take in the oak-hickory woods. As you make your way toward the top, note a wood platform and a fence that runs eastward across the dune (protecting the highly eroded south slope). As you approach the upper dune, the trail cuts back, then comes out of the trees as you push northward.

Emerge from the woods and onto the top of Mount Baldy—it feels like a different world. The wind-drifted sand creates a rolling surface dotted mostly with large clumps of marram and reed grasses. Wild grape vines mix with some of the grasses, all working to hold the dune together. A few cottonwoods grow nearer the woods. Walk across the sand towards the northernmost edge—the views are amazing. (Resist the urge to run down the front of the dune!) Once you've had your fill of the view, turn around and retrace your steps back down to the first trail junction at 0.65 mile. Turn right at the trail junction and navigate through the trees for 0.2 mile to the beach. As you descend some wooden steps to the shore, read the interpretive sign (about halfway down) about the starving beach below. Some small trees along the beach seem to split their roots—half are sunk in the shrinking sand, the other half are suspended in air. Gazing westward, you can take in unobstructed views of shoreline and the lake. Return as you came.

Options

Add another 2 miles (round-trip) to this hike by continuing from Mount Baldy west/southwest for about 1 mile to Central Beach. (Do not walk east/northeast; Mount Baldy is the easternmost trail in the national lakeshore.)

Directions

From downtown Chicago, drive east on I-90 and take Exit 21 for I-94 E; continue for 7.6 miles. Take Exit 22B and drive 11.2 miles on U.S. 20 E. Turn north at N. County Line Road and continue for 1 mile, then continue onto U.S. 12 E for 0.7 mile. Just before U.S. 12 curves east, take a slight left northeast onto Rice Street and into the lot at the end.

Public Transportation: Take the train from the Millennium Station in Chicago to the South Shore 11th Street Station (Michigan City, www.nictd.com). From W. 11th Street, turn right onto Buffalo Street. Turn left on W. 10th Street and walk one mile. Turn right on Sheridan Avenue, then left on W. 4th Street/US-12. Walk south, then west to turn right on Rice Street and the trailhead.

GPS Coordinates: 16 T 505894mE 4617039mN

Information and Contact

There is no fee. Dogs are allowed on leash. The park is open 7 A.M.–dusk daily. There are restrooms and water at the trailhead. Maps are available for download at www.nps.gov/indu. Fore more information, contact Mount Baldy, Rice Street/U.S. 12, Michigan City, IN 46360; or Indiana Dunes National Lakeshore/Dorothy Buell Memorial Visitor Center, 1420 Munson Road, Porter, IN 46304, 219/926-7561.

4 WEST BEACH TRAILS   BEST C

Indiana Dunes National Lakeshore, Indiana

Level: Easy/moderate   **Total Distance:** 3.5 miles round-trip

Hiking Time: 2 hours   **Elevation Change:** 270 feet

Summary: You get it all on the West Beach Trails – beachfront, sand dunes, boardwalks, oak savanna, and a stunning view down to Long Lake.

During the frenzy of mid-19th-century development, the fragile dunes, forests, and prairie of the Lake Michigan shore nearly disappeared completely. Conservation campaigns began around the turn of the 20th century and by the 1920s, a state park protected this valuable stretch of shoreline. It would be another 30 years before another conservation campaign resulted in the creation of the Indiana Dunes National Lakeshore. Today visitors can walk the dunes, wander through native bogs and marshland, hike through a historic farm and homestead, and enjoy the natural riches of these woods.

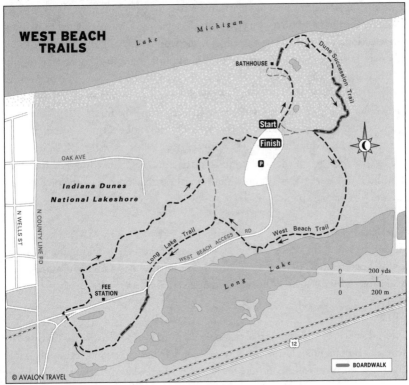

No summer in the Chicago area is complete without a trip to the Indiana shore—and that often means West Beach. The popular swimming beach is crowded all summer long, and is a wonderful place to begin exploring the wonders of the Indiana Dunes National Lakeshore. West Beach has three short trails, which together make a pleasant 3.5-mile loop.

Begin by walking north along the wide, paved path to the bathhouse, then through the building towards the lake. At the sign for the Dune Succession Trail, pick up a brochure to will guide you along the numbered posts. The trail crosses the sand and begins climbing up along the dune in a sandy oak savanna. Clumps of marram grass here help slow dune erosion, as do the few cottonwoods, while the upper dune is wooded with pines, oak, and a few aspens. Follow the elaborate stairway and boardwalk system, crossing the last boardwalk and descending steps to a three-way trail junction at 0.8 mile. Turn south at the junction onto the West Beach Trail loop.

The trail heads south through a recovering savanna with just a few hardy grasses, scattered oaks, and even some prickly pear cactus. Watch for white-tailed deer along this stretch. The trail curves west along Long Lake's shore. At 1.3 miles is a short spur south to a viewing platform; watch for frogs and butterflies.

Cross the road and turn west again onto Long Lake Trail at a signed three-way intersection. The trail skirts the edge of the woods, curving south towards the lily pad–covered Long Lake before heading uphill and into the woods. Around 2 miles, boardwalks provide lovely views down to the lake—watch for great blue or green heron. Long Lake Trail curves back eastward after crossing the road and then enters shady oak woods with dense ferns covering the forest floor. There are deep ravines north and a pond farther south as the trail continues. Emerge near the top of a sand dune at 3.2 miles, with spectacular views of the lakeshore. The trail skirts the edge of the vegetation atop the dune before heading north downhill. Follow the trail as it curves slightly southeast back down to the picnic area adjacent to the parking lot.

Options

Spend the day at the beach and get an overview of the area by hiking the 1.4-mile Dune Succession Trail. The brochure and numbered posts make it informative and fun, and the system of boardwalks and stairways are a nice change of pace.

Directions

From downtown Chicago, drive east on I-90 to Exit 17 for I-65/U.S. 12/U.S. 20 towards Indianapolis/Dunes Highway. Keep left toward U.S. 12/U.S. 20 E for 0.9 mile. Turn east and continue on U.S. 12 (Dunes Hwy.) for 4.4 miles. Turn

West Beach shoreline, swimming beach, and trail marker

north at County Line Road. Drive 0.2 mile and turn east on Main Street, reaching the main parking lots in 1.1 miles. Walk north to the information sign and sidewalk at the end of the lot, then continue to the beach house.

Public Transportation: From Millennium Station, take the South Shore Line from Chicago. From the Portage/Ogden Dunes Station, walk west on U.S. 12 W for 1.9 miles and turn north onto County Line Road. Walk 0.2 mile north to Main Street and turn east. Continue another 0.2 mile, picking up the trail where it crosses the road in front of the park entrance. The total distance to the park from the station is 2.3 miles.

GPS Coordinates: 16 T 482631mE 4607662mN

Information and Contact

The summer entrance fee is $6 per vehicle or $1 for hikers or bikes. Dogs are not allowed on the beach, however the Long Lake Trail is open to dogs on a six-foot leash. From Memorial Day to Labor Day, the park is open 9 A.M.–dusk daily. The rest of the year, the park is open 6 A.M.–sunset daily for hikers and cyclists; vehicles are allowed 7 A.M.–dusk daily. Restrooms are available year-round. For more information and map downloads, please contact Indiana Dunes National Lakeshore, West Beach, N. County Line Road/West Beach Road, Portage, IN 46368, 219/926-7561 (press 2 for beach information), www.nps.gov/indu.

5 COWLES BOG TRAIL
Indiana Dunes National Lakeshore, Indiana

Level: Easy/moderate

Total Distance: 4.7 miles round-trip

Hiking Time: 2-2.5 hours

Elevation Change: 240 feet

Summary: The trails of Cowles Bog guide you on a quiet walk through black oak savanna, wetlands, and dunes.

Along 15 miles of diverse Lake Michigan shoreline are the dunes, woods, and wetlands of Indiana Dunes National Lakeshore. In the early 20th century, botanist Henry Cowles recognized the value of these unique wetlands and he became a major impetus behind research and conservation efforts. Following decades of efforts of both local and national advocates, this collection of diverse natural resources became protected in 1966. Today, Cowles Bog is part of a large wetland complex undergoing restoration by the National Park Service. Prior to urbanization, the bog was home to a diverse array of plant and animal life. Although succession has largely eliminated the open-water bog of yesteryear, hikers can enjoy a look into the more recent past as they hike from the forest to the dunes.

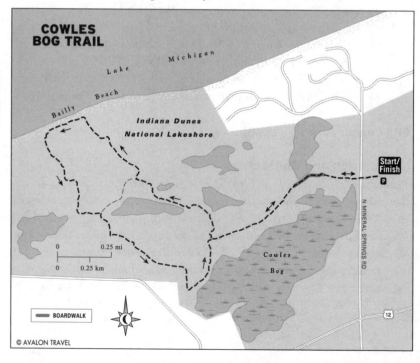

the steep return trail from Bailly Beach

From the trailhead, the Cowles Bog Trail cuts a straight swath through the black-oak woods for the first 0.87 mile. By midsummer the forest floor is overgrown with a tangle of vines, shrubs, and flowers. Watch for may apple, false Solomon's seal, toothwort, and various ferns. A boardwalk at 0.35 mile reminds you that you're hiking on wetlands. As maples change the forest canopy, more light filters down to the trail over the next 0.5 mile. At nearly 0.9 mile, turn north at a signed junction towards the beach.

The short uphill climb is just a preview of what's to come. Enjoy the rolling trail (and the woodland sunflowers) for the next 0.6 mile as you continue towards the lakeshore. Reaching the beach requires climbing the steep backside of the dune at 1.5 miles; it is a short climb, though, and the grasses and small oaks are only a slight distraction. As you crest the top of the dune, the sparkling blue lake provides more motivation. Drop over the other side of the dune, making your way down the sand and to the beach. One look at the fragile exposed tree roots and grasses as they cling tenuously to bits of sandy soil and you will gain a new perspective on the powerful erosion that takes place here.

After enjoying the lakeshore, head west 0.2 mile to pick up the trail again at around 2 miles. (There is an IDNL sign on the east side of the trail, and further along there is another marker, though it is nearly buried.) Soak in the dramatic views south across the marram grass to the thick black-oak forest. Prepare for another steep 0.2-mile climb up the dune—the trail is heavily eroded and slippery. When you reach the top, catch your breath, then begin hiking 0.5 mile downhill past mixed oak and pine. As the canopy thins, note some cottonwoods, beech, and a few pines mixed into the oak woods. Ignore the three-way trail junction at 2.7 miles, instead continuing along the southwest side of the wetland. The partially submerged trees lend these waters an eerie look. The trail turns south to a junction at 3.3 miles; turn left and head northeast past more watery ground. Cross a boardwalk through a low section, then turn east at a signed junction at 3.6 miles. You are now retracing your steps along the flat path to the trailhead. Check out the variety of flora on the south side of the trail—the moss-covered water and verdant ferns accentuate the white bark of the beech trees. Continue east to return to the trailhead.

Options

To shorten this hike by nearly 0.7 mile, skip the loop and instead do an out-and-back to the beach for a total of 4.0 miles round-trip. A nicer option would be to drive south down Mineral Springs Road to the Chellberg Farm. From there you can enjoy another 2 miles of hiking along the interpretive Bailly–Chellberg Trail.

Directions

From downtown Chicago, take I-94 E to merge onto I-80 E/I-94 E and continue for 29.4 miles. Exit on I-49 N and drive 3 miles to U.S. 12/Dunes Highway and go west. In 2 miles turn north on Mineral Springs Road. Drive 0.7 mile to a side road with a small sign for Cowles Bog, just ahead of the Dune Acres entrance. Turn east and drive to the lot at the end of the road; there is an information sign, map box, and outhouse. Walk west back down the road and cross Mineral Springs Road to reach the signed trailhead.

Public Transportation: Take the South Shore Line to Dunes Park Station. From the station, walk west on the Calumet Trail 1.5 miles, turning north on Mineral Springs Road. Walk 0.5 mile to the trailhead on the west side of the road.
GPS Coordinates: 16 T 492959mE 4610186mN

Information and Contact

There is no fee. Dogs on leash are allowed. The park is open 7 A.M.–dusk daily. Maps are available for download at www.nps.gov/indu. For more information, contact Cowles Bog, N. Mineral Springs Road, Chesterton, IN 46304; or the Dorothy Buell Memorial Visitor Center, 1420 Munson Road, Porter, IN 46304, 219/926-7561 (press 3 for information), www.nps.gov/indu.

6 BAILLY HOMESTEAD–CHELLBERG FARM TRAILS

BEST (

Indiana Dunes National Lakeshore, Indiana

Level: Easy/moderate

Hiking Time: 2–2.5 hours

Total Distance: 4.6 miles round-trip

Elevation Change: 190 feet

Summary: Explore the remnants of a historic homestead and farm on this hike through the restored prairie and wetlands of the Little Calumet River Trail.

Indiana Dunes National Lakeshore's 15,000 acres encompass a wide variety of habitats, including rugged sand dunes, hardwood forests, and wetlands. Before European fur traders arrived in this region, Native Americans traveled here along well-established routes. (Today, one of these routes is the Dunes Highway, which follows the former Calumet Beach Trail.) In 1822, Joseph Bailly built his trading post and homestead at the crossroads of these trails, linking communities of settlers. In 1855, the Chellbergs arrived from Sweden, building a homestead and

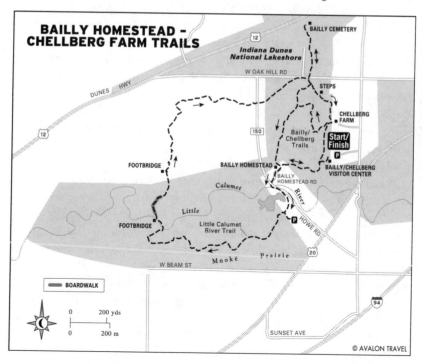

Bailly Homestead

establishing a farm in the area. Both historic sites have structures still standing, offering hikers an opportunity to walk back in time on a visit to both sites.

The defining natural feature of this former farm and homestead is a deep ravine that runs north–south for 0.5 mile before curving west towards the East Arm of the Little Calumet River. From the visitors center, walk south along the trail, downhill, and cross the ravine. The trail now heads west through dense forest, passing an old hand pump and other settlement signs along the way. Oak, shagbark hickory, and black cherry fill the woods; the forest floor is weedy and overgrown. Reach the Bailly Homestead around 0.3 mile; the restored buildings offer some insight into what life was like here nearly 200 years ago. Walk south across the property to reach the Little Calumet River Trail.

When you reach the road, turn left and walk southwest and uphill to the trailhead. Pass a sign and some huge bur oak, keeping right at a three-way intersection. Head south to the prairie, watching for woodpeckers in the woods. (The prairie has a sign explaining the restoration.) Lots of sparrows, goldfinches, and butterflies flutter along the grassland path, which has tall goldenrod growing along its edge. At 1.3 miles, enter the trees as the trail approaches the river. Keep left at a three-way intersection, crossing a wooden bridge that leads to a long boardwalk.

Around the boardwalk, look for arrowhead plants, birch trees, and lots of mushrooms growing on the deadwood. At 2 miles, a short wood footbridge leads the trail north. The trail curves east, crossing the road at 2.7 miles. At 3 miles, turn north and cross Oak Hill Road to reach the Bailly Cemetery. After circling the small, walled graveyard, return to the trail and continue south. The trail crosses a big ravine over a series of stairways and boardwalks. At 3.8 miles you will reach the edge of the Chellberg Farm, walking past fields and many outbuildings. When you leave the farm, turn west at a three-way junction to walk down to the edge of the ravine for a rolling 0.6-mile out-and-back stroll—this is an interesting walk through a secluded part of the property. When you reach a T junction at 4.2 miles, turn south and walk 0.6 mile back to the visitors center, passing the Bailly Homestead halfway along the trail. After returning to the main trail, turn south at 4.5 miles for a short walk along an avenue of trees and back to the start in 0.1 mile.

Options

Spend more time exploring the human history along this trail. The Bailly Chellberg property is divided into two separate areas with historic buildings. The Chellberg Farm includes a barn, a chicken house, and a maple sugar house. Seasonal programs explore daily life on the farm and may include activities such as making maple syrup. The Bailly Homestead includes several restored or recreated buildings, such as a two-story cabin, a kitchen/chapel, and a main house reflective of the 19th and early 20th centuries.

Directions

From downtown Chicago, drive east on I-90 to Exit 21 for I-94 E, then drive 7.6 miles. Take Exit 22B and drive 61.9 miles on U.S. 20 E. Turn north on Mineral Springs Road and continue 0.1 mile. Turn west at the entrance road and follow it to the parking lot. To reach the trailhead, walk past the interpretive signboard (in the southwest corner) and toward the visitors center. Walk through the building and down to the T intersection, marked with a trail sign.

GPS Coordinates: 16 T 492557mE 4607889mN

Information and Contact

There is no fee. Dogs are not allowed. The park is open 7 A.M.–sunset daily. For more information visit, contact Bailly Homestead, U.S. 20 and Mineral Springs Road, Porter, IN 46304; or Indiana Dunes National Lakeshore, Dorothy Buell Memorial Visitor Center, 1420 Munson Road, Porter, IN 46304, www.nps.gov/indu, 219/926-7561.

7 THREE PEAKS
Indiana Dunes State Park, Indiana

Level: Moderate   **Total Distance:** 1.7 miles round-trip

Hiking Time: 1 hour   **Elevation Change:** 320 feet

Summary: This short and intense three-peak hike serves as a wonderful introduction to Indiana Dunes State Park.

The dramatic terrain of the Indiana dunes was created in the wake of the retreating Wisconsin Glacier 14,000 years ago. Today the dunes, forests, and wetlands are part of the beautiful and unique landscape of Lake Michigan's southeast shore. After the Native Americans and European settlers tried to tame this land, industry boomed and significantly degraded the fragile landscape. However, in 1926, this portion of the lakeshore became Indiana Dunes State Park and was spared from further destruction. Today visitors come from near and far to enjoy this natural wonderland. Hiking the trails of this park is a great way to observe the work of nature's forces up close. The trailheads are located at the east end of the parking lot. The paved nature center path is on the left and the dirt trail is on the right. Stay right on the dirt trail and walk southeast past the nature center and turn north; the tall black oaks seem at odds with the sandy trail. Turn left at Post 8 and begin the first bit of climbing. The trail winds through the woods and uphill; stay on Trail 8 at the junction. Just before reaching 0.4 mile, the trail creeps up a wide, steep, sandy slope. You'll notice some ash and hickory mingled with the oaks and wild grape growing along the edge of the sand. Blue skies beckon ahead as you make your first summit atop 176-foot Mount Jackson in just under 0.5 mile. Walk past the summit post for rewarding lake views.

The trail continues north to the next summit—184-foot Mount Holden. Descend about 50 feet before climbing back up the somewhat steeper slope to the top of this peak. A break in the trees allows gazing down to the lake; clumps of dune grass intermingle with more wild grape vines. The trail cuts back southwest as it descends to a steep trail junction, crossing Trail 7. Continue southwest, keeping west at another trail junction around 0.8 mile to stay on Trail 8. Woodpeckers populate this heavily wooded section, as do some large tulip trees. With the aid of wooden steps—105 of them—reach the top of 192-foot Mount Tom, which has viewing platforms and interpretive signs. Turn north towards the lake and follow Trail 8 down the steps to the beach, crossing the foredune to the beach at

1 mile. The views of the Chicago skyline are incredible! Walk northeast and enjoy the shoreline, then turn back toward the trees and walk uphill toward a sign for Trails 4 and 7 at around 1.2 miles. Follow Trail 7 as it ascends and then crosses Trail 8 at a four-way junction at 1.36 miles. Stay on Trail 7 as it descends through scrubby woods; some trees may have bright yellow sulphur fungus growing on their trunks. At 1.6 miles, continue south on Trail 7 at the three-way junction to return to the nature center.

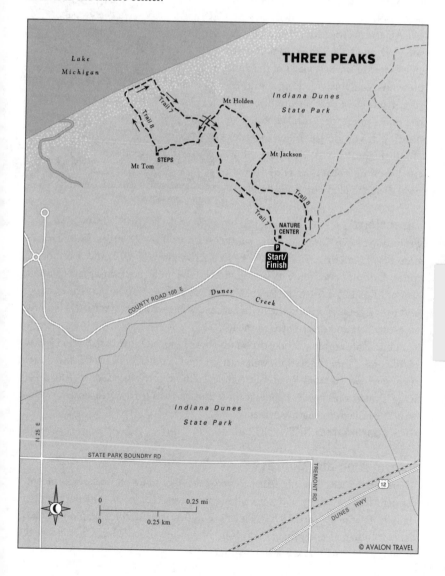

Options

Indiana Dunes State Park has many miles of trails. For a longer exploration, follow Trail 10 from the same trailhead. The loop heads west along a pretty wooded route, with great birding and wildlife, and crosses the Indian Portage Trail, a nod to the trade routes Native Americans used for generations. As you work your way around to the beach, enjoy some of the best views of the dune blowouts available. Walking south, return from the beach (as described in the main hike) for a total distance of 6 miles. If you do the hikes together, climb the peaks first, then just follow the beach northeast on Trail 10 for a total distance of about 6.3 miles.

© BARBARA I. BOND

view from Mount Tom

Directions

From downtown Chicago, drive southeast on I-90 for 28 miles. Take Exit 21 onto I-94 E and drive 7.6 miles. Take Exit 22B onto U.S. 20 E and drive for 3.7 miles. Exit on State Route 49 and go north for 1 mile, continuing north on N. County Road 25 E/N. State Route 49 into the park. Continue past the entrance and turn right just prior to the main beach lot. The nature center road is 0.6 mile east; turn left and drive north to the lot.

Public Transportation: Take the South Shore Line to Dunes Park Station (www. nictd.com). From the station, walk east on the Calumet Trail for 0.7 mile, then turn north on Tremont Road. In 0.5 mile Tremont turns into County Road 100 E. as it turns northwest. Follow it for 0.2 mile, then turn north/northeast and walk 0.1 mile to the nature center.

GPS Coordinates: 16 T 495832mE 4611747mN

Information and Contact

There is a resident entrance fee of $5 on weekends and $4 on weekdays; the nonresident fee is $7 daily. Dogs are allowed on a six-foot leash. The park is open daily from sunrise until 11 P.M. For more information and for map downloads, contact Indiana Dunes State Park, 1600 N. County Road 25 E, Chesterton, IN 46304, 219/926-1952, www.in.gov/dnr.

8 DUNE BLOWOUT-WOODLAND LOOP BEST (

Indiana Dunes State Park, Indiana

Level: Moderate

Total Distance: 4.0 miles round-trip

Hiking Time: 2 hours

Elevation Change: 125 feet

Summary: Enjoy spectacular views while walking along the edge of a blown-out sand dune.

As a landscape, the Indiana Dunes are a work in progress. For sand dunes, a combination of wind and heavy use wears away the sand and creates steep depressions called blowouts. Unfortunately, these naturally occurring changes have been hastened by human activities in some of the more popular areas. Other areas are for the birds—literally. Indiana Dunes has been designated an Important Birding Area by the National Audubon Society, as the woodland provides rich habitat for many species. Watch for red-headed and pileated woodpeckers, wood thrush, and various migratory birds such as warblers and flycatchers. Along the trail, you may spot gulls or loons on the lake or warblers in the trees.

From the trailhead, begin hiking east, keeping right at the first two three-way junctions. For the next 0.5 mile, enjoy the pleasant views south of the black oak woods. This area harbors a variety of different birds, including the stunning

© BARBARA I. BOND

northwest along the trail at Indiana Dunes State Park

redheaded woodpecker. At the first junction, ignore the "shortcut" trail and continue north, then east towards the dunes. The dune is visible through the trees on the left for a short distance. At 0.8 mile, turn north onto Trail 9 (numbered post 9) and head uphill in deep sand to reach the edge of the Beach House Blowout.

Amazing views greet you as you climb above the trees on the right. Marram grass edges the trail, and the trees thin until there is only a lone cottonwood on the grassy rolling dune. The trail dips and climbs again for a mile, following the contour of the dune edge until eventually heading north toward the trees; note

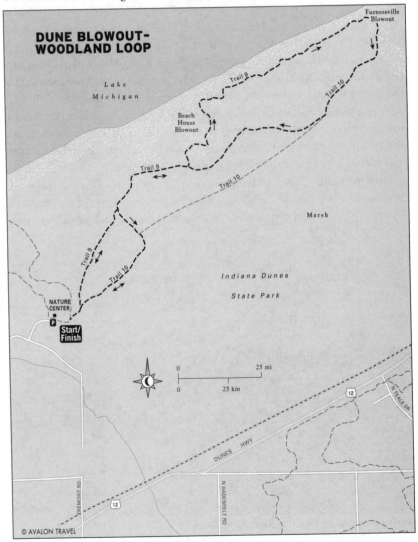

their exposed roots on this windswept section of dune. Turn east at nearly 1.2 miles. The next 0.7 mile is magical as the trail winds through black oak and hickory woods with unparalleled views of the lake. Watch for a weather station on the right (a white-tailed deer surprised me on the trail here). At 1.9 miles, turn right at another Trail 9 post and follow the trail as it descends south, then west, into the dense forest once more. Continue walking west, still in the deep woods, for another mile and keep left at the trail junction. At 3.1 miles, the trail turns south away from the dunes and quickly reaches a shortcut trail. Follow this trail southeast towards a marshy area; the trail cuts back west and south here to reach the Trail 10–Trail 9 junction at 3.7 miles. Retrace your steps the last 0.2 mile to the trailhead.

Options

For more great views and a longer hike, combine this trail with the short but challenging Three Peaks hike (see listing in this chapter). Hike the Three Peaks in the reverse direction by starting on Trail 7. After reaching the Trail 9–Trail 10 junction, follow the preceding directions for a total combined distance of 5.6 miles.

Directions

From Chicago, drive southeast on I-90 to Exit 21 for I-94 E; continue for 7.6 miles. Take Exit 22B onto U.S. 20 E and travel 3.7 miles. Exit on State Route 49 north and go 1 mile, continuing north on N. County Road 25 E/N. State Route 49 into the park. Continue past the entrance and just prior to the main beach parking lot, turn right. The nature center road is 0.6 mile east; turn left and drive north to the parking lot. To reach the trailhead, walk to the east end of the parking lot. The paved nature center path is on the left; the dirt trail is on the right.

Public Transportation: Take the Northern Indiana Commuter Transportation District (NICTD) South Shore Line from Chicago's Millennium Station to Dunes Park Station. From the station, walk east on the Calumet Trail for 0.7 mile and turn north on Tremont Road. In 0.5 mile, Tremont Road turns into County Road 100 E as it turns northwest. Follow the road for 0.2 mile, then turn north for 0.1 mile to the nature center. For transportation schedules, visit www.nictd.com.

GPS Coordinates: 16 T 495832mE 4611747mN

Information and Contact

The resident entrance fee is $5 on weekends, $4 on weekdays; the nonresident fee is $7 daily. Dogs are allowed on a six-foot leash. The park is open daily from sunrise to 11 P.M. For more information, contact Indiana Dunes State Park, 1600 North 25 E., Chesterton, IN 46304, 219/926-1952, www.in.gov/dnr.

9 LY-CO-KI-WE TRAIL

Indiana Dunes National Lakeshore, Indiana

Level: Moderate

Total Distance: 7.0 miles round-trip

Hiking Time: 4 hours

Elevation Change: 140 feet

Summary: The Ly-co-ki-we Trail travels across sandy ridges and wetlands, as well as through shady, fern-filled woodlands.

South of the Dunes Highway, between the Buell Visitor Center and Dunewood Campground, is the 9.4-mile Ly-co-ki-we Trail system. The central trails cross sand ridges and wetlands that remained behind when Lake Michigan receded over 11,000 years ago. Indiana Dunes National Lakeshore's large tract of wetland supports a variety of wildlife, including snakes and amphibians, muskrat, and damselfly.

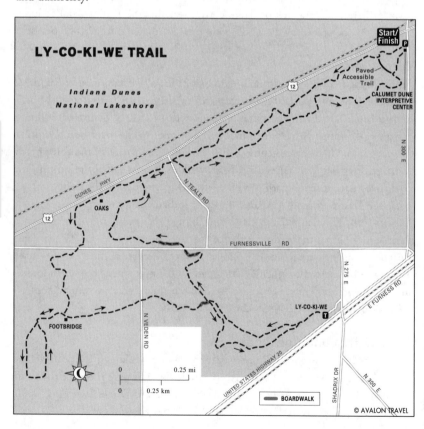

Begin your hike at the Calumet Dune Interpretive Center, where the 0.5-mile paved, wheelchair-accessible trail begins. Hike west from the center along the paved trail for a short distance, then keep right and take a dirt path into the woods. Plenty of black and white oak, black cherry, and hickory keep the trail well shaded. Ferns, false Solomon's seal, and poison ivy cover the forest floor, as do a variety of weeds. A snag along the trail sports a series of woodpecker holes. At 1 mile, pass a stand of white pine, then cross Teale Road as the trail continues west. Maples begin to fill the understory of tall oaks. At 1.4 miles, look for an opening and explore for a moment—the small oaks are partially buried in sand. The trail begins heading south, crossing Furnessville Road.

woodpecker nests

© BARBARA I. BOND

There is a three-way junction at 2.1 miles; keep west and begin hiking uphill. (You will return to cross the bridge on the east.) The trail cuts back south, still in the woods, passing another three-way junction. Continue following the main trail as it loops east, then north, and east once more. Cross a bridge at 2.8 miles and continue east for 0.6 mile. Cross a boardwalk, then keep right at a junction, reaching the main trailhead at nearly 4.1 miles. There are information signs, restrooms, drinking water, and a picnic shelter. In winter, there is a warming hut for cross-country skiers.

Back on the trail, keep right to continue on the loop. Turn right again at 4.6 miles. The trail descends as it approaches the wetlands; the fern cover increases and at 4.8 miles there is a boardwalk over the sensitive boggy ground. Cross the road and look for another low section protected by a boardwalk. Ferns litter the ground in all directions. Keep right at a junction at 5.2 miles. The trail opens up and you soon walk past the south side of that sandy opening (at 1.4 miles). Aspens await ahead, as do some huge bur oak.

Just past Teale Road, keep right and hike south, then east, into the very wet woods at the wetland's border. White-tailed deer like to wander through the woods here and woodpeckers flit from tree to tree. As the trail skirts the wetland, following the wooden posts with marked arrows will prevent you from getting wet feet. When you reach the paved path at about 6.6 miles, turn to cross the bridge and return to the parking lot in 0.25 mile.

Options
Ly-co-ki-we is fairly isolated. The best way to extend your hike is with a drive to the West Beach Trails (see listing in this chapter). Together, these two trails offer a pleasant 10.5-mile hike, or a shorter 8.5-mile option via the Dune Succession Trail.

Directions
From downtown Chicago, drive east on I-90/I-94; take Exit 21 to I-94 E and continue for 7.6 miles. Take Exit 22B and drive 6.4 miles on U.S. 20 E. Turn north on N. 300 E/Kemil Road. The old visitors center is in 0.8 mile on the west side of the road. Park in the lot and walk towards the building, turning right to pass the restrooms. The trailhead is to the north of the building. The loop hike returns south of the building, winding around the old visitors center.

GPS Coordinates: 16 T 499168mE 4612050mN

Information and Contact
There is no fee. Dogs are not allowed. The park is open 7 A.M.–sunset daily. For more information, contact Ly-co-ki-we and Calumet Dune Accessible Trail, U.S. 12 and Kemil Road, Chesterton, IN 46304; or Indiana Dunes National Lakeshore, Dorothy Buell Memorial Visitor Center, 1420 Munson Road, Porter, IN 46304, 219/395-8914, www.nps.gov/indu, 219/926-7561.

🔟 RIVER BLUFF-OXBOW TRAILS
Tippecanoe River State Park, Indiana

🧍 🔽 🦌 🧍

Level: Moderate   **Total Distance:** 9.6 miles round-trip

Hiking Time: 4.5-5 hours   **Elevation Change:** 190 feet

Summary: Pine plantations and river views await hikers exploring the trails of Tippecanoe River State Park.

Tippecanoe River State Park occupies 2,785 acres of woodland along 5 miles of its windy namesake waterway. Until the 1830s, this land was home to Native American tribes such as the Potawatomi, who used the rich natural resources to support their simple way of life. Once settlers arrived, farming and grazing took place until the 1930s, taking a toll on the land. The area became a state park in 1943 and is now a restoration and conservation site that provides a rich habitat for a multitude of birds and animals. Miles of trails, nature preserves, and campgrounds provide opportunities for outdoors enthusiasts. If you enjoy river views and the crunch of pine needles underfoot, then a visit to the trails of Tippecanoe River State Park is for you.

The River Bluff Trail (Trail 5) begins next to historic Tepicon Hall. Walk downhill past the building, turning south at the numbered post. (Numbered posts identify the trail and are well placed throughout the trail system.) Breathe

Tippecanoe River

in the pine-scented air as the trail winds in and out of pine plantations full of birds. I saw a barred owl early one morning; red-breasted nuthatches also frequent the area. The hardwood forest is full of tall oaks, with smaller maples and black cherry. Near 1.9 miles you'll pass a canoe camp and boat launch, then begin hiking towards the river.

Around 2.5 miles, a bench at the river's bend invites lingering. Continue north a short distance, keeping left at the trail junctions to stay near the river as the trail meanders. At 3.4 miles, you will have made a loop along the river's edge. Keep left

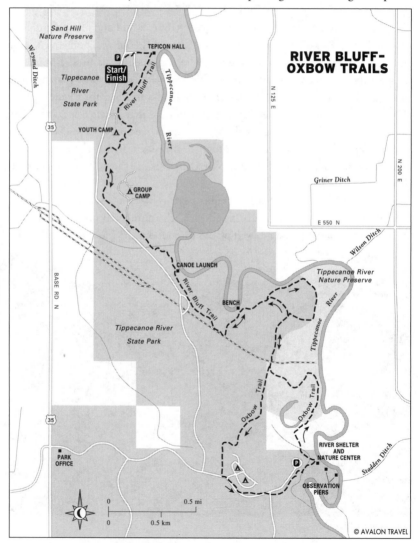

(south) at the junction on Trail 5, traveling through oak and hickory woods, then pines again, as you head toward a pair of trail junctions. The trail pops out into open grassland, then continues ahead through a four-way trail junction. Back in the trees, you'll reach a signed four-way junction with numbered posts and a nature preserve sign at 3.7 miles. Follow the signed arrows to continue south onto Trail 4, the Oxbow Trail (a 1.9-mile loop). Avoid turning sharply left or east, which is also Trail 4—that is your return route.

Trail 4 follows the southern edge of the campground, then the road, as it turns north towards the nature center. At 5.0 miles or so, walk north along the open grass, then cross the second bridge east of the nature center, where there are a number of river observation piers; there may be geese or ducks on the water.

Walk west and cross a grassy area north of the big parking lot to a nature preserve sign and stone footbridge at 5.5 miles. After passing some bur oak and birch trees, turn northeast along the water—you are now in the nature preserve, home to muskrat, beaver, and the Massasauga rattlesnake. The bottomland and marsh is a refreshing change from the woods. At about 6.3 miles is the signed trail junction; turn right to rejoin Trail 5. Continue north, crossing open grassland before returning to the woods. Keep left at the three-way junction (marked by a bench), then left again at another three-way at 6.8 miles. From here, retrace your steps 2.8 miles to the start.

Options

Another way to enjoy the wildlife and trails of Tippecanoe River is to hike in the two nature preserves. The Tippecanoe River Nature Preserve is best explored on the Oxbow Trail (Trail 4) from the nature center lot. To hike the maple and pine forests of the Sand Hill Nature Preserve, walk the Bluestem Trail from the north trail parking lot. The combined distance is 3.3 miles for the preserve trails.

Directions

From downtown Chicago, drive southeast on I-90 to Exit 17 for I-65/U.S. 12/U.S. 20 to merge onto I-65 S. Drive for 9 miles, then take Exit 253 for U.S. 30 and continue east for 37.4 miles. Take the U.S. 35 ramp for La Porte/Know and turn south onto U.S. 35 and drive 19.5 miles. The park entrance is on the east side of the road. Turn into the park and drive approximately 1 mile. Turn left and drive 2.6 miles to the parking lot on the left, just prior to the rent-a-camp cabins. Walk east past the Tepicon Building and restrooms; the trailhead for the River Bluff Trail will be on the right.

GPS Coordinates: 16 T 534017mE 4555179mN

Information and Contact

The resident entrance fee is $5 on weekends, $4 on weekdays; the nonresident fee is $7 daily. Dogs are allowed on a six-foot leash. Warning: There are abundant mosquitoes and ticks throughout summer; bring insect repellent and check dogs for ticks. For more information, contact Tippecanoe River State Park, 4200 N. U.S. 35, Winamac, IN 46996, 574/946-3213, www.in.gov/dnr.

RESOURCES

HIKING RESOURCES
National Park Service
Indiana Dunes National Lakeshore
1100 N. Mineral Springs Road
Porter, IN 46304
219/926-7561 (press 3 for visitor information)
www.nps.gov/indu

USDA Forest Service
Midewin National Tallgrass Prairie
30239 S. State Route 53
Wilmington, IL 60481
815/423-6370
www.fs.fed.us/mntp

Illinois Department of Natural Resources
http://dnr.state.il.us/lands/landmgt/parks

Buffalo Rock State Park
P.O. Box 2034
1300 N. 27th Road
Ottawa, IL 61350
815/433-2224

Castle Rock State Park
1365 W. Castle Road
Oregon, IL 61061
815/732-7329

Chain O' Lakes State Park
8916 Wilmot Road
Spring Grove, IL 60081
847/587-5512

Goose Lake Prairie State Natural Area
5010 N. Jugtown Road
Morris, IL 60450
815/942-2899

Hennepin Canal State Park
16006 875 E Street
Sheffield, IL 61361
815/454-2328

Illinois Beach State Park
Lake Front/Park Office
Zion, IL 60099
847/662-4811

James "Pate" Phillips State Park
2050 W. Stearns Road
Bartlett, IL 60103
847/608-3100

Lowden-Miller State Forest
1365 W. Castle Rock Road
Oregon, IL 61061
815/732-7329

Matthiesen State Park
P.O. Box 509
Utica, IL 61373
815/667-4868

Mississippi Palisades State Park
16327A State Route 84
Savanna, IL 61074
815/273-2731

Moraine Hills State Park
1510 S. River Road
McHenry, IL 60051
815/385-1624

Rock Cut State Park
7318 Harlem Road
Loves Park, IL 61111
815/885-3311

**Shabbona Lake State
Recreation Area**
4201 Shabbona Grove Road
Shabbona, IL 60550
815/824-2106

Starved Rock State Park
P.O. Box 509
Utica, IL 61373
815/667-4726

Volo Bog State Natural Area
28478 W. Brandenburg Road
Ingleside, IL 60041
815/344-1294

William G. Stratton State Park
401 Ottawa Street
Morris, IL 60450
815/942-0796

Indiana Department of Natural Resources
www.in.gov/dnr/parklake/2392.htm

Indiana Dunes State Park
1600 N. Route 25 East
Chesterton, IN 46304
219/926-1952

Tippecanoe River State Park
4200 N. U.S. 35
Winamac, IN 46996
574/946-3213

Michigan Department of Natural Resources and Environment
www.michigan.gov/dnre

Warren Dunes State Park
12032 Red Arrow Highway
Sawyer, MI 49125
269/426-4013

Wisconsin Department of Natural Resources
http://dnr.wi.gov

**Kettle Moraine State Forest,
Southern Unit**
S91 W39091 State Route 59
Eagle, WI 53119
262/594-6200

**Richard Bong State
Recreation Area**
26313 Burlington Road
Kansasville, WI 53139
262/878-5600

County Agencies and Local Organizations
**Berrien County Parks
Commission Office**
701 Main Street
St. Joseph, MI 49085
269/983-7111

Chicago Botanic Garden
Lake Cook Road
P.O. Box 400
Glencoe, IL 60022
847/835-5440

Chicago Park District
541 N. Fairbanks Court
Chicago, IL 60611
312/742-7529

**Forest Preserve District
of Cook County**
536 N. Harlem Avenue
River Forest, IL 60305
708/771-1190

**Forest Preserve District
of DuPage County**
3S580 Naperville Road
Wheaton, IL 60189-8761
630/933-7200

**Forest Preserve District
of Will County**
17540 W. Laraway Road
Joliet, IL 60433
815/727-8700

**Forest Preserve District
of Winnebago County**
5500 Northrock Drive
Rockford, IL 61103
815/877-6100

**Kane County Forest
Preserve District**
719 S. Batavia Avenue
Geneva, IL 60134
630/232-5980

**Lake County Forest
Preserve District**
2000 N. Milwaukee Avenue
Libertyville, IL 60048-1199
847/367-6640

**Lake Katherine Nature Center
and Botanic Gardens**
7402 W. Lake Katherine Drive
Palos Heights, IL 60463
708/361-1873

**McHenry County
Conservation District**
18410 U.S. 14
Woodstock, IL 60098
815/338-6223

Morton Arboretum
4100 State Route 53
Lisle, IL 60532
630/968-0074

Village of Lemont
418 Main Street
Lemont, IL 60439
630/257-1550

Map Sources
Trail and/or site maps are available
from the managing agency via download or email.

U.S. Geological Survey

www.usgs.gov/pubprod/
The USGS's 7.5-minute maps are available through the USGS website for download or purchase.

Public Transportation

The Chicago area has one of the most widely used public transportation systems in the United States. Most trains or buses allow bikes. Using bus or rail may be the easiest way to reach your hiking destination.

CTA

www.transitchicago.com
The Chicago Transit Authority is the region's largest provider of bus and rail service. Bikes are allowed.

Metra

http://metrarail.com
Metra is the regional rail service of northeastern Illinois. Trains run regularly from Chicago to suburban locations north, west, and south of the city. See the website for full schedules. Bikes are normally permitted on trains, but check the schedule for details.

Northern Indiana Commuter Transportation District

www.nictd.com
The Northern Indiana Commuter Transportation District operates the South Shore Line, which runs between Chicago and the Indiana shore. See the website for schedules. Bikes are not allowed on the South Shore Line.

PACE

www.pacebus.com
Pace is the suburban bus service. Bikes are allowed.

HIKING CLUBS AND CONSERVATION ORGANIZATIONS

Chicago Wilderness

www.chicagowilderness.org
8 S. Michigan Avenue, Suite 900
Chicago, IL 60603
312/580-2137
Chicago Wilderness is a regional alliance of organizations working to connect people and nature through their initiatives. Its website offers a large archive of hiking-related articles.

Forest Trails Hiking Club

www.foresttrailshc.com/
The Forest Trails Hiking Club has been active in the Chicago region since 1942. Contact the club via its website for a hike schedule or more information. They host a hike every weekend throughout the year.

Ice Age Trail Alliance

2110 Main Street
Cross Plains, WI 53528
800/227-0046
www.iceagetrail.org
The Ice Age Trail Alliance works with the National Park Service, Wisconsin Department of Natural Resources, and local entities to maintain and support the Ice Age National Scenic

Trail. The alliance sells a comprehensive map set and trail atlas and posts trail updates regularly on its website.

Illinois Audubon Society

www.chicagoaudubon.org/links.shtml
The Illinois Audubon Society has chapters throughout the Chicagoland region. See the websites for event and outing schedules.

Illinois Trails Conservancy

www.illtrails.com/index.htm
This organization maintains a statewide list of linear trails (paved and unpaved).

The Nature Conservancy

Illinois Chapter
www.nature.org/wherewework/
  northamerica/states/illinois/
  preserves/
The Nature Conservancy is working to preserve several important sites around the state.

The Prairie Club

135 Addison, Suite 212
Elmhurst, IL 60126
630/516-1277
http://theprairieclub.org
Since its founding in 1908, the Prairie Club has helped with conservation efforts around the region. See the club's website for a hike schedule.

Sierra Club

Illinois Chapter
http://illinois.sierraclub.org
The Sierra Club's chapters in Illinois, Wisconsin, and Indiana have active outing schedules. The "outings" webpage provides calendars. The Chicagoland area also has several smaller, local chapters.

Index

Acknowledgments

Thanks to my family for their support during another hiking book, and for even coming along once in a while! I couldn't have done it without you all.

The patient staff at Avalon Travel made this project go smoothly; thanks to Sabrina Young for encouragement and helpful suggestions.

Many employees and volunteers at managing agencies gave generously of their time, patiently answering my many questions. In particular thanks to Deborah Ripper, John Elliot, and Yvonne Woulfe, all at the Forest Preserve District of Cook County. Stacy Iwanicki of the Illinois DNR was kind enough to go out in the field with me one morning to point out the some of the unique flora and fauna at Volo Bog. George, at the Bartlett Nature Center, was extremely generous with his time as he shared some of his vast knowledge of butterflies and flowers at James "Pate" Phillips State Park.

And, thanks to all the folks who came hiking with me. I hope you had as much fun as I did!

Notes

Notes

Notes

Notes

www.moon.com

DESTINATIONS | ACTIVITIES | BLOGS | MAPS | BOOKS

MOON.COM is ready to help plan your next trip! Filled with fresh trip ideas and strategies, author interviews, informative travel blogs, a detailed map library, and descriptions of all the Moon guidebooks, Moon.com is all you need to get out and explore the world—or even places in your own backyard. While at Moon.com, sign up for our monthly e-newsletter for updates on new releases, travel tips, and expert advice from our on-the-go Moon authors. As always, when you travel with Moon, expect an experience that is uncommon and truly unique.

MOON IS ON FACEBOOK—BECOME A FAN!
JOIN THE MOON PHOTO GROUP ON FLICKR

YOUR ADVENTURE STARTS HERE

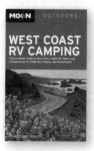

For campers, hikers, cyclists, anglers, boaters, and for those that like the comforts of an RV, Moon Outdoors guides are written by outdoor experts who offer well-researched info and insider tips.

For a complete list of guidebooks, visit Moon.com/books.

Moon Outdoors guidebooks are available through online booksellers,

MOON TAKE A HIKE CHICAGO

Avalon Travel
a member of the Perseus Books Group
1700 Fourth Street
Berkeley, CA 94710, USA
www.moon.com

Editor and Series Manager: Sabrina Young
Copy Editor: Maura Brown
Production and Graphics Coordinator:
   Domini Dragoone
Cover Designer: Domini Dragoone
Interior Designer: Darren Alessi
Map Editors: Brice Ticen, Albert Angulo
Cartographers: Albert Angulo, Kat Bennett,
   Kaitlin Jaffe, and Chris Henrick

ISBN-13: 978-1-59880-761-5
ISSN: 2158-7612

Printing History
1st Edition – May 2011
5 4 3 2 1

Front cover photo: Indiana Dunes National
   Lakeshore, © Getty/Stone/David Muench
Title page photo: Herrick Lake, © Barbara I.
   Bond
Table of Contents photos © Barbara I. Bond
Back cover photo: © Peter Cade / Getty Images

Printed in Canada by Friesens

Keeping Current

We are committed to making this book the most accurate and enjoyable hiking guide to Chicago. You can rest assured that every trail in this book has been carefully reviewed in an effort to keep this book as up-to-date as possible. However, by the time you read this book, some of the fees listed herein may have changed and trails may have closed unexpectedly.

   If you have a favorite gem you'd like to see included in the next edition, or see anything that needs updating, clarification, or correction, please drop us a line. Send your comments via email to feedback@moon.com, or use the address above.